THE CARNIVALS OF LIFE AND DEATH
MY PROFANE YOUTH, 1913–1935

James Shelby Downard's

The Carnivals of Life and Death
My Profane Youth, 1913–1935

Edited By Elana Freeland
Foreword By Adam Parfrey

Feral House

ᶤ

The Carnivals of Life and Death: My Profane Youth, 1913–1935
© 2006 James Shelby Downard

Original cover art by Danger
Cover and interior design by Parker Todd Brooks

ISBN 1-932595-15-5

Feral House
PO Box 39910
Los Angeles, CA 90039
USA

www.feralhouse.com

10 9 8 7 6 5 4 3 2 1

TABLE OF CONTENTS

Masonry and the Downardian Nightmare
By Adam Parfrey

"Because the dead and deadening scenery of the American city of dreadful night is so utterly devoid of mystery, so thoroughly flat-footed, sterile and infantile, so burdened with the illusory gloss of 'baseball-hot dogs-apple pie-and Chevrolet' that it is somehow outside the psycho-sexual domain. The eternal pagan psychodrama is escalated under these 'modern' conditions precisely because sorcery is not what twentieth century man can accept as real."
—James Shelby Downard, 'King-Kill 33°'

James Shelby Downard died before he could finish writing his life story. *The Carnivals of Life and Death* is only Part One, ending in 1935 when Shelby reached the age of 26.

Like the Wizard of Oz, Downard is a guru and a mystic and perhaps a bit of a mountebank, too. He inspired me to see beyond the deadening scenery of modern America and appreciate the magic of words, geography, and the secret underpinnings of American life in the twentieth century. I started to wonder, is it really all that organized and sophisticated, even in subconscious orbits? Who's behind the curtain, got his thumb on the scale? What if Downard was wrong, that it's all chaos and coincidence, and no one, but no one, is in charge? Would our situation be even more terrifying?

The establishment housekeepers of what we call reality would be fast to call Downard a kook. In fact, Downard possessed the typical characteristics of kookdom—frequent mailings of correspondence airing previously suppressed, mind-controlled memories in envelopes rubber-stamped with a quote from Ambrose Bierce: "My Country 'Tis of Thee/Sweet Land of Felony."

Among his advocates, James Shelby Downard is an almost mythic figure. Over the years, dozens of devoted fans wrote and emailed Feral House for yet more Downard. An Atlanta punk band called itself "King-Kill 33°" and Marilyn Manson wrote a song of the same name. Feral House published his work in the first printed edition of *Apocalypse Culture*, another essay in the revised *Apocalypse Culture*, a piece for Jim Keith's *Secret and Suppressed*, more strange thoughtforms in *Apocalypse Culture II* and a variant of this Introduction in my now out-of-print collection, *Cult Rapture*.

For the *Cult Rapture* piece "Riding the Downardian Nightmare," I flew to Memphis in the summer of 1994 to finally meet Mr. Downard in person. There were two failed attempts to film Shelby at Trinity Site, location of the first atomic bomb blast. What Downard has to say about the mystical meanings of the atomic bomb can be accessed today in the current in-print edition of *Apocalypse Culture*.

Memphis seemed the perfect place to find Shelby Downard, home to the occult temple Graceland, reflecting the King of Rock's quest for eternal life. The Memphis Convention Center is a huge pyramid (Masonry is obsessed with pyramidology), where developer Isaac Tigrett hangs photographs of Hindu Godman Sai Baba, and is said to possess a Mayan crystal skull situated in the pyramid center's power point.

Downard lived with his sister in an upper-middle-class brick two-story affair located near a man-made lake in an exclusive part of town. Shelby's sister, an elderly, D.A.R.-type woman, greets me at the front door with Southern hospitality, inviting me into the living room for a whiskey sour or mint julep—my choice. Downard, an octogenarian full of tics, wattles, and liver spots, comes down from his upstairs bedroom, eyes dancing with excitement.

After sis hands me a whiskey, Downard takes me aside and whispers into my ear: "She thinks she's my sister, you know. But she's not."

Around Shelby Downard, things are never what they seem. Having read a number of his essays full of recondite factoids, I expect his library to be filled with thousands of obscure books. Instead there's an old set of World Book encyclopedias, a dictionary, an abused set of *Man, Myth and Magic*, and a couple dozen tomes that could probably be found in any large used bookstore. Downard does not rely on many secondary materials for his research, but instead upon topographic and city maps to prepare for personal visits to sites of arcane and personal significance. Downard had a batlike intuition for navigating dark and hidden terrain that sometimes amazed experts.

Masonic Grand Lodge of Arizona meeting in a cave in the mine of the Copper Queen Consolidated Mining Company in Bisbee, Arizona, Nov. 12, 1897.

Just before I visited, Shelby convinced his niece to drive him to Kansas City to explore underground caves. (As seen in this book, Downard believes caves are fundamental to Masonic beliefs and ritualism, part of the secret history of the United States.) Upon their arrival in Kansas City, the local spelunking society informs Downard and niece that there was no such thing as a cave or caves beneath Kansas City. Then he makes friends with a helpful librarian who spends many hours leafing through maps and consulting with city employees. The librarian discovers to her surprise that many caves do indeed exist beneath the city. I ask Shelby if he's seen recent commemorative postage stamps celebrating sign language.

"Maybe it's my imagination," I tell Shelby, "or the U.S. has issued a couple stamps celebrating the devil's horns."

"Is that right?" says Downard, a bit dubiously. I flash him the symbol on the stamp and suddenly he's excited. "Cuckold, the sign of the horns! You sure now? This I've got to see!"

We enter a standard-issue post office. Clerks work in slow motion, patrons silently stand in line next to a shade duct-taped to thick greenish glass.

By contrast, the excited and chatty Downard seems the epitome of life.

A growling clerk barks us ahead to his window, and Downard requests the "devil stamps."

"Don't know what you mean," says the clerk.

"The hell you don't," says Downard.

"He means the deaf stamps," I intervene.

The clerk tears out a pair for our inspection. Downard lets out a war whoop, a gutbucket howl of recognition.

"You're right, you're right, by golly! The sign of the horns, the cuckold, the devil," he shouts triumphantly. "And it's printed there that it means 'I love you.' I love you! I love you! That's the way they love you all right." He laughs again, stomps and snorts.

We stop for lunch and read aloud an afternoon newspaper wire story about the National Reconnaissance Office (NRO), an intelligence agency that remained secret until 1992. Apparently a few members of Congress were upset that no one would tell them why and for whom a half-billion-dollar, million square-foot "Taj Mahal" was being constructed near Dulles Airport. NRO was forced to admit that their huge complex, half the size of the Pentagon itself, will store and analyze information gleaned from satellites and phone wiretaps.

Welcome to the dead and deadening world of spookland. With $50 billion spent yearly on intelligence agencies and the dissemination of misinformation, shall we curtly dismiss James Shelby Downard as a complete kook?

Like many others, I first became interested in the writings of James Shelby Downard because he seemed so delightfully insane. On closer inspection I noticed that his "madness" had its own undeniable logic.

In Downard's writings, the products of his subconscious bubble to the surface and catalyze painstaking research. The collision of the poetic against the logical remains the freshest approach to the field of conspiracy.

In 1986, when I was putting together the first edition of *Apocalypse Culture*, I first came across the writings of James Shelby Downard when they were brought to my attention by the controversial anti-Zionist writer Michael A. Hoffman II. It was remarkable to me that JFK's assassination, by 1987 a seemingly tired and over-examined subject, could receive such an astonishingly fresh treatment. Who but Downard could think of examining the symbolism behind Jack Ruby (né Jacob Rubenstein)? To paraphrase Downard: the gem business calls a fake ruby passing itself off as the real thing a "jack ruby." A ruby is a blood-red gemstone and is sometimes referred to as a bloodstone. Since the facts behind JFK's assassination must be concealed from the public, it makes sense that the man whose job it is to silence the patsy by spilling his blood would change his name to "Jack Ruby."

Why does Downard pick on the Masons? Aren't they merely a clownish fraternity of small businessmen who wear corny outfits? Downard says he isn't interested in tenderfoot recruits or the window dressing of Masonic philanthropy. He's interested in the government, business, and military leaders that are part of the inner elite.

For many years Downard moved slyly about the country in an Airstream trailer to avoid becoming a Masonic "Pharmakos" or scapegoat. Masonry enjoins the oath-taker that death will greet those who spill secrets. The costumes of the Knights Templar and the other elite Masonic factions are littered with skulls and bones and knives. Talk about mysteries: Death, the greatest one of all.

Back in his house, Downard hands me a file of old newspaper clippings with photographs of presidents and cabinet members decked out in ritual attire. So what? Isn't Masonry as American as apple pie? Didn't Masonry pull off the American revolution? Didn't G-Man (Grand Architect of the Universe Man) J. Edgar Hoover boast of being a 33° Mason? What about Yale's Skull and Bones Society with all those Bush family members? The All-Seeing-Eye (adopted as a symbol of Sarnoff's CBS network as well as for the Pinkerton security operation) is secured within the Masonic pyramid on the back of every dollar bill. The eye here represents the monitoring and control of society, and according to Shelby Downard, the pyramid represents the building of monuments to honor the Pharoahnic elite.

However benign Masonry might be, when I visited Shelby Downard, he was armed at all times and had an extra loaded Colt .45 by his bedside. He didn't want to be caught unawares by sadistic fraternal hijinks, a strange leitmotif in this book.

The skeptic, with his dust-dry religion of old-style scientific rationalism, will dismiss Downard's revelations as cherry-picking from the garden of fact in order to confirm preconceptions. The skeptic will likewise argue that once a scientist buys into a thesis, his data can be tilted to prove his theory. This sympathetic transformation of data occurs even in the physical sciences. If the scientist is not merely fudging data, this principle supports a magical conception of reality. If a belief is strong enough, can it make reality conform?

Downard's life story, the early years found within this book, was confided to me in person, on the phone, in the mail, and through several autobiographical epics published at Kinko's. The typed manuscript of one of these was word-processed by Elana Freedland, a British-based writer interested in abuses by governments worldwide.

So, what is this autobiography? An adventure story as told by Walter Mitty? After all, many of the events seem improbable at the very minimum. For a start, how could such a young boy become capable of taking down entire contingents of nasty, murderous Ku Klux Klanners? Did Shelby Downard really get called into the White House to meet with Franklin

Delano Roosevelt to discuss weird prophetic books he found with his name engraved on their covers? What about the escapades in Cuba that go beyond any movie starring Errol Flynn? Mix them all together and the rational mind rebels.

But then what about Downard family patents and Million Dollar Gold Certificates that check out on a Google search? Secret truths hang over this fascinating book like ectoplasm photographs from the late nineteenth century. What's true? What's not? The joy of reading this book is that it bitch-slaps your belief system to kingdom come.

On my visit, Downard accompanied me on a drive through the back roads of north Mississippi where he was going to show me hot spots used by secret societies for occult charades, which Shelby pronounced as "shah-raid," emphasizing the first syllable in his definitive Memphis inflection. "Their entire program is an ah-cult shah-raid." Shelby and I hit dead ends on what became something of a goose chase. But on our return to Memphis, Shelby fished out some intimate photographs, about a dozen of them seemingly from the '30s and '40s, of a beautiful woman he referred to as "The Great Whore." The photos make clear that Downard once owned the allegiance of this woman and later lost her. The intensity of this loss seemed to inform his worldview. In a moody voice, Downard tells me about the Great Whore drugging him with "abulic" and "amnesiac" drugs while she ran off to perform "sex rites" with famous and infamous men.

"I don't blame her for her nymphomania," says Shelby. "They had her wired up. One day I found a wire sticking out of her ass. I pulled it out. It's a long, thin wire and connected to the end of it is some microelectronic contraption. This was to get her in a constant state of sexual excitation. They implanted me, too."

James Shelby Downard died in 1996 at the age of 87, two years following my visit. There is no one else like him. I owe him thanks for inspiring me to investigate the details and fantastic convergences of life. Is paranoia another form of awareness, or just another form of mental illness? After reading *The Carnivals of Life and Death* I feel less capable of answering that question definitively.

Sorcerers and Specters

Some people might find the maelstrom of evil that surrounds us as too grave a matter to discuss in a satirical way. I offer this explanation for the joco-seriousness I occasionally employ: in a wake, truths are sometimes revealed in jest, and the melancholia of loss is overcome by drinking, feasting and dancing around the corpse from whom all individuality has fled. The American Establishment behaves like a possessed corpse, and thus my need to carry on its wake.

The U.S. government is monotonously proclaimed to be of, by, and for the people, but the administrations of our day—whether Republican or Democrat—are really quite dead. A police state specter has taken possession of the body politic, and this zombie-like cadaver goes far beyond the clichés of science fiction films and the anti-Communist blather that sustained us through the Cold War. The specter lurks in secrecy, silence and darkness symbolized by the *cave (vault, crypt, tomb, grave)* in Freemasonry—the shadow world that conceals the mysteries of Masonic sorcery.

The bureaucratic inverts of the Department of Justice and the Federal Bureau of Investigation suckle at the specter's pap, while the public is ballyhooed with slogans of alleged fidelity, bravery and integrity. The OSS/CIA perverts have worked hard to thwart every principle of morality within their reach. Such amorality fits some Treasury agents to a T—the Greek letter *tau*, which symbolically is associated with crescent moon and star symbolism, as once depicted on badges worn by federal marshals. The sex-and-death rituals remain so well hidden in the good ol' U.S. of A.

The police state specter started out with a little sudsing of dirty political laundry, and just a bit of brainwashing here and there. Then the specter went into the possession business full time, and via mind control, the possessed became owned body and mind. A hideous mystery of lust is part of the game, and some unfortunates are used in orgiastic witchcraft rites where, in a condition resembling that of erotic robots, they perform will-less sex acts.

Cloaked sex-and-death rituals conforming to age-old sex magick creeds have been given the added touch of American ingenuity: they've been modernized by mad doctors who practice scientific sorcery as police specter helpers. In some rites victims are dosed with so-called abulic[1] drugs and are sexually stimulated by way of biotelemetry implants. [See Chapter 27, "Mind Molestation."]

Like "Love Potion No. 9" of the old rock 'n' roll song, the victims dosed with abulic drugs are every bit as effective as Circean potions were to ancient Greeks. Such *toloache*-mimetic concoctions have been used by sorcerers for ages. Mystical sex circuses with powerless victims are typical of witchcraft sex magick orgies that have always been performed in *Call to Chaos* rites.

People of all races are used in "sexathons" that aim at nothing more than racial blood mixing. The cry of voodoo witches at these assemblies has always been *Mislet! Mislet! Mislet! —Mix! Mix! Mix!* The United States, long hailed as the "melting pot," now emerges as a witch's cauldron in the sooty murk of these terminal times.

The witchcraft of public policy is practiced for the purpose of influencing human destiny, and sex and death rituals are part of the GAOTU cult that has employed "occult sciences" for ages. The plan is to bring all people together and make all as one—with the exception of the chosen elite, of course. According to said Master Plan, the mythology of Revelations will be followed like Tinker-Toy instructions: a time of tribulation will come first, after which survivors will be made "one" via a post-tribulation "rapture" spawned by the technical sorcery of having their brain pleasure centers titillated magnetically so that all will cum together. Those who are thus epiphanized will become nothing more than humanoid servomechanisms.

The computerized possession process is so far in its process that I am going to imagine that more traditional spirits such as fiends, devils, demons, and *dybbuks* are enraged at the possession concession being monopolized by the police state crowd. As you may or may not have heard, supernatural spirits

---

[1] *Abulia* or *aboulia*: a loss or impairment in the ability to perform voluntary actions, show initiative, or make decisions. From the Greek *a-* and *boule*, meaning *without will*.

of possession relish *soul food*, and we ain't talkin' about sow belly or collards, but more like *filet of soul* deep-fried in the fires of hell.

Of Cowans and Coffins

As I have alluded, the joco-serious humor in this study is far more purposeful than might at first be thought. The word *humor* (*humour*) actually means mood, but in the old physiology referred to blood or *sanguinity*, and was one of the four cardinal humours that contained the other three (*cholera, melancholia, phlegma*), which by their relative proportions were supposed to determine one's temperament. In studying word use, we find that a bloody temperament was the humour displayed by people attending the Circus Maximus of ancient Rome.

Life is often likened to a circus or carnival, and in the so-called carnival of life, I can say that I have walked the Crooked Mile (the Midway) as a real straight man. It hasn't been easy, for it seems that everyone is more than a little bent and I haven't fit in.

The Hierarchy of the cult of GAOTU evidently declared me to be an outsider, a Cowan—one who knows too much for his own good—and a very knowing one at that, damn my hide. Another such term they use is *profane*, from the two Latin words *pro* and *fanum*, meaning before or outside the temple. Reputedly, a person declared profane in ancient times was not allowed into the temple to see what was going on, just as nowadays the so-called profane are not permitted to witness Masonic Temple Rites—not that he'd be missing much most of the time. Cowans are persecuted, used as scapegoats, and sometimes tortured and/or killed.

Because of my forbidden knowledge, I have been betrayed, cheated, robbed, drugged, poisoned and surreptitiously fed stuff that even wretched carnival geeks would have scorned. Whenever I attempted to get away from it all, I found that I couldn't make out what was what, given that I was in the mystical darkness of the Masonic hoodwink.

The fact is that I was in a *cul de sac* along that ol' Crooked Mile. I mentally retraced my steps to see where I might possibly have gone wrong as I struggled on. There came a time when it seemed that I could dance no farther and the dead end that I faced reeked of finality. I considered then the eschatological/scatological aspects of the whole terminal trip, and when I mentally saw that crap-littered road of life, I realized that a maze had caught up with me. As in the play *The Labyrinth* (*Le Dedale*, 1913) by Paul Hervieu, a coffin seemed to be the only way out. However, after some thinking about coffin conditions and Ishmael's gloomy cogitation in *Moby Dick* when Queequeg's coffin seems to have rallied him to live yet a bit more:

> "...But now that he had apparently made every preparation for death; now that his coffin was proved a good fit, Queequeg suddenly rallied; soon there seemed no need of the carpenter's box: and thereupon, when some expressed their delighted surprise, he, in substance, said that the cause of his sudden convalescence was this;—at a critical moment, he had just recalled a little duty ashore, which he was leaving undone; and therefore had changed his mind about dying: he could not die yet, he averred. They asked him, then, whether to live or die was a matter of his own sovereign will and pleasure. He answered, certainly. In a word, it was Queequeg's conceit, that if a man made up his mind to live, mere sickness could not kill him: nothing but a whale, or a gale, or some violent, ungovernable, unintelligent destroyer of that sort..."
>
> —*Moby Dick, Chapter CX*

I too rallied while walking past coffin warehouses and decided that attaching myself to that way out might not be the best route for me at that time. Given the morbid alternative, I wanted another chance at the Midway, and started searching the interstices of my memories to see if I could recall some exit along the way that I might have overlooked.

The *Elus* and Their Sub-Contractors

In an area that can be described as a limbo of memories, I teased out thoughts that were innocent enough, but seemed to be on the threshold of other memories that were real hellers. I began to examine each and every innocent-appearing memory carefully, suspecting that they might not be all that they seemed, given that some of the memories didn't have genuine connections or antecedents, which made me wonder if they were concealing something.

While rummaging through that limbo, I found a genuine old memory with valid connections, and with that memory came a teardrop through which I got a glimpse of frightful memories from the long-dead past and, perhaps more importantly, recognized the past for the *corpus mysticum* that it is. When my mystical past revealed how it had *really* occurred, it became a horrendous thing cloaked in iniquity, that old now-you-see-it-now-you-don't that preserves the criminal Mysteries of Masonic oz art (M *oz art*).

I had been fooled so long and so thoroughly that I did not at first remember that an assassination contract had been put out on me long ago. In fact, in my cradle days it was originally assigned to a group called the *Elus* (elected), who shall be known here as the prime contractors. They failed to fulfill their assignment, due, I suppose, to the vicissitudes of their lives and occupational hazards. They were, you see, given to ritualism in their assassination efforts, and that is doing it the hard way, as they say in crap-shooting.

The Hierarchy subcontracted my hit. The operatives were so numerous that it seems that just about everybody had a piece of the action. The various ways they were paid off are so fantastic that you wouldn't believe it if I told you, which this book attempts to do.

Take my word for it: the Carnival of Death sure does play off against the Carnival of Life. While it might be said that in the Carnival of Life I wasn't "with it," when it came to the Carnival of Death, my performances have been second to none. The ringmaster of the Carnival of Death is, of course, the Angel of Death, the angel that other angels won't play with. So perhaps the Angel of Death had empathy for me as a fellow outsider, for I have lived with the shadow of death on me for so long that it is like my very own shadow.

"Me and my shadow
Strolling down the avenue
Me and my shadow
Not a soul to tell our troubles to
And when it's twelve o'clock
We climb the stair
We never knock
For nobody's there
All alone and feeling blue
Me and my shadow…"

— "Me and My Shadow" by Billy Rose, Al Jolson, and Dave Dreyer, 1927

Of Sheep and Goats

In ancient times, a rabbi would perform the mumbo-jumbo now called expiatory rites and transfer Hebrew misdeeds to a goat. After being abused as a wicked thing, the "scapegoat" was then rolled down a mountain to its death. If the unfortunate animal survived, it was allowed to wander away, if it was still able to do so. This *caper emissarius* (emissary goat) of misdeeds and evils became identified with the so-called "Demon of the Dry Places," also known as "Azazel" by William Tyndale (1492–1536), English translator of the Bible and ace Hebraist.

While ritual trafficking with such sacrificial animals is very ancient, human beings also were used as assignees of sin. Human scapegoats (Gk., *pharmakos*) are known to have suffered greatly in expiatory rites that ranged from physical and mental abuse to death by drowning, crucifixion, and other priestly procedures. Wayward souls, too—the black sheep of fine families—are often drafted to play the role of scape-person.

Here's a story about such a black sheep. Once upon a time, a little boy was thrown to a pack of wolves when he was just his mother's little lamb. And when this swarthy sheep was promoted to scapegoat and rolled time and again to his near death, he gored some of the rollers when they were least expecting it. What's more, instead of wandering off, he stuck around to fight it out.

It is an axiom in magic that occult (hidden) knowledge is achieved from suffering. Thus it follows that a human scapegoat who somehow manages to survive the cruelty inflicted upon him would have occult knowledge. At the very least, a surviving scapegoat should know a thing or two about his tormentors. I have undergone years of ritualistic oppression, and while I don't claim to have gained supreme occult knowledge from the long ordeal, I sure as hell know about sorcerers in high places, as well as their overall Great Deception that varies as socioeconomic and political structures change.

The Sorcery of Computerized Mind Control

The latest, greatest evil is a science rooted in the occult and developed by way of electrophysiology, cybernetics, biotelemetry/radiotelemetry, etc., into a monstrosity of computerized mind control. The esoteric origins of these seemingly neutral technologies can be seen in specialized Masonic lore such as the various lodge scams of Cagliostro, Egyptian Masonry, Mesmeric Masonry, Universal Harmony, and earlier in Gnosticism, Jewish Kabbalism, and particularly alchemy—all of which are somewhat similar to the degree that they treat a force or energy that might best be described as resembling electromagnetism.

Radiotelemetry is the science of automatic measurement and transmission of data by radio from remote sources. Its primary use is for surveillance ("remote monitoring") in a variety of forms, some seemingly benign, all devious. Tracking was first done by monitoring on-the-body transmitters with a directional antenna; next, a method of location was developed similar to LORAN (Long-Range Navigation), which determined the positions of ships by the use of intersecting electronic signals. I should call attention to the fact that in LORAN a technical problem arose by which "slave station" and "master station" transmissions became reversed—that is, the "slave" would occasionally get into the position of the "master" station. I call this the Spartacus Effect.

Medical telemetries such as radiocardiography and radioencephalography sound humane enough, but are they? Biotelemetric experiments start with pasting electrodes to animal or human bodies, then move on to implantation of electrodes, such as the primitive one that was embedded in me. It has long been known that pain or pleasure can be produced through electrical stimulation of the nervous system; eventually, it was realized that the same thing could be done by implanting a radiotelemetry-controlled device to produce electrical stimuli capable of causing not only pain or pleasure, but even death.

Today, magnetic resonance imaging (MRI) has made it possible to take a fingerprint of your brain, which means that remote monitoring might not even require implants anymore. Indeed, biotelemetry has always been about monitoring not just the vital signs of wretched animal and human guinea pigs, but what they are *seeing, feeling,* and *thinking* as well.

When radiotelemetry and biotelemetry began to look like a go, the creeps at the LORAN Center had the brainstorm of subjugating with their cybernetic hardware. As hideous as their scheme seemed, it was at first limited to the pain-pleasure gambit plus surveillance, and the absolute horror that has now materialized was not earlier within their grasp. In order for that to develop, it was necessary to discover the nature of the *radiant mind power* that coexists with the electrical functions of brain and body, and the means for transmitting and receiving that energy. Mind control finally became an actuality where human servomechanisms served under remote control.

The insiders knew, of course, that such a slave-master relationship would at long last put into the hands of a dominant superclass the means of absolute control over manpower, wealth, and natural resources of the entire world, as set forth in the Master Plan. However, the people engaged in mind control experiments did not foresee the real nature of radiant mind power or the force whereby mental operations could produce telepathy, telekinesis, and psychokinesis.

Where would scientists look for information on radiant mind power? It would be logical to investigate the findings of people engaged in psychic research, particularly extrasensory perception, and even to examine the alleged psychic powers of so-called primitives and animals, such as the "eye" of Scottish border collies, that can reputedly immobilize sheep with a glance. This quest was accomplished with the help of government intelligence agencies and elite families, such as the Huxleys. All information on electrophysiology, cybernetics, and computerology was examined, including the fact that binary coding works for programming brains almost as well as it does for programming computers, making biotelemetric link-ups very "cybernetic." Thus the groundwork was laid for computerized control of minds, the rationale being that it was all for the benefit of humankind. To be fair, only a select few of those working on the projects had any idea of what their research would eventually be used for. What the public coffers did not pick up was gratefully paid by private foundations for the most part governed by American and European elites who owed their fortunes to slaves, rum, and opium.

This well-oiled effort is similar to the atomic bomb project that never would have transpired if Franklin Delano Roosevelt had not had a great deal of arcane understanding, and thus become an ardent backer of the undertaking. Although Roosevelt is said to have been miffed that he did not get into the super-snooty Porcelain Club at *Hahvahd*, he appears to have been more than compensated when he later worked his way into what now passes for the Order of the Illuminati. He certainly shared the same ambitions of that secret clique that believes they are semi-divine shepherds of the profane human race or "sheeple." Besides having shepherd pretensions, high level Masons like Roosevelt identify with wolves, too, which surely has it both ways. In France, the male offspring of Masons are termed *louveteau* meaning wolf-son, indicating that those flock-watchers are wolves in shepherds' clothing. Truly, the man-wolves are dissimulators as adept at verbal image-shifting as the storied werewolves are at shape-shifting.

The Illuminati's Invisible Government is feverishly building worldwide supercomputer nets for surveillance and control, such as Intel's ASCI (Accelerated Strategic Computing Initiative) series at Lawrence Livermore, Los Alamos, and Sandia National Laboratories. This trend is moving in tandem with biological computing, or using DNA and proteins as the computing elements. A number of "master" stations are almost operative, with vast shoals of "slaves" yet to come. But with LORAN the Spartacus Effect has already occurred to some extent, and it now seems that at least one "slave" station is drawing a bead to zap the "master."

These central control stations have supercomputer brains of axiomatic system design, which means they are of a Euclidean Theorem type. The so-called 47th problem of Euclid is a major arcane symbol in the Master Mason degree is known as an axiomatic system.

I wonder if these supercomputer brains were able to prove by a chain of reasoning that they are, say, the God of Triangulation. By way of equilateral triangle symbolism, they might identify with Ammon Ra, who in his divinity was three-fold as Ammon-Mouth-Khon in heaven (the equilateral triangle) and Osiris-Isis-Horus on earth (the right triangle). As a result of such reasoning, supercomputers might just jump to the conclusion that they are the *deus ex machina* on the "stage of life"—like HAL in *2001: A Space Odyssey*—and as such no less than the controller of the Great Principle of Animated Existence. After arriving at this idea, such supercomputers might decide that they are a just and righteous god, and that some changes should be made here and now. Wouldn't surprise me a bit.

Screeing Past and Future Through A Teardrop

Once upon a time priests used drops of wine or ink to serve as mirrors into the past so that they could make prophecies to their devotees, which no doubt paid off in the collection plate. Past events were considered the channels by which the future could be ascertained, given that history repeats itself and the past is therefore the mirror of the future. Such truisms suggest that past and future have a *spiegelschrift* (mirror-writing) relationship with only a time differentiation, and that the present mirrors this reciprocity. This is the Egyptian Double House of Life belief: that by reflecting upon the past, one endeavors to gaze into the future and discover what is going on then and there.

While such a possibility must be considered, it would be good to remember that my glimpses of the past came through a teardrop and not wine or ink. Despite the efforts of evil people to expunge my memory, old recollections were able to persist because the Guardian of my memories was on the job. Memories often associate with emotions (humours) and therefore arrive in the present with mixed feelings. Mine associate with humor mixed with a little sadness. Since so many of my memories are of horrendous events, the humor associated with them may seem macabre.

There were incidents I could not remember after recognizing gaps (lacunae) among my memories, like cul-de-sacs in a maze that prevented me from following through their intricacies properly. Some memories seemed dreamlike and others like distant nightmares, and many are elusive of clear recall that it was difficult to decide if they were merely figments of imagination. On the surface, my inability to recall certain things might not seem unusual, but some memories were truly frightful and so it seemed odd that I could not recall them in their entirety. I knew that localized (lacunar) amnesia can be caused by injury, disease, drugs, systematic brainwashing, and old age, but many memories began to surface when I was young. I mentioned my elusive memories to a "friend" and was advised not to look backward but to live for today while trusting in the future that was in the hands of God. Well, I said that if the future is in God's hands, then no doubt the past is, too, and God shouldn't mind my special way of remembering His handiwork. So I kept struggling to look back.

Suddenly I remembered receiving a government check for one million dollars, but could not for the life of me reconstruct why I had gotten it or what I had done with it. The recollection of such strange largesse from the United States Treasury Department then triggered recall of other lesser sums of money and valuable possessions I once had, but as to what happened to them, zip. I did know that I had lived hand-to-mouth for many years, so to remember that such a great deal of mazuma had been mine was hard to believe or take. But while those losses bothered me, they didn't depress me as much as memory losses. My forgetfulness seemed more mysterious than Judge Joseph Force Crater's disappearance on August 6, 1930, which has been attributed to everything from abduction to time anomalies.

I remembered receiving the government check under a "cloak of security." Upon mentally trolling back, I recollected buying a secondhand but nifty Bugatti and parking it on a Washington, D.C. street before starting to walk somewhere. I remembered being in the Walter Reed Army Hospital and wondering why I was there, given that I wasn't eligible for treatment in a government hospital.

Mesmeric and Magnetic Masonry

It was then that I thought of hypnotism historically associated with Franz Anton Mesmer, specifically the Mesmeric Masonry he founded. Mesmeric Masonry in turn interfaced with Magnetic Masonry, Universal Harmony, and the Egyptian Masonry surveyed by Giuseppe "Cagliostro" Balsamo in his notorious Rite of Memphis-Misraim. All this had to do with "beast power" or "animal magnetism" as well as bioelectrical radiant energy and other aspects of the occult-psychic plague unleashed by these awful mind manipulators.

Masonic sorcery has been termed Solomonian Science, Mosaic Science, Occult Masonry, Theurgic Masonry, Rite of Memphis, Egyptian Masonry, Masonry of Cagliostro, Mesmeric Masonry (AKA Universal Harmony), Magnetic Masonry, etc. The practitioners of such sorcery, besides performing mystical rites and rituals, supposedly have knowledge of and use "the great force known to ancient people," called animal magnetism (bio-electrical radiant energy) by Franz Anton Mesmer (1733–1815).

Part of the story of Freemasonry's descent into sex magick and witchcraft lies somewhere between the Misraim Rite that swept Italy and France in 1805 and 1814 respectively, and the Memphis Rite that took hold in the United States in 1862. On June 4, 1872, John Yarker (1833–1913) bought permission to take the Memphis Rite to England. He then merged the Misraim and Memphis Rites into the Ancient and Primitive Rites of Memphis and Misraim (MM). On September 24, 1902, Theodor Reuss (1855–1923) then purchased permission from Yarker to install Ancient and Accepted Scottish Rite (AASR, 33 degrees) and irregular MM rites (90 and 97 degrees) in Germany. Through Reuss, Memphis-Misraim became the mother order of the Ordo Templi Orientis (OTO), a mix of Craft Masonry, AASR, MM and the sexual mysticism of Tantra. After Reuss' death, Aleister Crowley took the OTO and mystic Masonry further into the precincts of sex magick and satanic witchcraft.

When I thought back upon the style of early hypnotism called Mesmerism, I remembered something about the political intrigue with which Masonry has long been involved. I thought of the witch Cagliostro and how he and Mesmer were butt-buddies, as well as a probable agent of the Knights

wagon, fetching ice for people and delivering circulars. I figured I could keep warm and dry by sleeping in a garbage can filled with newspapers.

James Shelby Downard, five years of age, and friend.

The decision to run away came after considerable thought about the miserable way I was treated by members of my immediate family, in-laws, and outsiders. For example, my uncle Thomas Norman (1868–1918), married to my mother's sister Hetty, was a dyed-in-the-wool Southerner born in Cato, Mississippi. He had taken me to Hattiesburg, Mississippi and then to a crossroad settlement where he was born. I hadn't wanted to go and protested, but was still made to go. At the crossroads, I watched Ku Kluxers hang a man, and it seemed to me that I had been taken there specifically to see the hanging and be scared by it. It was while thinking about that hanging that I went to sleep on that Christmas Eve.

When I woke in the morning, the house was still quiet. I hollered for my mother, and then heard my parents come in the front door and come upstairs immediately. My mother stood in the sewing room while from their bedroom my father said, "Don't turn him loose yet." Then in a few seconds he said,

"Turn him loose," but my mother couldn't get one or more of the safety pins loose and my father had to come in and help her.

I crawled out of bed and ran to the fireplace where my Christmas stocking hung. There was no little red wagon and nothing in my Christmas stocking but switches and ashes. My mother then proceeded to switch me. My father left the room before the switching started, saying he didn't want to see it. Such punishment at Christmas was not uncommon for children in the past, and the only reason that incident is set forth here is that it has a place in a series of events that to some extent were planned.

For days I mulled over what had been done to me and made up my mind to get the little wagon at any cost. It was at that time that a man started standing on the corner on the same side of the street my home faced in Ardmore, Oklahoma. Every time I would go out of the house he would beckon to me, but I was scared and stayed in the yard, then would retreat into the house and watch him through the curtains. I called my mother's attention to the man and said that I was scared, but when she told me to go and see what he wanted, I did.

The man said he had some packages he wanted me to deliver and that he would pay me to do it. I told him that I would deliver the packages if he got me a little wagon that was in the store where the RCA plaster dog listened to his master's voice. He said to wait there, and he went and got the wagon. As he took several packages from the car he had been driving, he told me where to take them. Being so happy with my wagon, I didn't stop to wonder why he didn't deliver them himself. I made several deliveries before being arrested for delivering bootleg liquor.

After being arrested, I was taken home and released to my parents. I left my little wagon in our yard while I was scolded for what I had done. Mother cried or pretended to cry and talked about the shame I had brought on the family, etc. Then I was sent upstairs. The next day when I went outside, my wagon was gone. My mother told me that the man who had given it to me had come for it and said he was keeping it for me and I should come and get it if I wanted it. Mother then told me where he lived. I knew the house and thought it was vacant.

past me when I called out to him and told him to untie me. He was scared, and after untying me told me to run home.

There had been repeated flashes of lightning, like heat lightning. During the flashes, the deputy and I could see each other clearly. He wore a gun and I wondered why he had not arrested the men who planned to kill me. I told him as much. Again, he urged me to run and I told him that I was waiting for God to blow up the men who were going to kill me, that I had been under the house and had heard them talking. Then a flash of lightning struck a vacant lot adjoining the house where the men were and the dynamite under the house exploded.

I asked the deputy for his pistol and he said he couldn't let me have it. So I just reached out and took it from its holster and ran into the house. Two of the men staggered out of the kitchen, managing to get past the divan to the far wall. A second later the leader of the gang came out of the kitchen and was a sight to behold. His left eye was dangling on his cheek. He had his pistol in his hand and started shooting wildly. I hid behind the divan for a few seconds, then crawled out the door and ran home where I got a German officer's spiked helmet (*pickelhaube*) that a Dr. Von Keller had given me.

With the spiked helmet, I ran back to where the explosion had occurred. The men who had planned to kill me were now laid out side-by-side, face up, in the grass. The deputy took me aside and made me promise that I would not tell anyone about his part in what had happened, reminding me that he had protested the plan to kill me and had untied me. I agreed. I examined the bodies of the dead men who had all been shot. Then I marched back and forth in front of the bodies, cursing the Jew who had tried to have me murdered. A man standing around pointed out that the three dead men had their genitalia cut off, which he called pricks and balls. The cutting off of genitalia was not uncommon in the West at that time, though not as common as scalping had previously been.

The deputy's story was that he had gone to the house to inquire about something or other and as he was leaving lightning struck near the house, and then the explosion occurred. It was decided that an electrical charge from the lightning went through damp ground and set off a stick of dynamite that had been carelessly left around. The explosion was called an act of God.

Since the men were shot, too, it was asserted that one of them had gone berserk from the pain of his wounds and in a blind frenzy had shot the other men and then himself. The severed genitalia was attributed to the explosion. How much the explosion story became public record is a matter of conjecture, but I do know that it was a matter of record that I was arrested for delivering bootleg whiskey. The deputy who arrested me for bootlegging was the same deputy at the house with the men who planned to murder me, all of whom were Ku Kluxers.

Shortly after that incident, a woman came to my home and offered me Seventy-five cents to take a lunch pail to her husband at a wagon yard. I didn't want to leave the house, but my mother said it would be a nice way to earn some money and so I went, after first demanding getting paid. On my way to the wagon yard, I opened the pail and found it contained garbage. However, since I had been paid to deliver the lunch pail, I went on to the wagon yard, feeling a little uneasy about the garbage I was delivering, but seventy-five cents was a lot of money to me. I had gone back to the chicken house the day after the explosion and found the dynamite that had not been removed, so I cut the fuse off one to about an inch in length and took it with me.

When I got to the wagon yard, I hid by the watering trough and yelled for the man to come and get the pail. He came out of his office with a shotgun, and two men with guns came out of the area where the feed was kept. Shooting started, so I lit the fuse on the dynamite stick and threw it high in the air over the heads of the three men where it exploded. According to a newspaper story written about the incident, all three men were killed in a shootout. But the truth was concealed by the secrecy, silence, and darkness of the Masonic hoodwink that covered Ardmore like a pall.

Chapter 2

My Little Alice Blue Gown and Golems
Ardmore, Oklahoma, 1918

Witchcraft rites have long transpired in Ardmore under cover of ordinary affairs performed night and day. However, it is not just Ardmore; such rites take place all over the country in various guises. Some of their (dis)guises are so adroit that many people have embraced their appearance without being aware of their sorcerous substance, which means they are unconsciously practicing witchcraft though they would be the first to express shock and dismay if ever they really understood what they were doing.

People think themselves free of witchcraft entertain ideas based on the Old Religion whose atavistic revivals are upheld by both consensus reality and an occult transmission called *contagion* by Sir James Frazer which bolsters these beliefs.

But there's the tendency to dismiss as gullible those who do affirm the proliferation of covert witchcraft rites throughout the world. In actuality, the most naïve people refuse to understand that the material world is only a cover for a perpetual spiritual battle for the minds of men. Control over the minds of men is the highest and greatest control, alongside of which money, fame, and other powers are so many heaps of straw and ash. *The* control mechanism is a hidden thing, a subtle thing, and wishful thinkers overlook it.

Something chose me at an early age without inquiring into my wishes in the matter, and I have ever after been burdened by an awareness of the waste, evil, and treachery that is perpetrated on this earth in the guise of "current events" and "everyday happenings." Unlike wishful thinkers, I cannot pretend these things are not there, and ultimately, none of us should pretend, because whatever we close our eyes to we will one day have to face in all its full form and fury.

Quite a while after the three men died in the "shootout," some men came to see my mother. After they left, Mother explained to me that they were "good friends" who knew that some bad people were trying to hurt us, and if I would just do something that they wanted me to do, everything would be all right. All I had to do was dress in a certain way and walk up Main Street at a certain time to a music store where I would be met by men and taken someplace where I would do something that wouldn't hurt me, and after that the attempts to hurt us would stop. Mother then asked if I would do whatever it was they wanted me to do for her, and of course I said that I would. She then started to make a small blue dress and when I asked her about it, she called it "Alice Blue." I was to wear it when I walked from Bloody Caddo Street up Main Street to the music store where the plaster dog listened to his master's voice.

That night shortly before twelve, I was dressed in the little Alice Blue gown. I picked up my dead grandmother's sealskin muff that went with her sealskin coat and hid my dead grandfather's loaded pistol in the muff. Mother said I couldn't take the muff and I said I wouldn't go without it and so was allowed to take it. Minutes later, three men came for me in a car and took me to Bloody Caddo Street and Main. There, they put me out and told me to walk up Main Street to the music store.

Not a single store light or streetlight was on from Bloody Caddo to the music store, and not a person or car was on the street. I walked up Main Street with considerable confidence. When I got to the music store, I started examining the plaster dog that was said to listen to his master's voice. Almost immediately, a car with three men drove up. One of them got out and ordered me to get in the car. I said I didn't want to. He then jerked me in the direction of the car and when I pulled away, threatened me with a pistol. I then pointed the open end of the sealskin muff at him and pulled the trigger. I was tempted to shoot the other two men, but instead permitted one of them to get out of the car and help the wounded man into the car. They drove away fast and I stalked home. Mother wanted the full details of what had happened, but I didn't want to talk to her. I went to bed immediately and got a good night's sleep. In the morning she scolded me for ruining

Grandmother's sealskin muff but asked no questions. When I asked her what had become of my little Alice Blue gown, she turned deadly pale.

Some time later, she said that because I hadn't cooperated with the people who were trying to help us the night I ruined her muff, I had to do one more thing. Everything would be all right if I would just played dead, like playing possum, and allowed myself to be taken someplace for a born-again ceremony. I asked when the game would begin and she said, "Tonight."

Not trusting her, I went to get Grandfather's pistol but discovered it was gone. I looked for another weapon, and all I could find was my mother's sewing scissors, which I put under my blouse. Shortly after that, Mother gave me some pills to take and had me get into my trundle bed. I pretended to swallow the pills but held them under my tongue, as I did just about any medicine she insisted I take. Once it was dark in the sewing room, I spit the pills out. I was wide awake but playing possum when I heard some men talking to my mother. One of them came into the dark sewing room to give me some liquid to drink. I held it in my mouth and pretended to swallow it, then played possum again. After a few minutes, three men carried me in a sheet out to a car. I was then taken to a funeral home, put on what was supposed to be a bier, and covered with the sheet I had been carried in. The three men then went outside to stand by the door and talk. I could hear them clearly; they were worried about something. One of them declared that if anything went wrong, he knew they would be killed; the other two reassured him as they kept their vigil.

As I lay there, I started to get an erection, which I considered to be an affliction, having been told by a man called Steamroller who operated a steamroller for my father that if it happened very often, I would not grow. I somehow had the idea that it was because I was so small that people treated me so badly, so having an erection was a serious thing to me. I had also been told that the closed foreskin was the cause of my unwanted erections. So taking hold of the foreskin, I stretched it as far as I could and cut the foreskin off with the scissor I had brought with me as a weapon. But I missed a small piece of the foreskin, and when I tried to cut it, the pain was unbearable. It seemed that every nerve in my body went through that unsevered piece of skin, and it made me scream.

One of the men almost shouted, "My God, what was that? I'm getting out of here."

I took off the sheet and struggled up. Every movement hurt. I put the sheet over my head and body and went to the door to face the men, but they weren't there. Starting for home, I cried, groaning and screaming continually; lights went on in houses as I passed. (Mother's response the next day was, "You disturbed everyone on your way home with your unseemly performance.") When I got home, Mother called a doctor who managed to cut the little piece of attached foreskin without hurting me. He said I had done an almost perfect circumcision operation.

Some months after that ordeal, I was walking in the middle of F Street past the home of Max Westheimer who was sitting on his porch. Suddenly, he rushed out into the street and grabbed me. I didn't struggle much, for Mother and Father had me fooled into believing he was a family friend. He took a lipstick and printed something on my forehead, then with a handkerchief tried to erase the first letter he had printed. I wanted to see what he had done, so I kicked him in the leg and he turned me loose. I ran home and looked in a mirror, but since I hadn't learned my ABCs yet, I couldn't decipher what was on my forehead. Both Mother and Father looked at what he had done, then Father called him and talked for quite a while with him. Later, I was told that he had printed EMETH on my forehead, and that EMETH in Hebrew means truth. EMETH was and is the name of the Temple of Reformed Jews in Ardmore. A long time later, I learned that while EMETH is said to mean truth, METH means DEATH, and both EMETH and METH have to do with the making and killing of *golems*. *Golem* is a Hebrew word synonymous with *homunculus*, an artificial human being created by supernatural or magical means, and is referred to in the Old Testament (Psalms 139:16).

Cotton was alleged to have a very long staple and was used in the early telephone system to eliminate what was called crosstalk.

It was on St. Simons/Sea Island that a cabal of internationalists, known to some as the Bilderbergers, assembled in February 1967. (Their designation is due to a meeting on May 10, 1954 at the Bilderberg Hotel in Osterbeck in the Netherlands.) This cabal of internationalists is just one of the powerful assemblages of mysterious organizations that make up a web of conspiracy that covers the world. In most such organizations, there are those who really do not know what they are part of, or that a mysterious Hierarchy presides over the organization aptly described as a *Secret Combination*. Nor do they know that others in the organization they are in believe that there is an inherent natural order for governing society (the Divine Right of Kings, Manifest Destiny, etc.)

Some who attended the Bilderberger meetings were and are unofficial government advisors who secretly wield great power and influence (*eminence gris*), as were those who assembled at the Jekyll Island Hunt Club in 1910. Not all of those later intriguers belonged to the same specious brotherhood, but their lack of democratic principles and purposes were decidedly similar to those of the men who assembled at the Jekyll Island Hunt Club in 1910.

Watson, Holmes, and Bell

Rich and famous people were of course members and guests of the Jekyll Island Hunt Club, but nothing on Jekyll Island was what was represented by and to outsiders. The houses ("cottages") were not the type that anyone would associate with great wealth. The Jekyll Island Hotel wouldn't even have done credit to an average town in the good ol' USA.

There was, as you might suspect, a caste system among the people on Jekyll Island in which Alexander Graham Bell was pre-eminent, and when news got around in 1919 that he was to arrive, people acted as though they were expecting Christ.

Alexander Graham Bell (1847–1922) was born in Edinburgh, Scotland. In later years, he lived in Nova Scotia. On his estate at the Bras d'Or Lakes of Cape Breton, he went in for such stuff as trying to teach a dog to talk and breeding multi-nippled and twin-bearing sheep. Edinburgh has gone in for honorary titles for a long time.

Bell visited Jekyll Island in 1913 as a guest of Boston bankers, and by 1915 had a house there when the first transcontinental telephone line from New York to San Francisco was put into service and an open line connected Jekyll Island, New York City, Washington, D.C., Salem and Boston, Massachusetts. His house was not much; in those days of cheap labor and material, it should not have cost as much as ten thousand dollars to build. The furniture was cheap stuff, too. I am quite sure that Alexander Graham Bell never lived in the so-called Bell House.

A fantastic story revolved around the fact that Bell was supposedly seen at more than one place when the transcontinental call was put through: he was on Jekyll Island, or maybe one of the other places—who can say for sure? In truth, Bell had one or more look-alikes. His "son" looked enough like him to have been his twin, and his cousin Chichester A. Bell is said to have been made up at times to look remarkably like the famous Bell. The Bells "loved to play jokes on people" by switching identities, something like Edwin P. Grosvenor and his "identical twin," who were also part of the Bell clan.

Bell was granted telephone patent No. 174,465 on March 3, 1876, and the first telephone exchange was put into operation in Boston, Massachusetts on May 17, 1877. The telephone exchange switchboard was connected to six banks or "financial houses" which during the day enabled those institutions to communicate with each other, but at night was a burglar alarm system. In fact, the telephone exchange was in the office of Edwin Thomas *Holmes* who was in the burglar alarm business.

It is now common knowledge that Thomas Augustus *Watson* of Salem, Massachusetts assisted Bell in inventing the telephone. It should also be noted that Bell's laboratory was in Salem, a place of witchcraft significance. When Watson was married, he settled in East Braintree, Massachusetts. The term Brain Tree was once a widely used term for the nervous system, and the nervous system was often compared to a telephone system, with the central nervous system likened to an automatic switchboard relaying messages to and

When it finally got around that Cock Robin was dead, I was told that Bell had invented a machine that could bring him back to life. I am not spoofing when I say that Bell had brought a contraption into his house and showed it to several men. He claimed that with this device he could hear a person think. I had busted in on that group with Bell's dog, about which it was said that Bell had taught it to talk. I was then told that Bell was going to bring Cock Robin back to life and the resurrection was to take place at midnight at a large-frame building possibly two blocks from the Jekyll Island Hotel.

At midnight, the corpse or someone pretending to be a corpse was put on a bier in the main room and covered with a sheet. I was watching it closely, given that I had been told that when Cock Robin would be brought back to life he would tell who shot him and I didn't want to miss a word of what he had to say. There were candles around the bier in sufficient number to light that part of the room, but the light was not bright enough for me to see the faces of the people standing not very far from the bier. I was peeking through a window out of which a piece of glass had been broken.

After some mumbo-jumbo, a man lit a candle from one of the candles and moved to the head of the bier where he apparently started to raise the part of the sheet that covered the head of the "corpse." At that point in the ceremony, I hollered like some banshees are reputed to do and immediately a dog close by started to howl, too, then others took up the howling. Maybe Bell's dog put them up to it, for I guess that he might be considered a *bell-wether*, for he even wore a bell on his collar. When they got into full swing, shooting started. It was afterwards explained to me that someone had fired a shotgun to quiet the dogs and possibly that is so, for I did hear a loud shout some distance from the frame building. But shooting went on in the frame building, too, and it was as though the first shot was a signal. People started running and I suspect that the "corpse" got to the door first.

It was explained to me later that the story that Cock Robin had just been wounded, as well as that Bell was going to bring him back to life, were both told to get the killer to reveal himself. It might be that the resurrection story and ceremony were partially concocted for such reasons, but why did Ku

Kluxers dressed in their sheets secretly bury a corpse or something representing a corpse the day following the said resurrection rite?

The Million Dollar Gold Certificates

Shortly before that burial, "Colonel" William Joseph Simmons (AKA "Colonel" William S. Simmons) had arrived at the Jekyll Island Hotel with a lady called Elizabeth Ann (Tyler). They were treated with great deference and people said he was "the great Wizard" and that he had brought a number of men with him who were camped in the southern part of the island where the Grand Dragon was. "Colonel" Simmons had filed a Petition for Incorporation of the Ku Klux Klan in Georgia with the Secretary of State in October 1915, and it was granted shortly thereafter. Besides being head of that Order in the United States, "Colonel" Simmons was a York Rite Mason and a Knight Templar, as well as having been an organizer and solicitor for the Woodmen of the World and then professor of Southern history at Lanier University. Here was the Ku Kluxer in the marshes of Glynn on Jekyll Island. Perhaps he recited "The Marshes of Glynn," the poem by Sidney Lanier (1842–1881), an old-time Ku Kluxer:

> ... Ay, now, when my soul all day hath drunken the soul of the oak,
> And my heart is at ease from men, and the wearisome sound of the stroke
> Of the scythe of time and the trowel of trade is low,
> And belief overmasters doubt, and I know that I know,
> And my spirit is grown to a lordly great compass within,
> That the length and the breadth and the sweep of the marshes of Glynn
> Will work me no fear like the fear they have wrought me of yore
> When length was fatigue, and when breadth was but bitterness sore,
> And when terror and shrinking and dreary unnamable pain
> Drew over me out of the merciless miles of the plain—
> Oh, now, unafraid, I am fain to face
> The vast sweet visage of space.
> To the edge of the wood I am drawn, I am drawn,
> Where the gray beach glimmering runs, as a belt of the dawn,
> For a mete and a mark
> To the forest-dark...

Elizabeth Ann left shortly after arriving, but she made an impressive entrance and was an impressive woman. Elizabeth Ann Tyler was the public relations genius and co-owner with Imperial Kleagle Edward Young Clarke of the Southern Publicity Association that had managed membership drives for the Red Cross and YMCA prior to managing the Ku Klux Klan membership drive.

About the time that "Colonel" Simmons appeared at the Jekyll Island Hotel, Gaston B. Means came, too. Others called him a Secret Service agent, but according to other stories, he was a private detective in 1919 and later became an agent of the Bureau of Investigation, which officially became the Federal Bureau of Investigation (FBI) in 1935. He was one of numerous criminals who were brought into the FBI, and were later were to some extent exposed. Jekyll Island history states that a man named Vail had wired Means to come to the island. Whether that Vail was a relative of Alfred L. Lewis Vail (1807–1859), or whether the old man was reanimated from his grave to send a wire, I don't know. But I do know that Means could not have gotten to the island from Washington, D.C. as quickly as he was supposed to, so perhaps he was hiding in the weeds of the Glynn Marsh or encamped with the Ku Kluxers on the island. In either event, I find it interesting that a Vail—a name associated with Samuel Morse (1791–1872) and the Western Union Telegraph Company—was on Jekyll Island where Alexander Graham Bell was supposed to have been when the first continental telephone call was made, and that Bell was supposed to have been there when the wire was sent. In fact, I find it as interesting as that the Jekyll Island Hunt Club elite was on the island out of season in such numbers.

Almost immediately after "Colonel" Simmons arrived at the hotel, he and Gaston B. Means and another man went into the room used for gambling. After a short time, "Colonel" Simmons came out and went to Bell's house. I followed him. Bell was there, and when I started to follow them, "Colonel" Simmons protested but Bell said it was all right for me to be there. Upstairs, Bell and Simmons stood in front of the window through which the mystic current supposedly passed and faced each other in a seemingly hostile way. Each held a so-called Million Dollar or Multi-Million Dollar Gold Certificate. I had seen this phony money before. A "guest" had shown me such a Certificate a day or two before, saying at the time that I might have one someday. Bell held one in his right hand and Simmons one in his left. Then at some signal, either given or felt, they made contact through that phony money.

It is strange how emotionally influenced people are by that phony money. I have seen expressions of hate, fear, affection, concupiscence, and satisfaction on the faces of people during and after such "face-offs," which I have witnessed a number of times since that day. But never have they taken place to my knowledge in a place where there was alleged to be a mystical current. Samuel L. Clemens (Mark Twain) obtained a copyright on a book in 1892 called *The Million Pound Bank Note,* telling of how the sight of the bank note, as well as the reputation of the holder, influenced people. Well, the influence that the Million Pound Bank Note had on people can't hold a candle to the influence that "Gold Certificates" have on people. For example, consider Bell's and Simmons' actions and reactions:

A moment or two after contact and most certainly some transference of energy, they both put up the Gold Certificates they were holding and Simmons proceeded to suck Bell's dong. Simmons was most certainly allowed to keep the Gold Certificate because of the oral contact with Bell's genitals, for in other such confrontations the dominant person takes the phony money of the other. Now, what Bell was it? Was it Alexander Graham Bell, his son, or his cousin Chichester?

After the Bell & Simmons sex scene, I followed Simmons to the hotel where the desk clerk told me that the Sheriff wanted to talk to me. A man coming down the steps approached and showed me something scrawled across two pages in the hotel register. I was asked if I had done it. I doubt if I could read or write at that time; maybe with the help of pictures I could make out dog, cat, and rat or something similar, but someone or other was supposed to have said that they saw me writing, "Who Killed Cock Robin?" I had come into the hotel shouting out what I had seen done to Bell, so there and then I proceeded to tell the Sheriff what had happened. Then a couple of deputies questioned me about the hotel register and Cock Robin, and I guess they were all quickly satisfied that I could not read or write much. I learned many years later that the Brunswick, Glynn County, Georgia Sheriff and deputies "investigating" the Killing of Cock Robin were all Ku Kluxers.

A veil of secrecy, silence, and darkness of the Masonic hoodwink concealed things that happened on Jekyll Island, and the Glynn County Sheriff Department participated in the hoodwink. If they didn't actively participate, then they condoned or permitted it. For example, the servants on Jekyll Island were rounded up and taken to a tennis court where they were lectured on the benignity of their employers, the Jekyll Island elite and their inherent greatness and goodness. Alexander Graham Bell was represented as being the epitome of the elite and referred to as a prince among men as well as the veritable prince of the world. The servants were told how fortunate they were to serve such people, for that in itself showed them to be among the chosen. At the close of the lecture, they were instructed not to reveal that Mr. Bell was on the island at the time of the shooting; then they were asked to take an oath that they would not reveal any of the personal affairs of the people they served. The connection between the oath and Mr. Bell's whereabouts was made quite apparent to the servants, and each and every one of them was promised a sum of money which was to be a gift directly related to the benignity of their employers.

Shortly after the tennis court oath was administered, things quieted down and people started to leave or go into hiding. The "guests" started to thin out, but I am sure that each and every one had been there longer than the two weeks' limit. The tennis court oath may in fact have been just more Jekyll Island fun and games, given that a tennis court oath has to do with a historical political event, *The World Toast at Tennis* (1620), a play produced for the public stage in London "By the Prince and His Servants." The play had to do with Deviltry, and the Devil was depicted as being the same as the one shown in *News From Scotland* illustrations of Edinburgh origin. The Devil is of course said to be the Prince of This World, and his Servants were somehow Tennis Court-oriented in that mystical Play. (Tennis, anyone?)

After the death of Cock Robin, "Count" Eugenio took me to the home of Richard Crane of toilet fame. Crane or someone pretending to be him seemed very attentive to me and asked me a number of times if I needed to go to the bathroom. When I said I did, he showed me several bathrooms and told me that I could use any one I wanted, so I ran to one and proceeded to piss on the floor, walls, and towels. I don't know how a tiny bladder could have held so much. I was angry at all the Jekyll Island people for my having been choked and forced to crawl out of the hotel, and pissing was intended for everyone on Jekyll Island.

J.P. Morgan Sr. (1837–1913) was of course dead, and years later I heard that J.P. Morgan Jr. never stayed on Jekyll Island but on his yacht Corsair, and would fly the Jolly Roger (Skull & Bones) flag whenever near or passing Jekyll Island. Certainly in 1919 no one to my knowledge mentioned the name Morgan or many other prominent people. The only name that seemed to matter was Bell, and the old telephone equipment from the first transcontinental telephone call in the hotel was treated as a sacred fetish. It and the Jekyll Island Hotel registration books were on display for a number of years. The only book missing was the one in which WHO KILLED COCK ROBIN is scrawled. I have heard that it has become a secret and valuable holding of Klan-Masons in Atlanta, Georgia.

Chapter 4

The Land of Enchantment
Columbus, New Mexico, 1919–1920

*M*other, the "Count" and I left Jekyll Island the day after I was taken
to the Crane house and went to Florida where we visited a number
of places seemingly as tourists, ending with John Ringling at the Hotel
Verona (the Ringling Hotel) in Sarasota, Florida. In 1912, Ringling had
acquired tracts of land between Cornish and Ardmore, Oklahoma, some of
which proved to be in the Healdton and Fox oil fields. The first oil well was
brought in on August 13, 1913 at Healdton. On a tract of land that
Ringling had near Cornish (now gone), a town called Ringling was built.
Ringling had also joined with an oilman called Jake Hamon (1873–1920)
of Lawton and Ardmore to build the Ringling Railroad that went from
Ardmore to Ringling and then to Healdton. A silver spike was driven by
Hamon and Ringling in July 1913 to mark the start of the railroad.

Hamon acquired a common-law wife named Clara who prior to meeting
her husband had done stenographic work for my father. I assume that it was
by way of Hamon that Father and Mother became acquainted with Ringling,
but I have no idea how "Count" Eugenio met him. In any event, Mother and
the "Count" were greeted as friends when we arrived at the Ringling residence in Sarasota. I don't recall seeing my mother and the "Count" until we
were ready to leave Sarasota, for I stayed with Ringling and sat up until midnight watching a high-stakes poker game that he presided over and came out
as a big winner. Ringling was a Mason and a Ku Kluxer, but as far as I can
remember the only thing he did contrary to my welfare was to insist that I
puff on a cigar he handed me.

There were two strange things about that poker game. The first is that
the game room in which it was held was almost identical to the game room
in the Ca D'Zan (House of John, now owned by the State of Florida) that

Ringling would not build until 1925–26. Secondly, the men talked about the shooting death of Hamon, and yet Jake would not be shot until the following year. Clara "Hamon" was alleged to have shot him in the Randol Hotel on Main Street in Ardmore, a hundred yards from the Ardmore Hotel where they had previously lived. Actually, he was shot on the mezzanine of the Ardmore Hotel, after which men immediately carried him to the Randol Hotel. I know because I was there. He was shot with a .25 automatic formerly owned by Lilly Langtry, the Jersey Lilly. The bullet was said to have lodged in Jake's liver and supposedly it took him some time to die, so he could have testified against her if he had so desired. There was a time when I would have been willing to bet that the "law man" who admitted giving Clara the .25 automatic had been in the poker game with Ringling the previous year, and that he and two others who had been in that game were the ones who carried the wounded Hamon from the Ardmore Hotel to the Randol Hotel.

Mother, the "Count" and I left Sarasota the next day and went to Miami and on to Key West where we ended in Chase, Florida on Sugar Loaf Key. In 1901, Dr. H.F. More of the U.S. Bureau of Fisheries had established an experimental station on Sugar Loaf Key to experiment with growing sponges. In 1906, Charles W. Chase ("Charley"), a showman from England, persuaded his brother George and a Henry Bate from London to buy the Sugar Loaf Key property from Dr. J.V. Harris who had possession of the More property, having organized the Florida Sponge & Fruit Company. By 1912, a small settlement called Chase was on Sugar Loaf Key. The company started to fail during World War I because England "froze foreign assets." Soon after the war, Chase contracted with Tatum Brothers of Miami to sell shares in the company. R.C. Perky, Sr. was reputedly assigned the stock-selling account. Perky was unable to get people to buy the stock and the company went into bankruptcy in 1919. Perky then reputedly bought the company holdings on Sugar Loaf Key and changed the name of Chase to Perky.

Florida Sponge & Fruit Company employed as many as a hundred men in the "sponge plant." Often there was discord among the men. Pete Chase, son of Charley, was deputy sheriff of Chase. His job was purportedly to drive people off from stealing sponges. Deputy Chase enforced the law in

Keystone Kops fashion, which might have been humorous had there not been something evil permeating the operation.

There weren't many people at Chase in 1919 when I was there, and those who were there, with the exception of laborers, were engaged in operating electrical devices on which were electrodes, meters, graphs, etc. These men talked not of sponges but of magnetism, memory, magnetic fluid, memory reels, and the "Baloney Society" or Societe de Biologia. A man called D'Arsonval was there and his name was used time and time again. There was also talk about the Jekyll Island Club having burned down, along with the word arson. I remember wondering if D'Arsonval had burned down the club.

I also wondered if D'Arsonval had a magnetic crown, for there was talk at Chase of such a crown that could make people do things. I also wondered why, when looking at graphs and meters, the men would sometimes say, "the centipedes are coming" or "some centipedes are here now," because I didn't see any centipedes where they were looking. In back of the building where the men were working, huge black centipedes were kept in cages with electrical devices on them. A woman they called "the centipede woman" lived in a tiny house a short distance who believed she could communicate with the centipedes and actually had a centipede constantly on her dress. The cruelty toward the woman was the epitome of evil; they taunted her and told her that her mind that was half centipede and would soon be all centipede.

One of the men took me to the cage where the centipedes clung to wire mesh and said he wanted me to go in. I was scared, of course. Then he threw a switch and all of the centipedes fell to the floor, stunned by electrical current.

While I was somewhat interested in the centipedes, I was more interested in the ice-making machine. The ice was deep green and after it was frozen was moved on what I called a chute-chute. One day a workman tried to get me in between two pieces of ice coming down the chute and in so doing was crushed.

Things began to fall apart at Chase. Whether the people engaged in sponge research got ptomaine poisoning or some other type of poisoning, I choose to think the centipedes got them. I don't believe that there are any records of centipedes being poisonous enough to kill grown human beings, with the possible exception of *Scolopendra obscura* which I know from experience to be a very peculiar type of centipede. Some people at Chase went out of their minds and were physically ill; some died. Two or three—one of whom said his name was D'Arsonval—got into a rowboat and took off, believing they could row to France. When Dr. Harris arrived at Chase to treat the poisoned people, he immediately had "the centipede woman" taken to the mental hospital in Key West. There is a Central American Indian myth that long ago centipedes developed a mystical power with which they started to take over the world, and they would have done it if not for an army of iguanas that showed up and ate them. They have a ritual based on that old myth in which members of the tribe pretend to be iguanas and eat or pretend to eat centipedes.

The most likely theory regarding the breakdown of Chase, however, is microwave poisoning. There was a large and very high steel tower on the property purportedly used for broadcasting as late as 1938. Old-timers on the Key refer to these structures as "mind control towers."

Mother, "Count" Eugenio, and I left Chase soon after Dr. Harris arrived and went briefly to Key West. Dr. Harris and the "Sheriff" questioned me about things that had occurred at Chase while I was there, and I am sure that I talked chiefly about the poor woman in the cage with the centipedes.

From Key West we went to Cuba and then began what unknowing people might consider a magical sightseeing trip—Haiti, Nassau, the Virgin Islands, the Greater Antilles, Lesser Antilles, West Indies and the Bahamas—but which actually was mapped and detailed in the triptych codebook along with formulated and scheduled events, enough to make anyone who didn't know better embrace theories of determinism. Afterward, we returned to the United States via Mexico City, with a number of stopovers on the way. Every place we went, there were occurrences that in their nature went far beyond ordinary understanding.

When we arrived in Columbus, New Mexico, we checked into the Hoover Hotel. Almost immediately, Mother met Deputy Jack Thomas whom she and her family knew when he was an orphan in the Fort Stockton, Texas area, where he had lived with a number of families. My mother's family had a "sheep ranch" at Coryell, Texas until the sheep died from black tongue; then, they acquired another place near San Angelo. Somewhere along the line, Jack Thomas stayed for a short time with them and only left because they were having difficulty making ends meet. Mother's older half-sister Lilly was married to Frank Lantz who had a huge ranch in Ozona, Texas, where Mother stayed for considerable periods of time. While she stayed on the Lantz ranch, she occasionally saw Jack in Fort Stockton, as Frank and Lilly went there on buying trips and would take her along.

We had only been in Columbus a short time before Mother told me that she and the "Count" were going to have to leave Columbus for a while, and that while they were gone I must not attempt to get in touch with my father or anyone else in Ardmore. She said Jack Thomas would be around to watch over me, but no sooner had they left than Jack left, too. My mother had allegedly left some jewelry with the hotel manager to cover my food and lodging, but immediately after Jack left, the manager's attitude toward me changed. Previously, he had entreated me to sleep with him and even prepared a few decent meals for me, although most of the time I was forced to eat apple butter and bread. But then he ordered me to sleep in bed with him, and when I refused he threatened me and repeatedly did such cruel things as taking the covers off the bed I was sleeping in and removing the rubber hose that connected the gas jet to the stove. Gas was produced by a generator in the back of the hotel. In order to stay warm, I cut the mattress and crawled into the cotton stuffing at night, and in the morning would turn the mattress so the cut wouldn't be seen.

The manager put me in a room at the top of the stairs that can best be described as a death trap. Its one window had a shutter that the manager nailed shut after I had been there a short while. Then he stopped feeding me, saying that the jewelry that my mother had left with him was not valuable enough for him to give me food, so I took the little money I had and bought a paper barrel of ginger snaps and ate them along with what was left of a jar of apple butter that I took from the manager's room.

When my money was gone, the hotel manager discovered the hole in the mattress by noticing that some cotton clung to my clothes after I rose. He went downstairs to get a heavy whip with a bull prick handle on it, and while he was gone, I took the door key. When he returned, saying he was going to beat me to within an inch of my life, he ordered me to come to him. I refused, and when he started to walk toward me, I ran over the top of the bed and into the hall, slamming the door behind me and locking him in the room. He pounded on the door, demanding that I open it, but I just turned on the gas that went into the room and waited. When I could smell the gas coming from under the door, I stood to one side and tossed a lit match toward the bottom of the door. A loud explosion blew the door loose from its hinges. I looked at the unconscious man and then went downstairs and took a blanket from his room; had I taken more blankets, my life would have been much easier for some time after that.

With my blanket around me, I left the hotel and moved to a deserted adobe just a little to the west of Columbus, on the road that was the old Mexican boundary line road.

For what seemed an eternity, I existed in that adobe under conditions that were indescribably dreadful. I scavenged for food. At night I would build a little fire, kneel on gunny sacks in a fetal position, and cover up entirely with the blanket, comforting myself by sucking my thumb. I could sleep very little and managed as best I could to keep the fire going. In the mornings I would search for food, which included fresh cattle droppings. In fact, I existed like a coyote. One day early in the morning, I saw a coyote some distance from the adobe and followed it when it left, and in that way would find things to eat. Every morning for a while a coyote, which I believe was the same one, would be in the same spot, apparently waiting for me.

No one can ever make me believe that everyone in Columbus or Polomas, Mexico, its twin town across the border, didn't know where I was and the way I existed, but no one offered any help. One day I followed my coyote to the carcass of a dead cow just a short distance from the border. When I started to eat part of it, a man who was probably a customs agent shouted and the coyote ran away. I walked up to the man and he told me that the carcass had been poisoned. Then he turned and walked off. The next morning, thinking that he might have told me the carcass was poisoned to keep me from eating, I returned to the carcass and saw a number of dead coyotes near it. I never saw my coyote friend again.

After the explosion, the manager of the hotel had been taken to Deming to the hospital. Seeking retaliation, I went to a water pump in back of the hotel to see if I could get the shooting device with one bullet in it that was on the pump, but found there was no way I could get it off. Shortly after that, when I was trying to get firewood by prying up a board from the bottom layer of adobe bricks of the little shack I stayed in, I discovered a rattlesnake stiff with cold. It could hardly move. Taking pity on it, I took it into the adobe, put it by the fire, and covered it with the gunny sack which I no longer used; I wore knickerbockers and had no stockings, so kneeling on the gunny sack chafed my legs. The snake stayed under the sacks by the fire for a number of days. I often looked at it to see how it was doing and wondered how I could get food for it.

Then a man sent by the hotel manager drove up to my adobe and stalked in. He announced that he was going to get me for what I had done to his friend, and that he had been given a pistol to do it with but didn't need a pistol to do what he was going to do. I told him that I was going to put a spell on him and have a snake bite him, that it was under the gunny sacks, and that he had better get out. He said he wasn't scared of such stuff and picked up the gunny sack to show me, and my snake bit him in the face. He was so scared and in such pain that he didn't even try to prevent me from picking up a stick that I had for the fire and hitting him in the head until it knocked him unconscious. I took his pistol and what money he had, then poured water on him from the barrel of rainwater just outside the door. When he regained consciousness and started begging for help, I got him to his feet and into the car he came in with. He managed to get back to the road and to Columbus where someone I hear took him to Deming. He survived.

Having money now from the man who came to kill me, I went to the store to buy food, but the manager refused to sell me any and ordered me out of the store. Then and there, I threatened to kill him, and he most certainly thought I meant to do it. He said he didn't know that I had any money and had been ordered not to let me have any food. So I bought food of the type that a small child might buy: a gallon of cherries, candy, a huge container of mustard, bread, a barrel of ginger snaps, etc. I put the things into one of my gunny sacks with a board partly supporting the weight and dragged the load back to the adobe shack.

What then occurred most certainly set things in motion for my leaving that dreadful place. Jack Thomas came back to town shortly after the food I had was gone and told me that my mother would be there soon. Then he took me to a café, but I wouldn't go inside. I felt that a trap had been set for me. Jack said he would bring food out to me and asked what I wanted. I told him bread with mustard on it. He went into the café and came out with the bread and mustard, and I stood in the middle of the road gobbling it down. Jack said, "I am going to call you Mr. Mustard." Years later, he told me that he had put a whole jar of mustard on the bread he had bought me.

Mother returned to Columbus a few days after that. She brought some clothes for me and in the adobe shack washed me in water from the barrel of drinking water in which wiggling things swam about. We then walked down the main street of Columbus to the train that was undoubtedly being held for us by Jack and another man who most certainly was the sheriff or a deputy. When we got to the train, I turned and loudly cursed the town and the people in it. Mother then asked me if I had a gun and I said I did, and she made me give it to Jack before she would let me get on the train. She later told me that I should always remember that Jack had helped us when we needed help, and she also told me she hadn't deserted me when she left me in Columbus but that a powerful man named Manby in Taos, New Mexico had held her prisoner. He was the head of a secret society and everyone was scared of him.

Chapter 6

The Blue Front Café on Bloody Elm
Dallas, Texas, 1922

lue is the color of masonry. The first three degrees of Freemasonry are known as Blue Masonry, and a master mason was once called a Blue Master. Now while blue is the color of what is known as the craft degrees, the color purple (which of course is the product of combining blue and red) is the hue of the Royal Arch Degree.

All of this information segues into an arcane concept known as Tavern Masonry, which may sound a bit preposterous to the uninitiated but then to such virgin ears much of what is contained in the Masonic order would seem as such, but people would be extremely foolish if they did not know that this sorcerous clowning was deadly serious and bore consequences and implications of evil far beyond what most might imagine. The legacy of Tavern Masonry extends even into the present, but its history is well documented. Many of the strategy-planning sessions of the American Revolution were held in Masonic temples that doubled as taverns. The list is lengthy: t7he Green Dragon Tavern, the Bunch of Grapes Tavern, the Apple Tree Tavern, and so forth. The Blue Front Café was part of this pattern.

While my sister went to visit former Ardmore residents now living in Bastrop, Louisiana, my mother suggested strongly that I find a job. Max Westheimer said that a job might be had for an enterprising young man—I was then eight—at the Blue Front Café. I informed Mother that I did not trust Westheimer and didn't want to work that summer whatsoever, that I very much preferred to play. Irritated, Mother claimed that Westheimer was a valued family friend and had been instrumental in our leaving Ardmore. She added that when I had knocked over the magnificent dessert, I had destroyed a $500 tablecloth and the Westheimers had said nothing about it.

My mother never hesitated to give me misinformation if it helped to make her point. While Max Westheimer could have paid $5,000 for table-cloths, I doubt that he had spent more than $20 on the one I upended the dessert onto. But still I ended up walking from Oakcliff over the Houston Street bridge to the Blue Front Café located on another sanguineous boulevard with a bloody appellation attached to it, like Caddo in Ardmore: Bloody Elm Street, a street that would go down in infamy in 1963.

Local legends differ on how this street came to have so grisly a moniker. Some said it was due to the whores, pimps, pawnshops and violence on upper Elm Street; others maintained that Elm got its reputation thanks to the industrial and railroad area that was loaded with violence. Still others claimed it had to do with a Negro ghetto where razor-wielding and gunplay were common, a section of Elm called "Ellum" and "Bloody Ellum."

As soon as I entered the Blue Front Café, a man asked me what right I had to be there.

"What right do you have to be here and by what right do you ask?" I shot back.

Almost immediately a bartender came to the front and asked what I wanted. I told him I had come in search of a job. He shouted out someone's name and announced my presence and intent. A man approached from the rear. I told him I was from Ardmore and mentioned Mr. Westheimer's name.

The proprietor called out loudly, "Anyone here know a Westheimer in Ardmore?"

It was customary in bars like the Blue Front and other near-beer joints in Oklahoma and Texas to holler, possibly as an expression of the patrons' camaraderie. The Blue Front struck me at the time as being a friendly café.

In reply to the proprietor's shout, one man replied just as loudly, "I might know him, I was in Ardmore once."

"That's good enough for me," replied the proprietor in a suitably stentorian tone.

Obviously, they were just having fun and I was pleased and relieved at the whimsical ambiance I was witnessing after my consistently harrowing ordeals in Ardmore. Also, the Blue Front sold near-beer and as tasty a roast beef sandwich as I have ever eaten.

a length of two-foot pipe and a hammer I had secreted into the Blue Front a couple of days before. I placed them on the bar and confronted the man behind it, demanding my wages. He said I'd have to wait and see the proprietor.

One of the men I had only seen in the Blue Front a few times before but who wore a continual smirk approached me. "I'm going to shoot you when you get out on the street," he informed me through his smirk.

"I'm going out on the street now," I responded, and we walked into the daylight with him behind me.

Once out on the street, I maneuvered myself so that my back was to the street and I was within reach of the skylight grill that he was then standing on. The man removed a .32-caliber revolver from his belt and challenged me to "Run!"

I had matches concealed in my hand and when his gruff voice shouted out the command to flee, I struck a match and threw it toward the grill but it fell short. Quickly, I stepped closer and tossed another lit match at it. An explosion was channeled straight up. The man who a moment before had been standing erect on the grill, menacing me with his revolver, was blown over to the front door of the Blue Front. Removing my pocket knife, I slit his nostril and then headed for the basement to extinguish the gas flow. The glass window was intact and I closed it after turning the gas pipe around.

Returning to the restaurant with my pipe and hammer in hand, I again demanded of the bartender my wages. He removed some coins from his pocket and gave them to me, saying, "It won't do you a bit of good because you're not even going to get home. They've brought in a professional to kill you."

With this news, I walked back out to the street where a crowd had gathered around an ambulance that had been called. Some of the bystanders had lime on them because the lime at the base of the skylight had been sucked out into the gas explosion where it rained down from the sky like surreal snow. I looked down at the man who had intended to kill me. I had slit his nostril because he had earlier informed me that he was intending to cut off my ears and nose, a threat often voiced in years past.

The wailing siren of the ambulance permeated the air as I walked down Bloody Elm Street toward Houston Street. Somewhere between the Blue

Front and the Houston Street bridge that linked Dallas and Oakcliff, I slipped a shotgun shell into my pipe. I had chosen the pipe with care, and the shell fitted as snugly as it would have fitted a shotgun. As I walked in the sun, I had the distinct impression that peril still stalked me and that my rendezvous with the cryptocracy's *thanatos* men was far from over. Walking bravely but trembling inside, I proceeded down Bloody Elm Street to Houston Street and down Houston toward the viaduct. I was ready for I knew not what, for that part of Bloody Elm that I had traversed had no people or cars on it that were visible to me, and Houston was of similar appearance. Under such circumstances, there was nothing to do but what must be done, and that was to go on.

The Tom Mix Charade

The drama that was about to be enacted on the bridge spanning the Trinity River was part of the so-called eternal pagan psychodrama of which Freemasonry is an indisputable part. Bridges and their symbolism form an important segment in the Mysteries, and in ancient times people were well aware that every bridge had a spirit that required placation in some way. Unquestionably, the cruel, crazy, perverse Freemasons were enacting a bridge charade with me as the intended victim in line with their dogmas about "Freedom of Passage" (FOP) and "Liberty of Passage" (LOP). Men who gathered at both ends of the bridge and who sent my intended assassin were Masons and Ku Kluxers.

When I got to the viaduct, I spied men on either side of it examining something beneath it. My attention was suddenly drawn to another group of men just off the bridge near several parked cars. As I was walking across the bridge, the men who had seemingly been examining the Trinity River made obscene gestures and shouted hateful imprecations in my direction. I turned and began to flee in the opposite direction, but this way was now blocked by other gesturing and shouting men. I wanted to climb over the bridge but this was impossible. I hesitated, temporarily at a loss as to what my plan of action would be.

The small crowd of men that formed on the Dallas side of the bridge parted to make way for a blue roadster which raced the length of the bridge to where I was standing. It executed a 180-degree turn on the middle of the bridge and came to a halt. The roadster's highly polished blue door swung open and out of it stepped a man wearing fancy cowboy clothes. He came across the bridge and took up a position on the sidewalk by the bridge railing about ten feet in front of me.

"Do you know who I am?" he asked.

"No," I responded.

"Why, I'm Tom Mix," he said.

"You don't look like Tom Mix to me," I said, "and I go to all his pictures. I love his horse Tony." The man seemed pleased with my statement.

"There is another Tom Mix, but I'm the real one," he responded.

"Your face looks thinner than the face of the Tom Mix I've seen in the pictures," I told him.

"Well, I've been in the hospital, but they released me so I could do this job," he volunteered. "You see, I'm going to shoot you one way or the other."

He was squinting and his pale skin seemed out of place in the Texas sun.

"C'mon over to the car, boy, and I'll give you something that will make you feel really good, something that makes me feel the way I do. If not, I will shoot you from here," he said, and it seemed as if he really meant to do it. He wore one holstered gun. I noticed then that the holster and revolver were both quite fancy and expensive-looking.

The crowd of men on the Oakcliff side of the bridge were now silent, their gestures stilled; behind me, the men were similarly disposed. Barricades must have been placed to keep traffic off the bridge. When I turned to face the ersatz Tom Mix, his gun was unholstered and pointing at the sidewalk. With one foot on the road and the other on the curb, my left side was higher than my right. I held the pipe with the shotgun shell in it with my left hand and wrapped a handkerchief around it. In my right hand, I held the hammer. The pipe was positioned so that the makeshift barrel end of it was pointing directly at the chest of "Tom Mix." I swung at the pipe with the hammer but missed. Despite the circumstances, I was not nervous, for this Tom Mix character was full of dope and apparently mistook my pipe gun for something more ordinary.

I swung the hammer again. There was a loud report as hammer met pipe. The speeding buckshot struck the impersonator in the upper chest. He dropped his revolver to the sidewalk and turned slightly, draping his upper body on the bridge railing. I thought he was perhaps only wounded since he didn't fall. I rushed and struck him with a severe blow of the hammer. Still he did not fall, so I grabbed him. I was amazed to see that he was extremely light for a grown man, really nothing more than skin and bones. His fancy brocaded shirt was padded. He wore a harness on his upper body and a con-traption that resembled football shoulder pads—devices that all contributed to the illusion that he had a chest of some proportion. Even his pants were padded. I guess the only apparel he wore that wasn't fake were his boots, and quite fancy they were, too. On closer inspection, I discovered that the huge belt buckle he wore had caught on the balustrade, preventing him from falling.

After examining the body of that pitiable creature, I dumped it over the bridge in full sight of the men who were standing in silence on both ends of the bridge. I loaded my pipe gun with another shell and retrieving the fancy, engraved pistol that "Tom Mix" had brandished, I started in the direction of the men nearest me, who let out a holler and ran unceremoniously down Houston Street. Before I knew it, the street was once again clear. I sauntered off the bridge and made my way to where the body lay below. A derelict who had been camping under the bridge was looking at it. He seemed in shock and I stopped only long enough to observe a horrible, needle-marked arm protruding from the sleeve of that now incongruously dressed make-believe man.

"I'm one, too," the derelict said.

From there, I proceeded to the Trinity River, little more than a glorified sewer, and swam and waded in it. I kept my hammer but left the pipe sub-merged in the muck of the riverbank. The bridge was clear at both ends now, with all the men gone who had menaced me. I noticed that their cars had also left the scene.

I arrived at the Starr Street apartment and as if by prearrangement met my mother in the yard where she turned the garden hose on me and washed me free of muck. After this, I went in the house to clean up. My father showed up and announced that we were immediately moving to another part of town. I am convinced that both of my parents knew more about the ordeal I had just passed through than they let on, but it was useless to try and obtain any confirmation from them. I also believe that my father was one of the men standing on the Oakcliff side of the bridge to bar my passage. I compare his being there—if indeed he was—with his presence when the Klansman nailed my hands to the *tau* cross analogue. What's more, I do not believe he was away on a business strip and only "happened" to turn up immediately after the conclusion of my ordeal. On several occasions, I had discovered that at a time when my father said he would be away on a "business trip," he was actually living near us in various apartments or houses. At those times, my mother saw my father often and cooperated in the charades that required his being "out of town on business."

I was glad to hear we were moving to another place, for fear had finally overtaken me and I was apprehensive about the possibility of men coming to get me. We moved with speed and ease. The Starr Street lodging had been furnished, so we needed only to pack our clothes and be on our way. Our new domicile was the Lemmon Avenue Apartments. My sister was enrolled at Bryan High School but then transferred to North Dallas High School, while I attended Travis grade school between McKinney and Cole, approximately four blocks from our apartment in the other direction. I had no idea at the time that what had transpired was part of the great Masonic hoodwink that concealed things that had happened and were about to happen.

Chapter 7

The Snake Charmer and the Three Assassins
Dallas, Texas, 1923

The best-laid schemes of mice and men... Yes, indeed, the best-laid schemes of Masonic sorcerers and others of the *Secret Combination*, including Ku Kluxers, go awry, as did the following ordeal concerning the snake charmer and the three assassins. Their mystical scenario was upset by a grateful snake, a water pistol loaded with Carbona, a brass key, and a pistol made of cast iron like that used in cap pistols.

Prior to my battle with the snake charmer and the three assassins, I had found a crude *crux ansata* (cross with a handle) or *ankh* in a concealed chamber beneath the foundation of a highway called Turtle Creek Boulevard. The *crux ansata* is a symbol of major importance in pre-Christian Egyptian religion, and is therefore an important Mystery sign for Masonic sorcerers. It is actually a type of *tau* (T) cross surmounted by an oval, regarded by the ancients as a symbol of life. When it is depicted with a serpent entwined around it, like the Caduceus of Mercury now used as an emblem of the medical profession, the serpent represents the principle of Eternity and the cross the principle of Life. A serpent on a *tau* cross is used in Knights Templar degrees, as in the Knight of the Brazen Serpent, a Scottish rite degree said to be traced to Numbers 21:9 wherein "Moses made a serpent of brass and put it on a pole."

The snake charmer identified himself by the name Elu, which literally means "elected." This name was charged with significance for me and tinged with more than a little irony. In the Third Degree of Freemasonry, a parable is taught concerning the architect of the Temple of Solomon, Hiram Abif. Hiram was assassinated by what masons call the Three Worthy Craftsmen or the Three Assassins. These assassins were in turn pursued by three others whose code names were *Elu* or *Elus* (plural). Hence, in the Third Degree centered on Hiram Abif, three assassins, and *elus,* we observe an elaborate charade predicated upon detection, punishment, and revenge. An instrument of such revenge was the *Elu* snake charmer, that is for sure. However, I can only speculate at this time as to whether the three men who confronted me after the nice snake swallowed the *Elu* symbolized the Three Assassins—alleged to have killed Hiram Abif, the so-called architect of the Temple of Solomon—or whether they symbolized the *Elus.*

When non-Masonic historians known as *cowans* (outsiders) and other impartial scholars and investigators discover the mystical Hiram assassination/*Elu* charade, members of the Masonic orders always claim that the mystical charade is strictly symbolic and has no relationship to actual current events or actions. That, of course, is part of the Masonic hoodwink, or bullshit.

But perhaps the most amazing thing was how I was consistently prepared in advance for every ordeal by "random" events that in retrospect proved not to have been random at all but actually invisible preparations. In this instance, it was after my mother insisted I go to a specific store and not the one nearest our apartment—and by so doing an *intuitive dread* arose within me that made me arm myself in a way uncannily specific to the task that would occur later.

One Saturday on the way home from picking up a roast for Mother, I saw in a vacant lot a colorfully painted circus wagon/truck, all set up for giving an exhibit of some kind. After pushing my way through the jostling, gaping, neck-craning spectators, I found a man who was acting as a snake charmer of the largest, most stupendous reptile I had ever seen. He called it a python but it must have been an anaconda, for pythons don't get that large. The snake charmer claimed that he had the python in his power and that it was therefore harmless. He was offering a ten dollar prize to any man strong and brave enough to hold part of the weight of the python—an estimated two-thirds—on either shoulder. A line was drawn on the serpent's body showing exactly how much had to be off the ground in order to claim the prize.

With some urging from the crowd, a man finally stepped forward and accepted the challenge, after which the carny snake charmer solicited side bets on whether or not the man could perform the feat. The challenger had great difficulty in picking up the forepart of the serpent, about seven feet from its head, in order to put it on his shoulder. Although he strained and grunted, for the life of him he could not hold the weight of the docile serpent that was no doubt drugged. Actually, that man might well have been a shill used to "milk the suckers."

While the challenger staggered away, I peered at the snake. It looked wretched to me—weak and hungry, not charmed. It had a very appealing cast to its eyes and I sympathized with it, so I covertly loosened the wrapping on the five-pound roast Mother was expecting and quickly thrust it at the snake. When it opened its gargantuan mouth, I saw it had no teeth. Gently, I put the meat in its mouth and it gobbled it down with one immense swallow. I seriously doubt that the snake had been fed anything substantial in a long time, which is why that poor snake looked at me with gratitude in its eyes. (Note: Pythons won't eat meat, but anacondas will.)

The snake charmer of course saw me feed it and became enraged. "How can I control this python with people feeding it?" he shouted, then resumed his game, asking for volunteers from among the spectators. Someone asked me if I wanted to try and before I knew it I said yes.

"How can you put that much weight of the python on your shoulder when a grown man can't even manage it?" the snake charmer asked.

"The snake and I have an understanding," I replied defiantly. The crowd howled with glee at the thought of so seemingly ludicrous a notion.

"Let him try it," someone shouted as the carnival atmosphere escalated.

The snake charmer acquiesced to the wishes of the audience and positioned me about seven feet from the snake's head in the same way as the man who had previously struggled to lift the snake. I started to gently lift the snake as it turned its head and looked at me. Then with my hands under its body, it slowly and gently started to raise the forepart of its body. I felt a not-so-heavy weight on my left shoulder as that magnificent, beautiful snake raised its body and seemingly rested its weight on my left shoulder, thrusting itself forward but somehow managing to keep its weight balanced on its tail. At this point, the snake turned its head and looked in the same direction I was looking: first, at the snake charmer who had an expression of dismay and shock on his face, then at the people smiling from ear-to-ear at the sight of so wondrous a feat.

There was a moment of stunned silence. Then someone punctuated the milieu with a whoop and a holler. "He's done it!" Indeed, the snake's body at the demarcated line was off the ground. Very little weight was on me. The only skill I had to manage was to steady the snake's balance while maintaining my awareness, inching my way backward so that the slight pressure on me by which balance was maintained would not be upset when I freed myself from the pressure.

The snake charmer started to stalk to the circus wagon/truck, shouting, "You will get no money out of me." But the crowd grew angry at the flagrant cheat and insisted that either the carny pay the boy or the crowd would "pay" the carny. With some reluctance, he handed me a ten dollar bill. I ran home with another roast and plenty of change.

About a week later—after I had found Masonic paraphernalia and burned it—I went to pick up a bottle of cleaning fluid called Carbona for my mother. She insisted I go to the little McKinney store across from Travis School, the only building to occupy a large pie-shaped wedge of vacant land that separated Travis School from Greenwood Cemetery. For some reason, I had foreboding and suggested to Mother that I go to a store closer by, but she persisted and so I went. To make the best of what might be a bad situation, I took along a possession that I then regarded as weaponry: a heavy brass key about two feet long made to open the locks on manhole covers and lift them.

En route to the McKinney store, I passed the circus wagon/truck of the snake charmer and found a McKinney store, and purchased not only the Carbona for Mother, but also a two-inch water pistol with a rubber bulb about the size of an eye-dropper with five sticks of almost unchewable gum rubber-banded to it for the reduced price of five cents.

When I came out of the store, I saw a large group of men on the street taking up positions near the play equipment at Travis School. Since I had only been in the store a few minutes, they must have sprinted into place. There was no traffic anywhere, which meant that the feeder streets had likely been blockaded. An ordeal was in the making such as had been made to occur on the Houston Street bridge. Weighing the recent events on the bridge with the fast-developing repeat scenario, I had the wit to improvise a weapon by loading the Carbona cleaning fluid into my water pistol. I then headed in the direction of home. As I approached the circus wagon/truck at the Sneed Street intersection, the snake charmer came out of his house wearing a fez that sported an emblem I had not seen before on a fez.

"You took my snakes," he shouted with a blood-curdling shout. "I will have you destroyed. I am an *Elu*."

For a moment I mistook his pronunciation and thought he said, "I am a Ballew." D.M. Ballew (1877–1922) was Sheriff Buck Garrett's deputy and friend in Ardmore, reputed to have killed a number of men. Without telling the snake charmer what I thought of him, I said, "I know Bud Ballew." The fez-hatted carny said nothing to this, so I asked, "How will you have me destroyed?"

"I am the last of those with *serpent power* and I'm going to put _____" (here he called out an indecipherable name) "on you."

I supposed he was referring to that beautiful snake of which I was fond and which I believed was fond of me. As I started to run past him he pulled out a pistol and pointed it at me. I too had a pistol, fully the equal of his, though he would have never believed it. I shot him in the eyes with my Carbona-loaded water pistol, and followed it up with a punch to his diaphragm while holding my pocket knife blade out.

The snake charmer fell face forward as if on cue. It was then that the wondrous creature, my beautiful snake friend, slithered across the yard of the carny's house. At once, a simultaneous thought seemed to pass through my mind and that of the snake because it pointed its head in the direction of where I was heading. I went to the nearby manhole cover and removed it with my giant brass key. I looked down into the hole and saw three tunnels heading off in different directions. I returned to the prone snake charmer and removed his clothing. While thus engaged, I glanced at the men gathered on McKinney and in the Travis School yard, who were watching me with a combination of horror and fascination.

The snake was close at hand, so I said, "See if you can get your rear part in that hole."

Whether the snake read my mind or words, I don't know, but it flipped its tail around and into the hole, and in about a second only one-third of its body was in the street. I then pushed the snake charmer toward the waiting, gaping mouth of my snake friend. It didn't take long for the creature to swallow the carny that had tormented it. After dining, the snake slithered down into the tunnels and I replaced the manhole cover but didn't lock it. Then I straightened up and faced the crowd of men still standing nearby. I yelled at them and made like I was starting for them, at which they scattered and ran. I set fire to the snake charmer's clothes, then thought I would have a look in his circus wagon/truck.

As I walked across the yard, I saw a coral snake with two tails, a gila monster, and a cobra that apparently had been born with parts of its organs in a skin sack outside its body. The cobra was upright and swaying back and forth. Suddenly, its head darted forward and touched my right hand. I thought it had attempted to bite me and missed, but when it opened its mouth I saw that it had no teeth. I was struck by deep sympathy for this poor creature that had had its teeth pulled and had to drag some of its entrails around in a skin sack whenever it moved. Without thinking, I bent down and kissed its head.

Immediately, the cobra, the double-tailed coral snake, and the gila monster went into some kind of ecstasy. The cobra wriggled and squirmed as it raised up as high as it could, while the smaller coral snake, standing on its tails, rose up higher than the cobra, fell and rose up again and again, and the gila monster squirmed on its back, as dogs are known to do, until it eventually had an orgasm.

I looked up McKinney Street. A black roadster that may have been a Model T approached, made a U-turn, then stopped. Three men got out and stood facing me. I had added the snake charmer's pistol to my arsenal, fabricated from cast iron and resembling a cheap starter's pistol that fires only blanks. But in fact this gun handled live ammo. The telltale mark of starter pistols that shoot only blanks is a steel rod inside the barrel; this pistol did not have such a rod, though the three men facing me probably did not know that.

I examined the bullets in the pistol; they were real. I then proceeded to the middle of the street. When I was about fifty feet from them, two of the men turned and walked to the yard of a corner house. One of them said something to me that I don't recall. The lone man remaining in the street had a pistol in his right hand and stood motionless. While the two men in the yard fiddled with a water faucet, I rushed toward the man in the street who shouted, "YOU SHALL NOT PASS!" He made a motion with his hands that I am at a loss to describe. I took this to be an opportune moment to attack and so shot him. The two men in the yard came toward me and I started to shoot them, too, but they threw their hands in the air and pleaded, "Don't!" I then permitted them to put the wounded man in the roadster. As they drove away, however, the man in the passenger seat turned and pointed a pistol in my direction. Before he could get off a shot, I shot and hit the driver, who still managed to continue to operate the roadster.

Despite the great noise and excitement, no one came out of the many homes lining the street. No automobiles or streetcars traversed McKinney, a busy metropolitan thoroughfare. I walked home without further incident and only stopped long enough to break the cast iron pistol apart on a concrete curb. Mother greeted me in a peculiar way, as though she had not expected to see me. I saw a strange, dream-like look in her misty eyes, as if she had been stupefied by something, and I wondered if she had been made aware of what had occurred.

As evening grew into night, I thought over the things that had happened at the Blue Front Café and in the adjoining Masonic lodge in the abandoned firehouse, as well as what had happened on the Houston Street bridge. It was a marvel how the Masons and Ku Kluxers were able to flout the laws of the country and get away with it, even to the extent of being able to blockade well-traveled city streets in order to do their dirty work. While thinking along these lines, I started to shake and shiver with cold, and so I got into bed, pulled the covers over my head, and assumed my fetal position for sleeping as I had so often done since my ordeal in Columbus, New Mexico.

Chapter 8

My First Gun

Dallas, Texas, 1924

Regarding the ineluctable perils to which I was exposed, "The Perils of Pauline," as portrayed by Pearl White, shaded into insignificance. Not only did my mother know the cast of characters who would bring about the charades that imperiled my life, but in the ordeal related below she made me loan out my shotgun so I would not have it when I needed it most. But such insights were far from me in those days, as I was not old enough yet to recognize the connections in the sequence of unpleasant and violent incidents that befell me. Nor did I recognize any association between the seemingly innocent things that would occur prior to my ordeals. The logical continuity of the rapidly occurring events utterly escaped me while they were happening. Remembering—*remembering*—is what has revealed patterns of events that point unerringly to the intelligence of the mystical Masonic hoodwink.

To show how relentlessly mystical charades permeated my life, I present the story of how I came to own my own shotgun. It has been said that America's gun culture grew with its gun industry, which may have some truth to it. Samuel Colt helped to move the gun from being thought of as a mere tool to being an object of romance with his advertising campaign for the Colt .45 in the two decades before the Civil War. With the mass production of guns in the mid-nineteenth century, as well as a more sophisticated technology, they became much easier to load between shots, were made more lethal, and America officially became the gun culture it still is today.

During my struggles to survive my ordeals, I developed some "situational ethics" that helped me to survive. Some are no doubt appalled by my "situational ethics," but no one should deny an individual's right to defend himself, much less the right of a child to do so. Out of necessity, I developed a cunning and creative arsenal of weapons with which to defend myself—a squirt gun, a brass key, sewing scissors, kitchen matches—but without the gun I never would have seen even my seventh birthday, which was why I looked forward to having a gun of my own.

The morning after the snake charmer ordeal, Mother gave me coffee and bread for breakfast, which was unusual. She often said coffee would stunt my growth, and as I was quite aware of being small, I never complained about not having it, though I really liked it. The next surprise was that she said she had been thinking it over and had decided that I could have a small shotgun, if it didn't cost too much. She had disposed of Grandfather's pistol, saying that she and my father had decided it wasn't safe to have a gun in the house, so talk of letting me have a shotgun was a major concession.

Some time before lunch, we went to Montgomery and Ward's. Mother asked the salesman how much single-shot, small-gauge shotguns cost. He put a .20-gauge shotgun on the counter and told her the price. She then asked if he thought I was big enough to have such a gun, at which I told him I would just as soon have a .410. The salesman then looked over at a well-dressed Negro wearing a pistol and standing maybe fifteen feet from the gun counter, and launched into a talk with Mother about a young boy having a shotgun.

Disgusted by the way things were going, I too looked at the Negro and vaguely wondered if I had ever seen a Negro wearing a gun before. Was he a deputy? But then I couldn't recall ever seeing a Negro deputy. So I walked over to him and asked him what he thought of my having a gun. He said he not only approved but would get me any kind of gun I wanted. He said he knew about me, he had seen me on the bridge and could hardly believe what he had seen. I believed him but wondered why I hadn't seen a black face among all the white faces on both sides of the bridge. I asked him what his name was and he said, "James Amos." I asked if he were a deputy and he demurred. I then asked him if he would come to the gun counter and tell my mother that he thought it was all right for me to have a shotgun, and so he did, even telling her that he would buy it for me.

The salesman asked him who he was and he produced some identification, showing it first to Mother and then the salesman. Mother thanked him for offering to pay for the gun, but said it wasn't necessary. Then she told the salesman she would take the gun and put money on the counter. The salesman took the shotgun apart, wrapped it up, and handed it to me. I thanked James Amos warmly, and Mother and I left the store. Outside, I told mother that I didn't remember ever seeing a Negro wearing a gun and asked her if he was a deputy or what, and she said that he was a detective. She wouldn't tell me any more about James Amos, and as far as I can remember I didn't see him again for years.

About that time, Mother obtained the services of a Negro washerwoman who had a house on Lemmon Avenue in a Negro area that bordered on Bloody Ellum, where the so-called "freedmen" had settled in some numbers after the War between the States. Our wash always came back spotless and ironed to perfection, and I joked with Mother, saying, "Your Negro washerwoman must have taken this wash to the best laundry in Dallas for you," which, I realized later, may well have been true. When Mother had more dirty laundry, she took me in a taxi to the Negro woman's house, telling the white taxi driver to wait for us. The Negro woman greeted us graciously at the door. Mother gave her some type of pastry she had made and we entered her house. Once inside, the woman started to show me around.

In her kitchen was a wood-burning stove on which irons were getting hot. There was also an ironing board and a wicker basket with clothes to be ironed in it. She took us out into the backyard where a large iron cauldron filled with soapy water was boiling over a wood fire. It reminded me of the cauldrons in which African cannibals reputedly boiled missionaries and into which Mexican witches sometimes put human body parts and blood.

The Negro woman said, "I use lye soap to wash with and I make it myself." She then lifted dirty clothes with a well-used broom handle and dropped them into the water, poking them ever deeper.

She was very cordial to me, but as we were leaving, I said to Mother, "I wonder how many miles she got out of her broom before she started using its handle the way she does."

We then got in the taxi where the driver sat in stony silence and went home.

As we were getting out and Mother paid him, he said, "I wouldn't go to that place again if I were you."

Several days passed, when the telephone rang. After talking a while and saying she would see what she could do, Mother hung up and said to me, "The washerwoman says her neighbor is having some trouble with the Ku Klux Klan and needs help. Will you go and find out what is happening? Maybe you could take your shotgun and loan it to the poor man."

I said I would and took with me my unassembled shotgun that was still wrapped up and with it a handful of shells. I ran to the washerwoman's house and was so out of breath that I could hardly talk, but asked her where the man lived who was having trouble. She directed me to a house around the corner.

There were no Ku Kluxers at the house. I knocked politely but no one came to the door. I sat on a front step and assembled my shotgun, then went to the door again and knocked harder, saying, "I have come to help you, there is no one out here but me, open the door." Several minutes later, the door opened and a Negro man peered out but wouldn't let me in. I told him, "The Negro washerwoman around the corner called my mother and said you were having Klan trouble, so I am going to lend you my shotgun to defend yourself with in case they come back and try to hurt you before the police get here. Mother has called the police." (I of course assumed she had called the police, but she hadn't.) The Negro reached out and took the shotgun and shells, then closed the door without saying a word, much less thanking me. I stopped by the washerwoman's house and told her what I had done and how strangely her neighbor had acted, then walked home.

The next day, the very same thing happened. When I asked Mother if she had called the police, she said she had but added, "You know how the police are about Negroes in Dallas." I told her I didn't want to go back there again, and that the Negro had my shotgun and could defend himself. She begged me "for her sake," and so back I went. Once again, the Negro man didn't come to the door and once again I sat on the steps and tried to figure out what was going on. It was then that an old touring car with its top down drove up with two white men in Klan garb but without hoods. On the back seat were two round five-gallon tin containers with gasoline in them. I could tell because I could smell gasoline across the narrow sidewalk.

When the two Ku Kluxers got out of the car, I got some kitchen matches out of my pocket and continued to sit quietly on the steps. They were
smiling when they came up the steps, and just as they grabbed me one of
them said, "We have you now." Then they took me to the back of the car as
I pretended to struggle. They tied my wrists with one end of a rope that was
possibly thirty feet long; the other end was tied to the back of the car. While
all of this was going on, Negroes gathered across Lemmon Avenue on both
corners but did nothing; they just watched what was going on.

One of the Ku Kluxers told me that they were going to drive slowly down
Haskel and for me to stand where I was until all the slack was out of the rope
or they would shoot me. So I stood where I was until the slack was out of
the rope and they started pulling me behind the car. It was then that the
Negroes on both corners of the street started walking across the street to
block the car's passage. The Ku Kluxer in the passenger seat stood up and
shouted, "We are taking him to be burnt on a cross," and pointing a pistol
at the crowd, continued shouting, "Get out of the way, I will shoot anyone
who tries to stop us."

That was when I ran forward but stopped just before getting to the car.
Leaning down, I struck one of the matches. In those days, you could strike
them anywhere, so the match blazed up and I tossed it on top of one of the
gasoline containers. The top of the container caught fire, and when I saw that
I yelled to the Negroes who were close to the car to get back. I ran backward
to the far end of the rope and fell face down.

Then there was an explosion. I looked around and saw that both Ku
Kluxers were on fire but had somehow gotten out of the car. They fell to the
pavement and started rolling around, and it was then that I yelled to the
Negroes to try and help them. Bravely, they did as they were asked to do
while I untied my hands. By the time the Ku Kluxers' burning garb had been
put out, I had stalked away. I began to run as soon as I was out of sight.

When I got home, I waited expectantly to hear the sound of the black
mariah (police van) coming to get me, but it never came. The next morning
nothing was in the *Dallas Morning News* or *Dallas Dispatch* about what had happened, so I retraced my steps. I went to the washerwoman's house, but she
wasn't there. I went to the house of the Negro whom I thought I had helped;

he was there but again wouldn't come to the door, so I forced open the door to get my gun that was leaning against the wall to the side of the door. The fact of the matter was that I had been hoodwinked and the whole affair had been a mystical charade. The Negro who was supposed to have been threatened by the Klan was part of it, as was the Negro "washerwoman."

Back at home, I didn't even want to talk to my mother because I knew that knowingly or unknowingly she had played her part, too.

Around the same time, I bought a BB gun with money that I took from my father's inside coat pocket while he took his afternoon nap. The bills I took were part of the "garage money," yet another mystery in my parents' secret life that would resurface when we moved to Ohio. While on Lemmon Avenue, we had at least two garages, one of which housed our Reo automobile as well as various books that I was told were business records and books with unissued stock certificates in them. This garage was declared off-limits to me. One day, I managed to come into temporary possession of the key to that garage. In the course of my investigations, I came across a box about four feet wide and two and a half feet long. I pried off the lid and could scarcely believe the sight that lay before me, for in that box were stacks and stacks of crisp bills in various denominations wrapped with paper bands—two rows of stacks of currency. The amount must have been significant.

After taking out a couple of ten dollar bills and pocketing them, I carried the box and its contents into our apartment and displayed them to my parents who, for a change, were both home. I told them where I had found the money, and that it appeared to be uncirculated bills fresh from the mint. At first, they disavowed any knowledge of it. Then after they saw my skepticism, they launched into one wild tale after another. First, it was the "house money" from Ardmore, which they claimed had to be kept secret from the Lion Bonding Company of Kansas City that had a judgment against one of my father's paving companies in the wake of his inability to sell his "paving bonds." This made little sense to me even then and less so when I heard variations later, one of which was that Secret Service agents had said it was counterfeit money and confiscated it. Several days later, while Mother and Father were still trying to accommodate themselves to my discovery, the contents of the garage were destroyed in a fire. Oddly, the fire was confined to the books, records, and car, while the garage itself sustained only minor damage. Shortly after this, Father went on another of his "business trips."

I bought a new Benjamin single-shot BB gun from a hardware store adjacent to Highland Park, with an air pump whose pressure could be so increased that the air gun would shoot a BB quite hard. I immediately showed my mother the gun, telling her that I had gotten it by trading with my childhood chum, Billy Whyte, who resided with his mother and stepfather and seamstress grandmother across the street from our apartment building. Billy accompanied me on a number of adventures, not because I enjoyed his company but because, according to my personal code, this was simply how friends were to be treated. He was, in fact, a liability and placed my life in genuine peril on a number of occasions. In short, I did not recognize him for what he was.

The day after I'd shown the BB gun to my mother, she told me that my father hadn't slept well the previous night and that my moving around in the apartment would prevent him from a good nap. She wanted me to go and sit on the steps in front of the apartment house next door and show the vacant apartments to prospective renters, if possible, so that we might get a commission if I rented any of them. She said I could take my BB gun with me but that I must not shoot it while I was there.

I did as I was told and was sitting on the steps when a man drove up and stopped in front of the apartment house. I asked him if he wanted to rent an apartment. (At that time, every apartment in the complex except ours was vacant, and there were four apartments in every apartment house.) He said he didn't want to rent an apartment, but from the way I handled my gun he could tell I liked guns. He liked guns, too, he said. He was, in fact, going to see a rifle made by a gunsmith friend, and wondered if I would like to go with him to see it, it wasn't far. So I ran and asked Mother, who said I could go.

We drove to a nice-looking bungalow and walked right in. Inside was a small, well-equipped workshop with a lathe, power drill, etc. At the workbench sat a man I recognized, and immediately I was fearful. The man I came with said, "I brought this boy to see the wonderful rifle you made," at which the "gunsmith" pointed to a gun rack where there were a number of guns of different types. The man I came with picked up a heavy rifle, opened the chamber, and handed it to me. I could see that the rifle chambered cartridges with large casings, but I had only to look at the end of the barrel to see that the bullet shot was much smaller than its casing. I said as much and added that I would like to see the cartridges this gun shot.

The "gunsmith" then handed me a wooden bullet, huge on one end and small on the other, and said, "This is the type of bullet it shoots. I make my own. We will go out now and see how the rifle shoots." He then picked up some real bullets in a box on the workbench. I protested that I couldn't go with them, that I had to go home and if the man who had brought me couldn't take me home, I would run home because I knew my mother was expecting me. My protestations didn't help in the least. They then escorted me to the car, letting me take my BB gun along as if they considered it harmless. We drove to a vacant field not far from where I had bought the BB gun, and walked into the field, the "gunsmith" carrying his "wonderful rifle" and I my BB gun.

In the field, a peculiar thing happened. The man who had enticed me to go with him to see the "wonderful rifle" said, "I don't want to see it" and left. Almost immediately, a man wearing a pistol appeared out of nowhere, took his place, and just as quickly walked away, saying, "I don't want to see it." The "gunsmith" then put the stock of his wonderful rifle under his upper right arm, took from his coat pocket a fez with some type of emblem on it, and announced that he was going to shoot me but that I could try to run away if I wanted. So I ran maybe as much as fifty feet, then turned and faced him. My BB gun was well pumped with only one BB in it, and that was all it took to take out the gunsmith's eyeball. And so the attempt of the three assassins to murder me failed again, and the "gunsmith" should have done what his friends did who said they didn't want to see it.

Chapter 9

Cagliostro's Treasure House

Dallas, Texas, 1925

Yet again, reality would be altered, this time through my playmate William "Billy" Whyte. A stage was set upon which I was fated to play a role in yet another scene in a long occult drama. Always at the conclusion of the dramas to which I was subjected, I would wonder about my mother's role in it. *Had she intentionally set me up?* I would ask myself, and then answer, *Of course not, my mother loves me.*

Behind Billy's house across the alleyway was a duplex owned by a man living in one half while the other half was kept vacant. For a time, I had been employed by this man as groundsboy and he had cheated me of my wages. One day, Billy somehow obtained a key to the vacant duplex, and when we entered, we found a fantastic mélange of incredible objects. This duplex housed everything from fatal trap doors and murderous dummies to serious *objets d'art.* There was an Egyptian mummy and sarcophagus, an Iron Maiden, a magnificent antique table, a functional crossbow, a whip with a bull prick handle, and a commode and porcelain chamber pot with the portrait of a man in the bottom of it. There was also a startlingly handsome cane in an expensive-looking ebony hardwood box lined with velvet.

One item that hovered somewhere between the ridiculous and sublime was another fancy commode as magnificent as any used in the most aristocratic French bedrooms. On and around this commode were yellowed circulars announcing the coming of "Cagliostro the Magician" to a theater whose name I did not recognize. I opened the commode and placed the circulars into the slop jar, much to Billy's dismay. I surmised that the man who owned this veritable treasure house was none other than the same Cagliostro whose feats of illusion were advertised on the commode.

What warranted closer inspection, however, were three contraptions. One was a door with a lintel, posts and sill uprighted by means of two cross-pieces parallel to the sill. It had a cleaver on it that could be cocked by compressing a spring. When so cocked, the cleaver would be released when the door was opened and the sill depressed by stepping on it. There was also a doorpost mechanism that would release the cleaver and prevent it from slashing a person going through the doorway. The next contraption was an intricate device consisting of a cast-iron water pump on which was affixed a shooting mechanism that would fire a projectile when the handle of the pump was worked. The final minor wonder—at least to boyish eyes—was a ventriloquist's dummy that had concealed within it a large, heavy spring-mounted knife-blade that stabbed outwardly with tremendous force when a trigger on the doll was activated. Then, when the blade of the clandestine weapon was pressed, it vanished into the corpus of the dummy.

Soon after our discovery of the treasure house, Billy's stepfather—an employee in the sales department at Briggs Weaver Company and a Freemason—approached me about joining the Order of DeMolay, the Masonic youth branch. I was almost thirteen, the age Masons recruit youths for the juvenile section of their great criminal brotherhood. During his recruitment pitch, he mentioned that instruction would be given in the other half of the duplex owned by Cagliostro. Had I known something about the notoriety surrounding DeMolay and the cognate Masonic trickster Cagliostro, I might have besieged Billy's stepfather with questions and skepticism. But I consented to join and by this assent was ushered into the presence of the man who called himself Cagliostro, though he immediately told me to call him Beppo.

Two other boys and I reported for DeMolay instruction at Cagliostro's duplex. Immediately, a man I had never seen before began a question-and-answer ritual by asking if we knew Solomon. I related that I had read something about the judgment of Solomon and his reputed wisdom and prudence. Throughout the session, I was silently thinking about the deadly "toys" in the house and what I was doing in that booby-trapped treasure domain. When it was over, I ran the short distance home in the dark with suspicions and apprehensions pursuing me.

I was extremely reluctant to go back, but was encouraged to do so by my mother. Before leaving, however, I secreted a thick *Saturday Evening Post* under my shirt front, thinking the whole time about the dummy with the knife blade. The second meeting began in much the same way as the first, until we were told to close our eyes tightly. I pretended to, but squinted to watch the man's actions. He placed the dummy on his knee in the fashion of a stage ventriloquist, then ordered us to open our eyes. After a few minutes of doing a ventriloquist's routine meant to impart some portion of DeMolay gnosis, he passed the doll to one of the other candidates to hold with the dummy's head resting on his left shoulder. I gazed intently to see if the man was going to trigger the hidden blade, which he did not.

Now the toy was passed to me. I held it in the same manner as the other boy, but almost as soon as I had assumed the correct position, in a darting motion the boy triggered the doll. I felt a heavy thud strike my chest where the blade had struck the thick magazine. The two boys and adult looked at each other in amazement as I suppressed any sound of surprise or discomfort and just sat there, pretending all was well and nothing had happened.

The man took back the dummy and before quickly pressing the knife-blade back into place ordered us to shut our eyes once again. Squinting, I watched him pass the doll to the boy who had tried to stab me. As soon as he did, I reached over and triggered the blade. The boy's face went instantly white. He froze, and beads of sweat materialized on his forehead. The man and other boy pulled the doll off the injured youth and opened his shirt. For some reason, only the tip of the blade had penetrated the boy's flesh to a depth of about one inch so there was only a small amount of blood and a superficial wound. The three of them scurried out the door and drove off in the man's car.

Indeed, the DeMolay instruction was another perfidious charade.

The next day, I reentered Cagliostro's treasure house to secret away the sword-cane which I then hid in tall grass in the alley near the duplex. The next phase of my plan involved the seemingly innocuous gesture of asking the boy who lived near the alley on Travis Street to accompany me skating. He agreed, and in the course of our walk to a choice skating area he retrieved the sword-cane without realizing that the cane was a disguised sword. I offered to purchase it from him and he agreed. I took it home with me, then displayed my prize to Billy who, I surmise, promptly informed the man who fancied himself a latter-day Cagliostro. As soon as the stage illusionist learned of my booty, he marched up the stairs to my home and demanded to see me, but I was not at home. Some days later, Mother insisted that I meet with him, so I headed to his home. It appears that she telephoned him to warn him of my impending arrival, for no sooner had I walked onto his yard than he came rushing out at me with pistol in hand. I continued walking boldly toward him until we stood face to face.

"You have my sword-cane and I want it back," he glowered.

"I don't have your old cane," I told him, which was true; I'd given it away. I was fuming with anger. Not only had this man cheated me of my rightful wages for lawn chores, but he was undoubtedly part of the strategem to injure me by means of the ventriloquist's dummy.

"I am the magician Cagliostro. I am going to kill you!" he shouted as he raised his pistol and pointed it at me.

It is a traditional ruse of psychological warfare that during life-and-death confrontations, combatants compare themselves to some force or announce that they are a type of powerful animal that can overcome anyone (even children do this in imitation of adult patterns). Perhaps I did not know what a magician actually was or who Cagliostro symbolized, but I was determined to overcome that "Beppo" creature, so I shouted, "I am the devil and YOU are about to die." Almost immediately, there was a noise that sounded like a shot. Beppo dropped his gun to the ground and walked slowly back to his house.

A Cole Street passerby exclaimed, "Wasn't that a shot?"

"It sounded like a shot to me," I said.

As Beppo entered his house, I picked his pistol up off the ground. On closer inspection, it turned out to be yet another of the wonders that seemed to accompany this magician the way paper adheres to glue. It was fabricated out of bakelite, an early forerunner of modern-day plastics. The barrel was huge for a pistol, with the circumference of a .12-gauge shotgun. It carried a clip holding several projectiles as large as CO_2 cylinders such as those used to make fizzy water. I removed one and observed that it was tipped with a hollow needle that did not come off when I tried to extract it but which emitted a drop of fluid under pressure. I replaced the projectile in the clip and fired the gun at the horizon. Sparks flew from the upper part of the clip and followed the trajectory of the projectile with ease about a hundred feet. I was enraged that "Beppo" Cagliostro had intended to shoot me with so fearsome and diabolical a contraption.

Removing the remaining hypodermic projectile from the pistol, I concealed it in one hand and carried the firearm in the other. As I entered the house, I encountered Cagliostro's sentry who had positioned himself by the stairwell with a clear view of both front and rear entries. (This was the same man who had played the "gunsmith.")

"Where is Beppo?" I asked him.

"Upstairs on the phone," was the gruff reply. I started up the stairs. "Hey!" the sentry shouted. "No one goes up there armed. Hand over that pistol now." I complied, keeping the needle-bullet carefully concealed in my other hand.

I ran up the stairs two at a time and reached the second floor where Beppo stood by a bed in a room slightly off the staircase, speaking on the telephone. He dropped the phone when he saw me.

"Come in here," he ordered in a fierce tone. As I approached him, he grabbed my left wrist. His grip was powerful and he started twisting my arm as though to throw me on the bed. I struggled to free myself and was able to stick him with the bullet hypodermic as I shoved him toward the bed. Quickly grabbing the telephone receiver by the cord, I hit him with it, then turned and ran down the stairs past the sentry who only made a pretense of trying to prevent me from leaving.

Two days later, the *Dallas Morning News* reported that in the course of a burglary, the owner of a Lemmon East home had surprised two thieves and was shot and killed by them. Following the story was the announcement of the victim's funeral, which was to be conducted by the Masonic order.

Cagliostro's sentry paid a call on me, but I was not at home. According to my mother, he informed her that the deceased "liked and admired me." Although I would not be permitted at the lodge funeral, as a "matter of respect" the sentry insisted that I come to the corner of Cole and Lemmon Streets where the funeral car procession would assemble. Just before the procession departed, I would be signaled to come forward.

Naturally, I wanted to have nothing further to do with the magician or his cronies, dead or alive. But Mother repeatedly insisted, "Won't you do this for me?" So when it came time for the funeral, I was standing at the corner wondering what would happen next. At the signal from the sentry, I ran across the street and asked him what would be required of me; the hearse and mourners' cars were just pulling away. He handed me a paper and ordered me to give it to a man sitting in the back seat of an open touring car between two men; it would be the last car in the procession. He then left, running up the street and barking something out to men in the two cars preceding the one he entered.

I trotted over to the appointed car and jumped on the running board. I extended the paper to the designated man, using my right hand to retain my grip on the moving automobile. The man I offered the paper to paid no attention to it but grabbed my left hand, endeavoring to pull me into the vehicle. I struggled desperately to get free. "We know you killed him and we are going to take you out and bury you with him," he said menacingly.

Frantically, I let go of my hold on the car, and steadying myself solely with my legs and knees, I reached into my back pocket for my switchblade. Popping the blade out, I slashed my assailant and inflicted a deep gash on his hand. He released me as he cried out. His two companions on either side of him just stared like dummies or as if drugged. I jumped from the running board, knife still in hand, and cursed them all.

The funeral procession then came to a screeching halt, as though all the cars including the hearse were connected and had run into a stone wall. For a moment, it seemed as if they might all attack me. Instead, a tall man in black got out of the lead car just behind the hearse, faced me in a ceremonial manner, and shouted something I did not catch. He then reentered the car and the funeral proceeded without the rear car carrying the man with the wounded hand, which sped off at the first right-hand turn.

Once again, in line with the occult pattern of Masonic sorcery, no other traffic was to be seen on Lemmon and Cole during the ordeal, nor were there any policemen about, unless they too were concealed within the procession.

Chapter 10

Re-Traumatization and Radiesthesia
Dallas, Texas, 1925

In 1925, when I was twelve, my family and I moved from Lemmon Avenue to Throckmorton Street in nearby Oaklawn, a Dallas suburb. We had lived in Oakcliff before. The *oak* may have been a signal that onomancy (divination through names) was going on. Next door to us was Houston Elementary School where I was fond of "Miss Haskell," my teacher or substitute teacher or who knows who she was, for she played a strange role in re-traumatizing me. Still, I thank her for teaching me to recite "Abu Ben Adam" by James Henry Leigh Hunt (1784–1859):

Abu Ben Adam (may his tribe increase)
Awoke one night from a deep dream of peace
And saw, within the moonlight of his room
Making it rich, like a lily in bloom
An angel writing in a book of gold.
Exceeding peace had made Abu Ben Adam bold
And to the presence in his room he said
"What writest thou?"
The vision raised its head
And with a look of all sweet accord
Answered, "The names of those who love the Lord."
"And is mine one?" said Abu.
"Nay not so," replied the Angel.
Abu spoke more low
But cheerily still and said, "I pray thee then
Write me as one that loves his fellow-men."
The angel wrote and vanished. The next night
It came again with awaking light
And showed the names of whom love of God had blessed.
And lo! Ben Adam's name led all the rest.

In those days, school children in the Lone Star State were indoctrinated with what is known as Texas history; maybe they still are. This indoctrination was chiefly oriented toward the alleged exploits of men known as "Texas heroes" during the war with Mexico that resulted in the separation of Texas from Mexico. Contrarily, "Miss Haskell" devoted much time to reviewing the life and actions of Pancho Villa and the invasion of Columbus, New Mexico by the band of greasers he commanded. As a feature of this history lesson, an inexpensive "field trip" to Columbus was organized for some children, including me. For me to make such a trip was quite fantastic because Mother incessantly talked about how poor we were. Besides "Miss Haskell," two other teachers went along.

When we arrived in Columbus, we were hurriedly driven around town in a bus, after which I was immediately separated from the other children who were taken to Deming to stay at a hotel while I was boarded with some greasers. No sooner was I left in Columbus than the entire past episode of my previous existence in that dreadful place came rushing into my consciousness, including my mother's role in setting it up. It was all happening again! My previous stay in Columbus when I was six had been a child's worst nightmare. I had lived in the manner of a feral child, scavenging and eating cattle droppings, helped only by a coyote and a snake. I remembered riding a stick horse up onto one of the Tres Hermanas mountains that overlooked Columbus, and imagining that I was the fifth horseman of the apocalypse and cursing the evil people of that area and all others like them.

The greaser woman I was boarded with made me a peanut butter sandwich, and after eating it, I told her I was still hungry, to which she said, "That is all we have and that is all you get. You are not wanted here, anyway." I then stole a butcher knife from her kitchen, thinking that once again I was going to have to fight to survive. That night I slept in a shed instead of her house. I am quite sure she called "Miss Haskell," who came to get me and dropped the pretense of a school-sponsored "educational trip." I was immediately returned to Dallas and home.

My last memory of "Miss Haskell" is when she kept me after school a few days later, declaring that she was going to give me "a good talking-to." Being kept after school was nothing unusual for me. At Travis Elementary, I'd had to wear a dunce cap until I had declared, "This is no dunce cap when I put it on, but a wizard's hat, for I am the real Wizard of Oz." So "Miss Haskell" said, "I know about you and who you are. I know the frightful things you have done and I will say this here and now: If a grown man had done such things, it might be said that he was a brave man defending himself, but for a child to do such things is frightful. Can't you see the difference and how horrible it is?" Her statement drifted between the bounds of a declaration and a question, until she added, "You are a monster!"

Then, it was my turn. "I don't think it is very smart of you to know about me, Miss Haskell, since I'm in your class and I live next door to the school. Anyway, what is horrible is the way I have been and am treated, and as for me being a monster, you might add that I am a nice, kind-hearted, friendly monster, and as for me being a child, believe me, I am no child. They wouldn't let me be one." I then stalked out of the room.

Mother had several regular men callers at our house on Throckmorton. One was a former Ardmore acquaintance who was then an insurance adjuster in Dallas and "dropped in to have coffee" repeatedly with her, both before and after our house on Throckmorton was set on fire. Then there was Judge Felix D. Robertson, who in the 1924 gubernatorial race was the publicly acknowledged Klan-backed candidate defeated by Miriam A. "Ma" Ferguson for the Democratic nomination, which then was as good as being elected in Texas. Why Mother would let such a man as Judge Robertson into our house made for another mystery. I am quite sure he was instrumental in my being taken to revisit Columbus, New Mexico, just as he got a "friend" to take me to Houston, Texas to purportedly compete in the Texas marble tournament but ended up locking me in a shabby room in a cheap hotel without food until it was almost time for the tournament to start. I called the hotel desk on the telephone, the only place I could call from the room, and asked the clerk to unlock the door, at which he said, "Your father said that you are a problem child and that he has urgent business to attend to and not to permit you to leave the room until he returns."

I told the clerk, "That man who brought me to Houston to play in the marble tournament is not my father but a friend of Judge Felix Robertson who arranged for him to bring me," to which the clerk responded, "If he is a friend of Judge Robertson, then I can't afford to unlock the door."

Since my appeals were useless, I then climbed through the transom over the door—nothing short of a miracle, even though I was small and strong. An attempt was made to prevent me from leaving the hotel when I entered the lobby, but with threats and agility I managed to escape. I then located where the tournament was being held. What happened there was a complicated mystery that I won't attempt to tell at this time.

The house on Throckmorton Street caught fire and extensive damage was sustained to the roof, so we moved yet again, this time to Douglas Street into one of the so-called shotgun houses about a block from the Houston School's yard. All of the houses seemed empty except for the one we resided in, and the whole effect was that of living in the middle of a ghost town. We had replaced our burned Reo car (from the previous fire) with a Hupmobile touring car.

My sister had graduated from North Dallas High School, spent time studying at Southern Methodist University and teaching at the elementary school level, and was now preparing to attend the Western College for Women in Oxford, Ohio. Though my sister and I had called the same place home for years, I was as unaware of her life as she was of mine. All I knew throughout the years, according to my mother's report, was that she was a very fine student and quite popular. I could see for myself that she was pretty, and Mother explained her numerous absences by saying she was studying, out on a date, visiting friends, etc.

A man moved into the neighborhood but made no attempt to furnish his place or even live in it. He just took over occupancy for one apparent reason: to keep a three-pig javelina herd in a pen adjacent to our garage. He mistreated them and only fed and watered them occasionally, but Mother and I gave them proper care at times. The man also kept a meat grinder on his back porch, similar to the one I had seen at the Blue Front Café; it was at least two feet high, not including the butcher block attachment.

One day I observed the man perform a bizarre ritual: walking back and forth from the meat grinder to the javelina pen, he threatened and cursed the pigs, brandishing a pistol all the while, then walked over to the house we lived in and touched the water faucet protruding from the side of the house. The ritual he was performing had to do with the belief that there is a magnetic field around human and animal bodies—a commonly held belief in witchcraft, Masonic sorcery, and the "science" of radiesthesia. Thus, he was performing a mystical charade by threatening and cursing the pigs and then walking over to touch our water faucet.

On another occasion, the sadistic, superstitious man learned that I had given food and water to the javelinas and spoke abusively to me, swearing that I would end up in the meat grinder along with the herd if I persisted in my actions. I related his threat to my mother who shrugged it off with a laugh, saying the man would never do a thing like that. I told her about him threatening the javelinas with a pistol and cursing them, and she said, "Some people just don't like javelinas." Nor did she attach any importance to the fact that he came over to our water faucet after he had performed the ritual; she said he probably just wanted to wash his hands, though he never turned the water on. Mother might not have taken the whole thing seriously, but the javelinas certainly did: they would go into a rage whenever they saw that man.

Detecting a pattern despite Mother's debunking, I cut a hole in the floor of my bedroom and ran wires to the outdoor faucet. The wires were, for the most part, concealed under the house, but a ground wire from a crystal radio set was openly attached to the faucet and had been there practically since the first day we moved in. I ran my wires to a switch and electrical plug that I plugged into the line. Then I waited in my room for a long time, taking a toilet break only once, waiting for the javelina man.

Finally, he came. Sure enough, as regular as clockwork, he went through the motions of his occult charade. After marching back and forth between the meat grinder and pigpen, he cursed the animals, then headed for the faucet. I tensed myself in readiness. What if he noticed the electrical wire on the faucet for the first time? What if my plan was discovered? He touched the faucet and I threw the switch. The current had him and held him! This was no quick shock that he could jump back from. He jerked and wiggled like a rag doll in a windstorm. I ran outside and looked at him. He was alive and his eyes were open, but set back in his head. I went inside, disconnected the wires, closed the hole in the floor, and summoned the ambulance.

The following day an electrician and telephone man came to inspect the wiring in our house. A number of scenarios and explanations for the shocking occurrence were bandied about before they concluded that the man had had a heart attack and only imagined he had been shocked. Mother and I continued to tend the animals in his absence.

After he recovered and returned, I went to ask after his health. But before I had done anything more than step onto my porch and mumble a few words, he drew a pistol and pointed it at me. "What happened at that water faucet was no accident, you son of a bitch!" he shouted. At the sound of his voice, the javelinas threw themselves against their wire pen that I managed to open by means of a string I had attached to the door of their shabby prison, and out they ran. Suffice it to say that the man was sufficiently distracted by the javelinas to never bother them or me again.

Chapter 11

Monster Manby and the Switcheroo
Taos, New Mexico, 1925

In a sense, the Million Dollar Gold Certificates touched every corner of my life and were a key to puzzling out why I was being used as a pawn in a tessellated game. The answer lay in the very concept of initiation. If such matters could be clearly and immediately understood by those not versed in the reality and techniques of Masonic sorcery, then we would all be initiates and there would be no compelling reason for Masons to insist on the fearsome security that is the hallmark of their craft, the craft of the crafty.

The concept of initiation is sometimes scoffed at as just a harmless or silly cover for adults playing at schoolboy nonsense, but if that is so, then one must attempt to fathom the recognized inner (esoteric) group of Masons who practice magnetic Masonry with a real and dangerous propensity toward mystical toponomy with its psychodramatic, earth-tessellation politics, economics, and all other forms of physical power and mental control, as claimed by the occult practitioners of geopolitics.

It is a matter of record that Arthur Rochford Manby of Taos, New Mexico had a secret society called the Self-Supporting Secret Service. It is alleged that he had paper money printed known as Million Dollar Gold Certificates. Manby was a Masonic conman who hoodwinked many people into believing that queer money was good. It is also alleged in Mexico that during his presidency, Porfirio Diaz (1830–1915) feared an imminent revolution and so sent all the gold held by the Mexican government to the United States for safekeeping, and that the Million Dollar Gold Certificates were issued by the U.S. government in return for Mexican gold. It is further alleged that no gold was sent to the United States, but that Felix Diaz, nephew of Porfirio, looted the Mexican Treasury, after which he and his cronies fled to the Philippines and then to Spain where they lived in luxurious fashion.

My sister's first fiancé, Charles Schalings, played a role in the continuing Masonic charades to which I was subjected. The son of a wealthy oilman with ranching interests, Charles was well set up in real estate with his brother-in-law, the premier realtor of Dallas. Both Charles and his father were Freemasons.

One night, my mother, sister, and I dined with Charles and his parents at their Fort Worth home that reminded me of a Southern mansion. After supper, Charles' father showed me one of those infamous Million Dollar Gold Certificates. Shortly afterward and seemingly "out of the blue," Charles invited me to accompany him to Taos, New Mexico where he was to meet up with the mystery man of that Land of Enchantment town, Arthur Rochford Manby, the same man who my mother claimed had held her prisoner when she left me in Columbus, New Mexico, though I did not remember that connection at the time. In my boyish way, I demanded a pair of boots as a condition for accompanying him, and Charles, by way of his father's suggestion, agreed.

All the way to New Mexico, we "roughed" it because Charles regarded himself as every inch a cowboy. As we drove, I marveled at the fact that his father had shown me one of those magic bills and didn't understand why. Upon our arrival in Taos, Charles and I proceeded immediately to Manby's palatial home where Charles was welcomed with enthusiasm. Immediately, an intense discussion ensued on the subject of the certificates. I paid very little attention to the conversation and busied myself with petting and feeding a large ravenous dog. I had the "privilege"—never underestimate the egomania of secret society honchos—of seeing both Charles and Manby "face off" antagonistically with phony money in their hands, just as Bell and "Colonel" Simmons had done on Jekyll Island.

We stayed at a motel and were about to leave for Columbus, New Mexico when we learned that Manby had been killed. Interestingly, his gravestone marker states that he died by decapitation on July 1, 1929, four years later. Yet Taos police records show that Manby died a natural death that summer, which I guess just tends to show that what is natural for some isn't nat-

On hearing that, I wished to be a thousand miles from that sinister house and that my mother had not again sent me into an ordeal that could not possibly resolve in my favor or that of the pitiable girl.

"Here, have a drink, kid," one of the "deputies" offered.

"No, thank you," I said.

"C'mon," he said, "take a drink! You're going to need it!"

At that, I bolted out of the house and ran toward the briars. When I fell, I tumbled and rolled into the berry patch where my shotgun was. Picking it up, I stood in the berry patch and looked back toward the house. The men came out and got into the black convertible roadster that bore a remarkable resemblance to the one that had taken up position on McKinney Avenue after the snake swallowed the snake charmer. Two of the men stood up and brandished their rifles. Both fired shots that hit near me.

"Don't make me go into the briar patch," I shouted like Brer Rabbit, and then returned their fire, not knowing what other recourse was available to me. Those men were the scum of the earth as well as desperate, surely a dangerous combination.

I crawled into one of the pig-made paths in the berry patch and encountered the giant boar. I asked him to be quiet, whimsically assuming he could understand me, petted him and said encouraging things to him as I peered out at the men who had by now driven near the briars. Being close to the ground in a blackberry patch, I could see through the leaves clearly while they camouflaged me perfectly.

The driver had not gotten out, but the two men with long guns had exited the car and split up, one to the left of the patch, the other circling to the right. Shaking and trembling, I gave a desperate slap without warning to the immense wild boar and sent him careening through the briars. Both men wheeled and shot in the direction of the sound. Then, I came out of the briars as one man was chambering another bullet.

Suffice it to say that the entire episode was suffused with a magical patina. All I can recall clearly is that those nice pigs got the three men in a manner that transcends ordinary understanding. The pigs and I became allies. They got the men and I got what was in their pockets, which included coins, currency, Million Dollar Gold Certificates, and three unusual pocketknives:

one large-bladed and rather ominous looking, used to castrate livestock; the second an electrician's knife; and the third with an ornate handle often seen in those days at horseracing tracks.

As I fished through their pockets, I noticed a girl watching. I did not at first associate her with the girl in the house, for she was attired differently. Her demeanor—though in what way I cannot rationally say—was in some respect altered, too. As I approached her, she said, "I saw the whole thing and I've been praying for you."

"How pretty you look in your dress," I replied. The dress fit her perfectly and reminded me of the stereotypical Sunday go-to-meeting dress that Western girls spruced up in on the traditional Sabbath. "What's your name, anyway?"

"Mary Farney. I took it out of the trunk," she said happily. "I feel good in this dress. I wonder if I should keep it. It belongs to the people who formerly occupied this house. However, they've been gone for a long time."

"By all means you should keep it, Mary Farney," I said emphatically, and then gave her a portion of the money I had expropriated from the "deputies" who had so cruelly abused her. I also gave her one of the Million Dollar Gold Certificates. At that time, I regarded the certificates as having a value roughly equal to that of a cigar store coupon.

She thanked me graciously and asked, "I'd like to take the car with me, if it is all right with you?"

"It doesn't matter to me, though it might get you into trouble."

"You don't understand. I paid for the car so it is really mine," she said as she strode toward the car with newfound confidence and vigor. Her eyes shone with an appealing luminosity quite in contrast to her dull and desperate look before. Impulsively, I yanked out the deputy badges I'd collected off the men and gave them to her as a memento. I have a vague recollection of her also retrieving their rifles. She opened the door to the roadster, then turned and faced me with as jaunty an air as any college girl could ever adopt.

"May I kiss you?" she asked, smiling sweetly.

"Yes," I said shyly, and she did.

I headed for home, wondering whether I'd be told to leave again or be welcomed now that I had money. I mused on the javelina feral boar, sows, and piglets and if they were grateful for what I had done for them. Was I destined to always befriend outcasts, being one myself?

As I approached the neighborhood, I began to imagine one of Mother's delicious meals. By the time I reached the door, I had a ravenous appetite. Purloined offering in hand, I approached Mother, who was overjoyed by the proffered booty—not the money, which she told me to keep, but the Million Dollar Gold Certificates. This puzzled me. After all her talk about how poor we were, why would she prefer bogus paper money coupons to the real thing? I dug into a steaming bowl of tender beef stew and she quizzed me on how I came to obtain the money and certificates. I stared at her, wondering if she had foreknowledge of my ordeal or exhibited any trace of deception, but she seemed innocent of subterfuge. My mother was a sphinx to me. After my searching stare, I relaxed the muscles in my face and smiled as I told her in a laconic and deadpan fashion, "A nice lady in the old house you sent me to let me have it."

A week or so later, our brief calm was broken by a storm. Mother answered a knock at our door. Overhearing angry female voices, I rushed to the door. Mary Farney stood there, her car parked at the curb. How she had located me was yet another puzzle. I told Mother that this was the lady who had let me have the money and certificates.

Reluctantly, Mother led Mary Farney into the dining room. As we seated ourselves, Mary said, "I understand that you are not wanted at home, Shelby, and I want you to come and live with me." I suppose sometime in the course of our trial together back in the briar patch, I had told Mary of my abandonment.

Mother was incensed. Trying to remain in my mother's good graces, I complimented her cooking, to which Mary insisted, "I can make it better!"

"Mary," I said, "Mother has decided to take me back," to which she hesitantly responded, "But Shelby... can you let me have some more of the Big Money, like you let me have before? I'll buy you the finest shotgun you've ever seen if you'll come with me."

Though intrigued by her offer, I shook my head and looked down at the table, not wishing to further antagonize Mother. Farney got up to leave and Mother escorted her to the door, shouting, "And don't come back!" When she returned to the dining room, she said, "Son, don't you know what kind of woman that is?" I was dumbfounded. I wasn't even sure what type of woman my own mother was, let alone Farney. What I did know was that something peculiar was going on which I could not understand.

Chapter 12

The Quarry

Louisville, Kentucky, 1926

I didn't realize that I owed my survival, time and again, not to my own strength but to certain imponderable forces that repeatedly rescued me from what can be described as death traps. Something appeared to be interested in saving me from my attackers.

Whenever I thought about Mary Farney and James Amos, I wondered why they should both have offered to get me any type of gun I wanted. Might they have been connected? Mary Farney was most certainly a poor little whore who had been raped and beaten by three evil men. Was she the same Mad Mary Farney who was reputedly very rich and said to be repeatedly involved in "mad escapades?" Possibly, the poor little whore had just taken her name. Then James Amos, the Negro gentleman who had helped me to get my .20-gauge shotgun—certainly he was a man of considerable standing to be able to carry a pistol openly and produce such startling identification.

In surveying such memories, I discovered a telling pattern in my mother's inaccurate comments and my father's ineffectual ways. I remembered how my father had acted both before and after my hands were nailed to the dead tree by the Masonic Ku Kluxers, letting me know that there was no real protection he could provide. I remembering him forbidding me ever to mention the name of "Count" Eugenio in our home. I did as he requested, not because of paternal fiat but out of sympathy for the man who happened to be my father and how disturbed he became by just the mention of that name. Certainly, "Count" Eugenio had been one of the architects of malignant death traps to which I was subjected and still managed to oppose and defeat, despite his "best-laid schemes," and what hold he had on my mother I will never know. But perhaps my father did.

While my father was helpless to protect me, my mother played the role of a credible raconteur skilled at mixing authentic information with misinformation with ease, "Count" Eugenio being a case in point. She had told me he was a German agent and that when he escaped from the Secret Service men who had staked out the railroad station, he had made it to New York City where he was finally apprehended. I raised my eyebrows in mock bewilderment, thinking that if that was so, he had set a record of some type, considering that I had witnessed his death at that railroad station, when he was stabbed and had his genitals stuffed into his mouth.

Her skill in mixing information with misinformation was also responsible for the anxiety I felt about the "garage money" that she and my father said had been confiscated and returned to the Treasury Department because it was counterfeit. When I had taken some of it and spent it on my BB gun, I agonized for months, waiting for a hulking Secret Service man to burst into our home and drag me away to prison as a counterfeiter. In order to overcome my anxiety, I took a ten dollar bill from a small "garage money" stash and marched trembling to a downtown bank. I presented it to a teller and asked if it was counterfeit, fully expecting to be arrested. As I stood quaking, he scrutinized it. Smiling, he passed it to a senior teller who then examined it with great care. Finally, the senior teller said, "Son, that ten-spot is as good as gold," to which the other teller nodded in agreement. I told them that there was a kid outside the bank who saw my ten dollar bill and said it was phony and wanted to trade me a dollar for it. The senior teller let out a chuckle and bent down toward me over the marble counter. "Son, you tell that boy that you know a crook when you see one." Seeing my look of puzzlement, he added, "Maybe you suspected that money because it is obviously fresh from the United States mint. That's new money that has never been in circulation." I went home and told my parents what the tellers had said, adding, "We were cheated out of our money by those crooked Secret Service men like Gaston Means." They did not respond.

Sometimes, I was able to speak out like that about my precocious past that I did not fully understand, though usually I kept my mouth shut. I desperately wanted to deal with all the jeopardy I was always placed in whenever I went on what on the surface appeared to be the most mundane and trivial of household errands.

Circumstances improved for my family after the pig herd got the "deputies" and I gave the Million Dollar Gold Certificates to Mother. As a result, some type of business arrangement was made with one Guy G. Rodebush, a Kansas City paving contractor, involving a patent or patents that my mother held. When a license for them was secured in Louisville, Kentucky, arrangements were made for my family to relocate there. While my sister continued to study in Oxford, Ohio, Father went ahead to Louisville to secure quarters while Mother and I followed by train.

Initially, we stayed in a suite in one of Louisville's finer apartment hotels, perhaps the very nicest. Father had ample groceries awaiting us, and as Mother expertly prepared our meal, Father left. I followed him out the door and watched with fascination as he took a self-service elevator, the first of its kind I thought I had ever seen. When Mother and I first rode it, it stopped about two feet above our floor and we had to jump to make our floor.

I had just returned to our suite to await my meal when two men boldly opened our door and headed straight for an end table and Mother's purse, which they proceeded to rifle. They displayed little interest in her money, demanding instead the Million Dollar Gold Certificates, and threatening us if Mother did not reveal where they were. At this, Mother bravely seized a pot of coffee she had on the boil and tossed it in the faces of both men. Because she heaved it with a motion similar to a roundhouse swing, the hot coffee effectively caught both men in the eyes. Screaming and staggering, the men groped their way out into the hallway while Mother called the front desk and demanded that a hotel detective be sent at once.

Hotel personnel and municipal police arrived shortly thereafter. But in the brief time between Mother's call and the arrival of the authorities, the intruders had disappeared. The police pounded on guests' doors and searched the establishment from basement to roof, but no sign of the hoodlums was detected until their bodies were located at the bottom of the elevator shaft. Mysteriously, they had fallen from our floor to their deaths. The next day, despite the protestations of the hotel manager, we moved to another hotel, after which we finally moved to an apartment on Douglas Avenue.

I enrolled at Belknap Elementary School, as well as Boy Scout Troop 22 that met at the Methodist church on Douglas Avenue and Bardstown Road. Scout and school friends and I frequented a nearby rock quarry where I discovered in the bedrock a large pipe protruding with a valve on it. Occasionally, a drop of water would drip out of it.

I took my studies and scouting seriously, especially the Boy Scout oath which in those days boys did not regard as trifling. Eventually, I visited the Louisville scouting headquarters and was introduced to Mr. Marion, who claimed he was from Charleston, South Carolina and a descendant of Francis Marion (1732–1795), the guerrilla fighter dubbed the Swamp Fox during the American Revolution. Mr. Marion's appearance was noteworthy: he had an androgynous demeanor with a face that the fairer sex often said was wasted on a man; in fact, his facial skin was as clear as the proverbial baby's butt—possibly due to some depilatory, or maybe it was just a case of his having the sharpest razor in town, I don't know. A medieval artist would have been happy to incorporate Mr. Marion's face into an angelic fresco. Despite my interest in scouting and my curious nature, I didn't get around to acceding to Mr. Marion's requests that I visit him at his home where he would "show me something I had never seen before."

On one occasion, Father permitted me to accompany him to a company that had purchased user rights on our patent. There, I met a man who may or may not have been an employee, but who was also some type of quarryman. He said that near my school was a rock quarry in which he was very interested, and then he asked me if I would inspect it for him. Why a businessman would ask a diminutive Boy Scout to go on such an expedition didn't occur to me at the time. I informed him that I had already been to the quarry and would tell him about it for free, but he insisted on giving me five dollars if I would go there again.

The next day, I set out for the quarry, taking with me a .32 Colt automatic pistol I had won in a punchboard game in a little Dallas café on Love Field Road; I also took my dismantled .20-gauge shotgun that James Amos had helped me to acquire. I brought the weapons for the purpose of amusing myself by setting up a target and plinking at it. When I arrived at the quarry, I spied two men standing at a large gasoline-run water pump a short distance from the valved pipe I mentioned earlier. When I approached them, one remarked, "We're going to pump the water out of this here quarry."

"What for?" I asked. "It isn't doing any harm. What's more, there is no place to pump water, nor enough hose to do the job."

My insights infuriated the two men. "Listen, kid," one of the men said, "if you want to be allowed to watch, you had better keep your mouth shut. Now stand over there," and the man indicated a spot about thirty paces away.

So I took up my position and immediately noticed that a gunman had appeared on the south rim of the quarry and was aiming a rifle at me. I ran for the water pump as a shot landed behind me. Drawing my Colt .32, I ordered the two pumpers to get over near the side of the quarry pit. As they did so, I knelt down in the shadow of the quarry's rim and quickly snapped the shotgun pieces together in a matter of seconds; I had practiced it for fun several times a week for some time. As the two men hunkered down, they tried to cajole me into believing that the rifleman had not been trying to hit me, for he was a crack shot and could have done so if he had wanted to.

Turning sideways as they spoke, I was able to eye them and keep a sight line on the rifleman's position. However, he was no longer where he had been. It was reasonable to assume that he had taken up a new position on the edge of the quarry where he could shoot me with ease even if he were far from being a crack shot. I briefly considered scurrying across the quarry to take up a new position. As I weighed my options, the two men now tried to convince me that they had no knowledge of the ambush and were merely hired to get me to stand by the quarry wall. So, they had been expecting me.

I secured them with a chain to the water pipe after making certain threats. Then, as I might be shot if I tried to walk out, I decided to scale the quarry wall at the same place I had climbed it earlier while playing and exploring. If I was right about where the gunman was, he would be able to see me in the act of climbing by just changing his position by twenty or thirty feet. I again threatened the men if they revealed my whereabouts when I started to climb the quarry wall.

With great speed, I climbed the wall, urged on every second by the realization that I could be shot. Finally, after terrifying seconds that seemed much longer, I reached the top of the rim. Just as I surmised, there was the

enced with Alexander Graham Bell on Jekyll Island, but I could not decipher it at the time.

The next day Mother, "Charles," and I began our trip to the pipeline. Charles said that he planned to meet with a wealthy investor who was partially financing the construction of the pipeline; he said that he and his family were considering buying in with the investor. En route to the pipeline, we "coincidentally" passed the house of Mr. Marion. Impulsively, I said that I wanted to stop there for a few minutes on our way back because Mr. Marion had said he had something he wanted to show me.

The pipeline was huge, and just as immense was the valve on it. While Mother waited in the car some distance from the pipeline, "Charles," a workman and I walked the pipeline. Charles walked further up the pipeline while the man and I returned to the huge valve. There, this workman opened the valve, grabbed me, and tried to shove my head into the pipe. I was terrified. I twisted and turned and by virtue of my flexibility overcame the man's superior physical strength. Freeing myself, I ran about twenty paces, then took out my nigger-shooter (slingshot) and wheeled around in combat stance. I shot a rock right between the workman's eyes, just like in David and Goliath, and followed it up by shooting him in both shoulders.

With my heart racing, I sprinted along the pipeline to where "Charles" stood. I told him that Mother and I were returning to Louisville and that he should come, too, unless he wanted to stay there and get back any way he could. He looked stunned as we walked to the car. Had it been a practical joke? And what was "Charles'" role in the affair, I wondered. I don't recall any conversation as we drove to Mr. Marion's house. However, I am reasonably sure that both Mother and "Charles" knew that something drastic had happened at the pipeline.

When we arrived at Mr. Marion's house, Mother and "Charles" stayed in the car while I ran up and knocked on the door. Mr. Marion answered the door as quickly as if he had been standing behind it, waiting for me. He invited me to come in, smiling his seemingly nice smile. I told him I could only stay a minute, that others were waiting for me in the car and I only stopped by to say hello. Mr. Marion offered to show me around, though there was little enough to see in that bleak house.

There was, however, a wood tunnel perhaps four feet high and three feet wide, going from the foyer toward the rear of the house, with a door on it that had a strong latch. I asked Mr. Marion about it, saying, "It looks like a gigantic rabbit trap to me. You don't have any rabbits that big around here, do you, Mr. Marion?"

"I'll show it to you later, but first I want to show you something else," he said.

So we went into what was intended to be a living room. On the floor was a shabby pallet, a chair, a floor lamp, and an end table with a book on it. Picking up the book and glancing through the pages, I saw many illustrations that interested me. I asked Mr. Marion about them.

"Those are by Dore," he said. The name Dore meant nothing to me. Taking the book from my hands, he opened to a certain picture. "That is you," he said, pointing to one of the plates, then turning a few pages he pointed to another illustration and said, "and that is me."

I assumed he was kidding, and as I knew Mother and "Charles" were waiting, I said that I had to leave. He insisted there was more to see. We then walked into what should have been the dining room. On a table was a sugar bowl and catsup bottle and nothing else in the entire room. In the kitchen, I saw where the wooden tunnel went out an open window far enough for the end of it to be over a large container used for garbage. From the kitchen we passed to the front of the house through a room in which there was no furniture, just an electrical cord plugged into a socket with the other end going into the tunnel. Surreptitiously, I pulled the plug.

When we entered the foyer, Mr. Marion opened the door to the tunnel and grabbed me, trying to force me into the tunnel. But being quite sure of myself, I told him to let me go and I would enter the tunnel by myself or he would be sorry. He let me go and I crawled into the tunnel. As soon as I was in, he locked the door and then said in a loud threatening voice, "Remember Diana Vaughn."

The name Diana Vaughn meant nothing to me then, but now I believe he was referring to the Charleston, South Carolina woman who practiced witchcraft for a while and testified that General Albert Pike, Grand

Commander of Scottish Rite Freemasonry, Southern Jurisdiction, had participated in witchcraft rites in Charleston in which she also took part.

I examined the door. Light was coming through cracks and while the door appeared quite strong, I knew I could get out that way or anywhere else in the tunnel because I was prepared as all good Scouts should be: I had my .32 automatic, Scout knives, a small flashlight, and my Scout hatchet dangling in a scabbard in Scout fashion, so I knew that I could knock a hole in the tunnel anywhere I wanted to and possibly shoot anyone who tried to stop me, thinking of course of Mr. Marion.

I turned on my flashlight and could see a curtain hanging where the electrical cord in the adjacent room entered the tunnel. I crawled along the tunnel to it and timidly raised the curtain. There I saw a mechanism that would best be described as an electrical/mechanical sledgehammer that would strike when electrically triggered by pressure on a board on the floor of the tunnel beneath the instrument. Although I was confident that I had disconnected the electricity to it when I pulled the plug, I employed the blade of my hatchet to immobilize the sledgehammer part of the mechanism, then crawled under it. After getting safely past it, I removed my hatchet and crawled the remaining way to where the tunnel went through the window, and exited the death trap.

Hollering to Mother and "Charles" that I would only be a few minutes more, I took out my automatic and went back into the house by the front door. I found Mr. Marion in the living room, standing by the door to the death tunnel, reading or pretending to read a Bible. Opening the door to the tunnel, I ordered him to go into it. He hesitated and protested that it was all a mistake and he had to do what he did, adding, "I love you, they made me do it."

"You're darn right it was a mistake, and the mistake is all yours," I shouted at him. "Get in that damn box."

Mr. Marion reluctantly entered the trap of death. I locked the door behind him, then ran into the adjacent room and plugged in the electrical cord. I was quite sure that as large as he was, he would have difficulty turning around and forcing the door open. He would assume that since I had been able to crawl through safely, he could, too. I then ran happily out to the car where Mother chided me for being gone so long, but I didn't mind. While we drove home, I did a lot of thinking. The cruel, evil nature of the pipeline/valve incident and the weird plan to kill me in the tunnel smacked of freakishness, and I wondered why in the world anyone would want to hurt me, much less kill me.

Several days later, I checked on Mr. Marion at Louisville Scouting Headquarters. At first, no one seemed to know where he was. I called police headquarters and gave them Mr. Marion's home address. Later, one of the minor functionaries at Scout Headquarters told me that Mr. Marion had been sent to Charleston. I didn't question that, nor did I inquire as to whether Mr. Marion had gone on his own power or been shipped. I never saw him again, nor was anything said about him or the injured workman/watch-man at the pipeline. Neither was a random event, so neither left the usual traces that ordinary violent crimes leave behind. The planned attacks on me were covered up in such a way that it would have been impossible for either man, singularly or together, to have arranged; others were most certainly involved.

Chapter 14

Military Complicity in Conspiracies of Silence
Fort Thomas, Kentucky, 1929

There is always an enigmatic design behind ceremonial ordeals, but it was a long time before I learned the secret of it all. Concealment went hand in hand with the traumatic incidents and occult psychodramas. Such cover-ups inevitably require a large network of influential people so they can work effectively, even if only an inner elite is cognizant of the esoterics of what actually took place and why. The fact of the matter is that attempts have been made time and again to ritually murder me.

Most alarming about these conspiracies of silence is how entire agencies of government are complicit. The silence surrounding my Fort Thomas ordeal involved the War Department, Fort Thomas military personnel, and the local police force. It would have been difficult for the officers at the Fort and their superiors in the War Department to explain how it came to be that the Ku Klux Klan was permitted to hold a Klan rite on federal property, or why a death-trap door was installed on government property. It was more expedient for the conspirators to conceal rather than reveal and face the subsequent burden of explaining the bizarre revelations would demand. There is no doubt in my mind that all Fort Thomas personnel were to some degree in on the Masonic hoodwink that was perpetrated, either by being persuaded or intimidated into silence, or as active participants in the collusion of the KKK/Freemasonry/government interface, similar to when a large number of soldiers forced the Poet Laureate of Kentucky to suck them all off and then beat him almost to death.

While I do not recognize any pattern of symbolism in the traumatic incident involving the "whipping boy" Negro slave and his owner near Alexandria, what happened there is most certainly connected with the KKK ritual at Fort Thomas. The symbolism of the whip with the bull prick handle—besides being a hidden practical joke of sick humor—was central to the ritual of masculine power used in the mystical sex and death charade at the Fort. In days of yore, a bull pizzle (penis), besides being a sex symbol, was actually used as a whip. The sex symbolism of the bull prick-handled whip is as far from being funny as the deadly door, or as Masons are from the righteous front they present to hoodwinked people.

My sister married James Eley Robertson, not Charles. For a time, they made their home in Cincinnati, Ohio, then moved to Covington, Kentucky, a Cincinnati suburb. Before long, my parents and I also moved to Cincinnati, then relocated to Fort Thomas, Kentucky, just a few miles from Covington. As I was starting ninth grade at Highlands High School, we had to move immediately into a boarding house on South Fort Thomas Avenue.

Strangely, I knew I had been in that house before and told my parents as much, which they both denied. My principal lived just a few doors from the boarding house. I liked both him and his son and visited them in their home several times before I was told by the boy that his father had resigned. He also told me that his father had received my transcript and couldn't believe it—that it didn't read like a student's transcript. I was sad when they moved. Most students I came in contact with seemed withdrawn, with the exception of several friendly boys whom I saw sometimes after school and Saturdays, when I didn't go to Cincinnati to see a movie.

One Saturday, I bought a small garlic-spiced beef sausage. Miss Fanny, the proprietor of the boarding house, wouldn't let me keep it in the kitchen, so I thought I might keep it under Mother's and Father's bed in our room. When I looked under the bed, I found a wooden box about sixteen inches wide, twenty-four inches long, and ten inches deep—the same kind of box that had contained the "garage money" on Lemmon Avenue in Dallas. I forced the lid open and just as I suspected found bundles of new currency in two rows stacked end to end, with paper straps separating each bundle. On each strap was the name of some bank, and each bundle contained bills from twenty dollars to five hundred dollars—a lot of money.

When Mother and Father came in, I showed them the money. Father rushed out of the room, and Mother started telling me the old story I had heard before: that it was the money she had gotten from selling "her house," and that they were keeping it in the box because of a judgment that the Lion Bonding Company had against my father, etc. She also said that an apartment house was going to be built next door and that we would move into one of the apartments as soon as it was finished, after which she was going to see to it that I got some of the things I should have had in the past but they couldn't let me have then. I didn't push for more of an explanation and let the matter drop.

There was an old barn in back of the boarding house that was never locked. Both it and the boarding house were owned by Dr. Ross, a dentist with an office in Newport, Kentucky. As soon as I entered the barn, I was positive I had been in it before. My parents, of course, said it wasn't possible, but the more I explored in and around Fort Thomas, the more I was convinced that my parents were, as usual, misinforming me.

I made the acquaintance of a boy named Wade Hampton, a descendant of the military Hamptons—American Revolution General Wade Hampton (1752–1835) and his grandson Confederate General Wade Hampton (1818–1902), who was instrumental in founding the original Ku Klux Klan. One day, Wade took me to a picnic where there was a lot of homebrew and good things to eat. The picnic was held outside Silver Grove, Kentucky; during the Civil War, horse-drawn coaches had reputedly stopped there. I felt I had been on the grounds where the picnic was held, too.

There was to be a dogfight, and the two pitbulls that were supposed to fight were tied to iron stakes some distance from the picnic tables. I was able to surreptitiously feed, pet, and talk baby talk to them, and after I gave them a friendly introduction to each other, they decided they didn't really want to fight. When the owner of the dogs found out, he was furious and got even more so when all the bets were called off after I showed how the dogs didn't want to fight. So the dogs' owner and I quarreled.

Shortly after the picnic, Wade dropped a metal disk about the size of a silver dollar while we were walking on South Fort Thomas Avenue by the Fort Thomas military installation. I picked it up and saw that it was made of aluminum with a swastika on one side. He said it was a Klan emblem and then gave me a Klan recruiting talk. I told him about some of my experiences with the Ku Kluxers in Oklahoma and Texas, and expressed my dislike for the

Klan. Wade insisted that the Klan in Kentucky was unlike the Klan in other states, and then went on to say that I already knew a number of people in the Klan and proceeded to name names. All the men at the picnic were Klansmen, and the Klan often had good times like that. Because I liked Wade and believed what he said, I told him I would join.

However, a most foreboding incident occurred that loomed like an ominous tower at twilight over a desolate countryside. Paul Rogers was the son of the Fort Thomas military post chaplain. He and I sometimes played tennis at the post. Because rank has its privileges, Paul and I occasionally went to the officers' mess to feast on cake, pie, and ice cream. We also had the run of other areas at the post, such as the stable tack room and commissary, routinely off-limits to outsiders. While roaming around with Paul, I came across a lethally rigged trick door in the stable tack room, exactly like the door I had seen in the duplex of the imitation Cagliostro, a Ku Klux Klan/Freemason. I marveled at its similarity to the one in Dallas and examined it carefully. If it wasn't the same door, it was identical, which in itself is a one-in-a-million synchronicity. Oddly, Paul Rogers denied any knowledge of or interest in the deadly door, nor were my parents interested when I told them that the door at Fort Thomas was exactly like the one in Dallas.

I wondered whether mystical Ku Klux Klan/Freemasonry doings were taking place on "the dark and bloody ground" of Kentucky, too. Since I had so often been oblivious to the cruel and strange facts of my life, it didn't really dawn on me then that there was in the making a plan to maim or kill me. *Why would anyone want to hurt me?* was my foolish refrain borne of forgetfulness.

Then came the day that Wade Hampton told me to go at a certain time to the place where he had dropped the Klan emblem. He said it would be near there that I would be "naturalized," meaning initiated into the mysteries of the Ku Klux Klan. In parting, he also muttered something ambiguous that had about it an inference of warning: "You don't have to go if you don't want to." Naturally, I was curious about what Wade had told me about the Kentucky Klan and wanted to find out if it was what Wade said it was. Would this be a legitimate meeting of a different sort of Klansmen, a gathering of Thomas Dixon-style "heroic" Klansmen? If so, that would be a sight worth

seeing, for I had never known one. Intrigued by Wade's parting words, I pock-
eted my .32 Colt automatic and went to see what was what.

The area of town where I had my appointment was bounded on one side
by vacant land that was part of the Fort Thomas post property, separated
from South Fort Thomas Avenue by a fence. Directly across the avenue were
stores that provided light when they were open for business, and the area was
dimly lit at night by streetlights some distance away and lights from passing
cars. But when the stores were closed and there were no passing cars, it was a
shadowy area.

When I arrived, I was greeted by a surprising scene: Klansmen were gathering on the vacant strip of the Fort Thomas military post bordering South
Fort Thomas Avenue, part of which was so well-lighted that faces of
unhooded Ku Kluxers could be seen from some distance away. A streetlight
was on, but store lights were not. The campfire near the fence gave little light.
There was also a mock campfire made with sticks and blood-red electric light
bulbs intended to symbolize fire; the electricity for the bulbs came by way of
a long cable from an Army generator parked some distance from the mock
campfire. It was the mock campfire that made the area hauntingly blood-red.
Adding to the surreal ambience of it all were the tiered bleachers that had
been carried from the nearby armory, now filled with uniformed soldiers.
Standing at a right angle to the bleachers about thirty feet from the imitation
campfire stood two rows of Ku Kluxers, all in Klan garb, only one of whom
was hooded. Standing next to him was Chaplain Rogers, and I can only guess
that the hooded Ku Kluxer was Wade Hampton.

It was quite a surprise to see a meeting of Ku Kluxers in Klan garb with
uniformed soldiers there, too, right at the perimeter of a military fort in an
area adjacent to a public thoroughfare. But that was not the biggest surprise,
for there were Negroes crouched around the real campfire, and a short distance from where they were hunkered down was a death trap door that must
have been the one I saw in the stable tack room.

I tried to be inconspicuous as I climbed over the fence, but the Ku Kluxer
who was making a speech from the front lines of those in Klan garb shouted, "Stay where you are!" I didn't like the tone of his voice and thought he
might at least have said please, but I feigned immobility while slowly and

imperceptibly inching my way forward until I was between the hunkered Negroes and the death trap door. About the time I took up that position, the Ku Kluxer stopped talking and a man in street clothes came out from behind the death trap door and shoved a whip in my hand, saying, "You take off your shirt and you whip him." The whip had the aura of evil for me, as I had seen such a whip before. The handle was fashioned out of the stretched and dried penis of a bull, and the thongs indicated it was what is called a cat-of-nine-tails—the same kind of whip, if not the same, that the perverted hotel manager of the Hoover Hotel in Columbus, New Mexico had intended to whip me with—the same type of whip that I had seen in the servants' house of the Ku Klux Klan/Mason in Dallas.

By the available light, I could see the face and body of the intended victim distinctly. His face looked ugly and brutal, his body strong. He also looked unafraid as he got to his feet and took off his shirt. When he turned his back to me, I saw that his back was covered by a mass of scar tissue, probably from numerous previous beatings. I forced my eyes away so that I could maintain a surveillance of the Klansmen, soldiers, and man who had ordered the whipping. Not a single car had passed on South Fort Thomas Avenue since I had climbed the fence, which meant that the south portion of Fort Thomas Avenue had been blocked off, a feat that could only have been accomplished with the connivance of the police. Military officials must have also been in on the connivance, since the soldiers in the bleachers could hardly have been in attendance within the Fort's perimeter without an official nod from on high.

"Beat that nigger," screamed the man who had shoved the whip into my hands. There was no doubt that he bore animosity toward me, and though he was clad in civvies, he was either connected with the Klan or the military or both; otherwise, he would not have been able to wield such authority at a Klan gathering and on the premises of Fort Thomas.

About the Negro, I inquired, "What has he done?"

"You have no right to ask that. You are to do as you are told and you had better be quick about it," he barked.

The Negroes still crouched around the campfire as if in a stupor suddenly took some sticks out of a gunny sack and marshmallows out of a paper bag, and impaling the marshmallows on the sticks, began roasting them in the campfire. The Negro "whipping boy" spoke up: "I will take a beating from you or I will take a beating for you, I can't really say which."

Throwing the whip down, I shouted to the Klan, "You sons of bitches aren't going to beat anyone."

The whip was immediately picked up by the man who had shoved it into my hands and he disengaged the prick handle. "Take this," he said, handing me the bull prick handle, "and knock on that door!" He then motioned to the tricky portal that could be lethal to anyone going through it if they didn't know how to release the spring-driven cleaver mounted over the door on the other side.

I was quite angry by then and for some reason this new command triggered in me the intuition that the door was not simply identical to the Cagliostro imitator's door, but was the very same door. The nightmare complex of symbolism aimed at me constituted a veritable conspiratorial web of ritual props and designs calculated to degrade, defeat, and ritually kill me in accordance with age-old Masonic sorcery sacrifices. I strode toward the door with a grim determination to carry out an obligation to myself. I still carried the dried bull prick whip handle, but had no intention of knocking on the door with it. When I got to the door in the dark, I dropped the bull prick handle and took out my .32 Colt automatic, and with it I knocked on the door several times.

The head Klansman, still standing with the other Ku Kluxers in their Klan garb, shouted, "We know what you are knocking for. Enter!"

I shouted back, "You evil sons of bitches, you may know what I am knocking for, but you sure as hell don't know what I am knocking with!" Those perverted, brutal, evil men assumed I had knocked on that sinister door with the bull prick handle, so immediately after knocking on the door as I did, I put the Colt automatic in my waistband, then reached out with my right hand and threw the lever that released the cleaver on that death door trap. Opening the door and stepping through the mock doorway, I hollered, "COME ON, GANG!"

Once through the ritual death door, I headed toward the soldiers in the bleachers and the mock campfire that stood about midway. I stopped my approach fifteen feet from the mock campfire so that I could see both the Ku Kluxers in Klan garb and the soldiers. The head Ku Kluxer then started walking slowly toward the mock campfire. He was carrying a pistol but made no move to point it at me then. Obviously, he didn't know I was armed. I believe this Ku Kluxer was from Indianapolis, although Wade had told me that the Kentucky Klan was not connected with other Klans.

When he got to the mock campfire, the Ku Kluxer said, "We know how to handle a man like you." I cursed him, his progenitors, and all Ku Kluxers. A complete silence momentary filled that blood-red field. The soldiers stared, the Ku Kluxers in Klan garb still stood in tow lines, the Negroes were still at their campfire that needed poking up. Expectation was in the air, something was about to be resolved.

The head Ku Kluxer then started to raise his pistol, slowly and deliberately. Possibly the slowness was for stage effect, just to have some fun with me in the way some good ol' boys get their jollies. I had learned that when in real peril, if you are not quick then you are dead. So I shot him about the time he had raised his pistol waist high. I didn't shoot him between the eyes as I could have, but in a shoulder. He looked very startled but didn't fall or drop his pistol, so I shot him again and he fell on the mock campfire.

At the sound of the first shot, the Ku Kluxers broke their lines and started running. The soldiers stood up in the bleachers but didn't run. They acted stunned, but one soldier in the second row hollered, "We're coming!" and started gesticulating wildly for the others to follow him. I fired a shot over their heads and they scattered like a bunch of cockroaches, with the exception of that one soldier who did start toward me. I fired in his general direction and he got away fast.

I looked around for anyone who might attack me but the area was suddenly deserted, except for the Negroes who sat at their campfire moaning, chanting, swaying, and generally carrying on in their fashion. I went to the mock campfire and picked up the pistol that the Ku Kluxer had been carrying, then walked over to the Negroes. The "whipping boy" Negro was not there. I asked where he was, and was told that he had left with a white man. Thinking that the Negroes might have been scheduled for some type of humiliation, I asked them why they didn't try to defend themselves or at least run away. One of the miserable group said that they just couldn't. I asked them if they had weapons to fight the Ku Kluxers with and they said they didn't, so I took the bullets out of the .32 revolver that the head Ku Kluxer had been carrying, thinking I might need them, and tossed the revolver on the ground, telling them that if they were to get some bullets for it, they might be able to shoot at least some Ku Kluxers if they came for them again.

(Note: While the popular depiction of enmity between Negroes and the KKK is true, it is also true that some Negroes took part in Klan rituals as a sort of KKK auxiliary. In areas that the Ku Kluxers call Klan Country, they are the "boss niggers." It would seem that the Negroes involved in the Fort Thomas "naturalization" charade were so disposed. Had I made some attempt to whip the Negro "whipping boy" as I was ordered to do, I might have been manhandled by the entire group, for I believe that was to be the first part of the occult script for the night.)

I expected to be arrested by the military police before I could leave the boundary strip, and when that didn't happen, I expected to be arrested by the police on my way home. When I got home, I told my parents what had taken place and what I had to do to keep from being shot, expecting every minute to hear the wail of police sirens. But that didn't happen, nor did the police come to call during the days following. Still naïve, I attempted to alert the authorities about a U.S. Army base being misused for Ku Klux Klan rites. I wrote the War Department (now the Department of Defense) and the major Cincinnati newspapers that professed dedication to truth rather the same way some whores profess allegiance to monogamy. Everyone ignored me. I wrote the commanding officer of Fort Thomas and even tried to see him by visiting his home and office; he was "not in."

During my last attempt to contact the CO at the Fort, I came across a large bell about thirty paces from his front door. No one seemed to know why the bell was there or who had placed it there. I rang it repeatedly, and it must have been heard throughout much of Fort Thomas, so great a din did it emit. But not one person came to investigate just what the hell was going on. I might as well have been ringing it on the moon.

Wade Hampton failed to attend class for a number of days following the Klan fiasco at the Fort. It was easy to guess why he didn't—he worked and so attended school intermittently—and I assumed he couldn't face me. I had no actual evidence that Wade was part of the trap that had been set for me, nor that he was even there. Perhaps those goddamn Ku Kluxers had given Wade to understand that they really did intend to initiate ("naturalize") me. When he finally did show up at school, he turned completely pale when I asked him if he knew that the Klan had intended to maim or kill me. His guilty demeanor caused me to believe more and more that he was the Ku Kluxer in the hood, and it saddened me to think that he hadn't shouted a warning about the death trap door when I was ordered to enter it.

Several weeks later, my parents told me that they knew the whereabouts of the "whipping boy" Negro with the scarred back who had figured so prominently in the Klan ritual. I wanted to go and see that poor son of a bitch and find out if I could help him in any way, so I drove out to the farm road near Alexander, Kentucky that my parents told me about and found a wretched little shack. I honked my horn and out of the shack emerged a Negro who resembled countless hard-working Negro laborers who peopled those parts. As his face bore no resemblance to the mean-looking Negro I had confronted at the KKK gathering, I began by saying, "I am looking for a friend whom I haven't seen in some time."

"I'm the one you're looking for," he responded laconically.

"I'm sorry, I didn't recognize you. If you take off your shirt, I'll be able to determine if you are who you say you are."

With that, he unbuttoned his old-fashioned work shirt and turned his back to me. Unbelievable enough, there was no doubting the massive scars; in fact, fresh welts covered his back. This was the man.

"Who did that to you?" I asked him.

"The man that I'm with," he replied. I had expected him to indict the Klan, but instead he was apparently referring to his employer.

"Well, in that case you ought to leave this place and never come back."

"Where you figure I ought to go?" he asked me.

"Hell, man, any place you want to, but go!" I retorted.

"I always did have a hankerin' to go to Chicago, but ain't never had the money," he said plaintively.

Impulsively, I took out my billfold and fished out eighty dollars in cash, all that I had with me. In those days, eighty dollars would have gotten him to Chicago with money left over for food and lodging for three or four weeks or more. "Here, take it," I said, "and good luck to you."

The Negro smiled and took the money. "But I'm afraid I still can't get outta here 'cause that man over there in the field—he's the man I'm with— he won't let me go."

"If that man won't let you go, then you are being held in peonage, and if you don't understand what that means, it means SLAVERY! Now where is this son of a bitch who won't let you go? I want to talk to him," I said.

"He's in the next field there, across that barbed-wire fence," the Negro informed me.

With my Colt .32 in my trench coat pocket already, I got my single-shot .20-gauge out of my car, then walked down the farm road to the fence that was partially concealed by brush, weeds, and a few trees. I walked along the fence a short distance. Once I'd ascertained where the Negro's boss was, I put my shotgun down by a large bush, then crossed the fence and walked the remaining distance to a burly white man with cruel eyes. I thought he might be the man who had presided over the deadly door at the Klan rally, but I wasn't sure.

"I am a friend of the Negro who works for you. He wants to stop working for you and to leave, but he tells me you won't let him go," I said.

"Yeah, I saw you talking to my nigger. Any decent white man would come and speak to the white man first before talking to his nigger," the man replied in a menacing voice.

"You are holding that Negro in peonage. So now, let's go and have a talk with him and then we will see if you don't agree that it will be better to let him leave than for me to have you arrested," I said, without showing any sign of the anger I felt.

"You go on back and I'll be there shortly," he replied.

I then left him, re-crossed the fence, picked up my shotgun and walked back to the Negro's shack where he was still standing. Twenty minutes later, the white man came, riding a horse and toting a .12-gauge shotgun with pump action. He dismounted and stood directly across the farm road from me about twelve feet away, brazen and cocky.

I said, "Not only have you been holding this Negro in slavery, but you have beaten him."

He looked at me with his cruel little eyes and said, "Yeah, I guess I am pretty good at that, but I didn't do it all, I had some help." Then he reached around to the rear of the saddle and pulled out a whip like the one at the Klan rally, which made me more sure than ever that he was the Ku Kluxer who had ordered me to whip the Negro.

Meanwhile, the Negro was standing off to my left on the edge of the farm road, grinning, which seemed odd to me. Could I trust him, even though I was getting into all this trouble for his sake? So I could keep an eye on him and his boss at the same time, I asked him to move onto the farm road. Then I said to the white man, "You know, you are a regular Simon Legree."

He seemed pleased by my accusation. "Yeah, that's what they called me at Raiford," he said, laughing. I cursed him as he laughed, after which he tossed the whip to the Negro and said, "Beat him." As the Negro caught the whip, the white man quickly pointed his shotgun at me.

Before he or the Negro could do much of anything, I shouted and scared the horse into rearing, which in turn threw the man off guard enough that he lowered the muzzle of the shotgun. At that instant, I shot, then turned my attention to the Negro, who was no longer grinning but stricken with terror.

I commented strongly on how he had been willing to beat me and what that made me feel like doing to him. He mumbled some Negro chatter about never wanting to hurt me and how he and the other boys at Raiford knew how to beat on one another so they didn't hurt each other much when the man told them to do so. Whether or not he had intended to whip me severely, in retrospect I wish I had hurt him. Instead, I told him to get going and not come back.

Wiping the dust off of myself, I hopped in my car and drove home, unable to shake the futility of defending such Negroes. I had risked my life for him and all the while he had been in on the occult charade as a black-and-white mirror reflection of some sort of sadomasochistic ritual. I still felt the betrayal when I arrived home and fell exhausted into a chair. I recounted to my parents the full details of what had just transpired, hoping for some affinity or understanding. Instead, they were utterly unresponsive until I got to the part about giving the Negro eighty dollars to get to Chicago, at which point they raced out of the house declaring that they had to see if that poor Negro needed more help.

After they had gone, I remember thinking, What about me? Was it because I had always been able to survive the planned efforts to injure or kill me that made my family think I was invincible, so that they did not recognize or respond to what it was like for me to live like that? When they returned and said they had given that poor, unfortunate Negro a thousand dollars because he also had a family to relocate, I couldn't believe it. "What?" I exclaimed and shot off of the couch as if a lightning bolt had struck me. "A thousand dollars? Why, that son of a bitch was going to beat me with the same whip I had refused to beat him with, and was grinning at the idea of beating me. He was my enemy, and you gave him a thousand dollars?"

To which Father said, sounding like a recording and staring not at me but at some imaginary thing in his mind's eye, "That Negro man just couldn't help himself."

Now, a thousand dollars in those days was a lot of money. I had no doubt that my father had it, for at that time in his life I had witnessed how he routinely carried large sums of new money in envelopes in his breast pocket. Since they were the ones who had told me where to find the Negro, I asked them to tell me how they knew and if they knew he was working for the very Ku Kluxer who had ordered me to whip him at the Klan rally. They said they didn't want to go into that, but that I didn't need to worry about what had happened.

For a while, I believed that the Negro man had indeed gone to Chicago, as he was not at his shack, but several weeks later I saw him in Campbell County Courthouse in Alexandria, Kentucky. He had been arrested in Newport, a notorious town of "easy virtue," after a wild week of rotgut swilling and whoring. While still drunk, he had said he'd gotten the money for his "fun" from some "dumb white people"—at least that's what I was told by a tavern keeper who ran a speakeasy in what had been a funeral home near the courthouse in Newport. I went to the Alexandria courthouse for his trial; he was found not guilty of whatever charge had been brought against him. The secrecy, silence, and darkness of the Klan/Freemasonry hoodwink was in progress, and the trial was just a charade.

Chapter 15

"Déjà Vu"

Fort Thomas, Kentucky, 1930

emories often arrange themselves in a collage, though we want to believe that they are only "real" if they are logically associated. However, each time I would get a few old memories of things or events logically systematized, I recognized that there were variables in those arrangements that had to do with placing the event before it happened (*prochronism*) or after it happened (*metachronism*). It seemed to me that my mother and father were ultimately responsible for my not being able to arrange old memories in a proper order because of the misinformation they continually gave me.

The Monday, March 4, 1918 *Kentucky Post* of Covington, Kentucky contains a news item headed, "ALTAMONT HOTEL WILL BE A HOSPITAL: A deal whereby the U.S. government will take over the Altamont Hotel, Fort Thomas, for war hospital purposes was announced Monday."

If I had had that information while my parents and I were living in Fort Thomas, I might have realized that my memories of having been there before were not *déjà vu* at all. I recall inquiring about an old vacant building that was said to have been a hotel, for I had faint memories of being in it long ago. It was said to have been situated on Bivouac Street, but the building referred to as "the old hotel" was actually on an old concrete road now washed out in places, but once connected Bivouac with the Chesapeake & Ohio Railroad that paralleled the Ohio River. The concrete road stopped at the railroad tracks. I also inquired about a small railroad station that I remembered having once been to, but no one I spoke to in the area recalled it. The part of the old concrete road from Bivouac to about two hundred yards beyond the building referred to as "the old hotel" was torn up and destroyed in 1929. "The old hotel," in excellent condition in 1930, fronted the portion of the road that was torn up, a section now called Crown Street. An extension of

Crown Street, called Crown Point, has been built on the bed of the old concrete road and C&O railroad tracks.

Apparently, the name Rosemont was associated with at least part of the
concrete road that was torn up, for there was a sign there in 1930 to that
effect near the old building referred to as The Rosemont Hotel. That old
building was in excellent condition but too small to be a hotel. It might have
been used as a guest home, such as a Mexican *posada*, if some rooms were
added, but it could never have been used for a hotel as it was. Upon first seeing the building that was called "the old hotel," I knew that I had been there
at some time or other in the distant past, and that something important had
occurred there.

I walked the old steep concrete road to the railroad tracks numerous
times after that, recalling getting off of a train at a small railroad station with
a man and a woman that I then thought of as my parents, and being taken
to a horse-drawn coach where I sat by the driver while we drove to the building later referred to as "the old hotel." He had a long whip that he beat the
horses with, and kept his right foot on a metal box that had been taken off
the train. I was forcefully carried into "the old hotel" where a party was going
on that ended in violent fighting minutes later. I also had a faint memory of
a large building nearby, and a large rose garden. The Altamont Hotel purportedly had "150 rooms, Mostly with Private Baths," and in 1930 a man
called Garrison lived on Bivouac and cultivated a small rose garden on the
property of "the old hotel." Garrison was very hostile toward me.

As I asked questions, it was hard to reconcile my faint memories with the
incorrect answers given by people who should have known about the old
hotel, the building then standing, and the concrete road. The son of the principal at Highlands High School had tried to assist me before his father was
abruptly dismissed and they had to leave. When I told him about the team
of four horses that had a hard time pulling the coach up the steep concrete
road from the railroad to the hotel, he suggested that perhaps the horses were
shod with rubber shoes, adding that some horses that pulled streetcars were
so shod. He also told me that there had once been a sanitarium on Bivouac,
and when I said I didn't know what a sanitarium was, he explained that it was
where people with nervous disorders are treated.

In 1930, work got underway to demolish the building referred to as the old hotel. The work was done by three men, one of whom lived in a brick apartment building on Grand Avenue, about a block from South Fort Thomas Avenue. They worked only with hammers and crowbars to keep from damaging the lumber, they said, for according to them, they were given the old hotel building and everything in it in exchange for demolishing it and removing the debris. Due to the way they worked, and because they did other work, too, the project took considerable time.

While I had memories of having been in the building, I had nothing tangible to back up my faint memories. Then one day after the demolition was well underway, I entered the foyer. The instant I walked through the doorway, I knew there had been a small room behind the counter in the foyer, and that the door to the room had been sealed up. I remembered that in the little room had been a secret compartment where something was hidden. I walked around to see if there was another entry to the hidden room, but there wasn't. The very existence of the room had been hidden. *Why?* I asked myself.

The following day when the "carpenters" were not working, I entered and saw that work had begun on the foyer, which made it easy for me to break into the hidden room where the entrance to the room had been. In the hidden compartment I remembered, I found a locked Wells Fargo box like the one I had seen on the horse-drawn coach. I took the heavy box home, and when I picked the lock I found it half full of large gold coins, with a bundle of Confederate currency and part of an old stained Atlanta newspaper, on the front page of which was an article about a Wells Fargo hold-up done by someone with the same name as mine.

Immediately, I called my brother-in-law, James Eley Robertson, executive secretary to Mr. William Cooper Procter of Procter & Gamble—at least I believe he was executive secretary to Mr. Procter at that time; his advancement in the company was so rapid that by then he might have been manager and/or president of the Buckeye Cottonseed Oil Company, a subsidiary of Procter & Gamble. I told Jim what I had found and where I had found it, and about the newspaper article. He was, of course, amazed, and drove to Fort Thomas in record time. He was flabbergasted when he saw the treasure.

When he finished reading the article, he said, "You will have to give it back, it belongs to Wells Fargo."

"Hell, you say," I said, "the statute of limitations has long since run out on this loot if it was taken in the robbery reported in that article. The treasure belongs to me, although I believe that the three men who are wrecking the building are entitled to something," and I told him about the deal they had with the owner or owners of the building.

James Eley Robertson

Jim insisted there were laws covering the finding of treasures and asked my permission to let him keep the treasure until he could look them up and find out. So I let him take the Wells Fargo box to his apartment at 28 Wallace in Covington, where he put it in a hall closet. The first misfortune, which I did not know then, was that Jim had mentioned the treasure to a P&G lawyer before he ever left his office building. Weeks later, I agreed to Jim's second plea to allow Alex Howard, a friend and attorney, to take custody of the Wells Fargo box and its contents and get in touch with Wells Fargo to ascertain what their position might be. Before it was taken to Alex, I secretly took thirty-two gold coins from the box, tied them up in a red bandanna handkerchief, and hid the bundle.

The second misfortune was that Alex Howard's father was Eule Howard, a formidable prosecuting attorney whose "partner" was Harvey Myers, a lawyer who knew how to get things done; both were senior members of a premier law firm in that neck of the woods. Harvey Myers owned the house at 28 Wallace and lived above the apartment that my sister and brother-in-law rented from him. In the basement of that house, Myers had a concrete room where he kept pre-Prohibition wine. The room had a steel door that opened and closed electrically via a hidden switch.

Alex kept the Wells Fargo box on a table just to the right of the entrance to his office for several weeks. I only recall going to his office once when Alex was not there. His receptionist/secretary said that many people had come to see the treasure and everyone at the courthouse had heard about it. That peeved me, and not hearing from Alex worried me. My brother-in-law advised me not to hurry him, saying he was very thorough and it would take him some time to decide what should be done. Though I had consented to let Alex have custody of the treasure, I felt all along that what Jim called the honest and right thing to do was stupid. I had only given my consent for such stupidity because I liked my brother-in-law and didn't want to do anything that might upset him.

Finally, Jim said that he had received a letter from Wells Fargo. The treasure was going to have to be turned over to Wells Fargo and I should go and see Alex as soon as possible, but to call for an appointment first. When I saw Alex, he said he wanted me to read the letter from Wells Fargo, but when he looked for it, he couldn't find it and concluded he must have left it at home. I grew angry and asked him if he was my lawyer or a lawyer for Wells Fargo, and if he was, had he written the letter himself. Then, feeling I had been a little harsh, I changed my tone and said something like the following:

"Alex, it might not be safe to keep my treasure where you have it, much less to let people come in and see it. I am not saying that any clients of the Howard law firm are dishonest, for according to what I hear, they are exonerated before they ever come to trial or found innocent about the time the judge sees them. But the Howard law firm might have some prospective clients who might be unduly tempted to take a gold coin or two if they looked into the open Wells Fargo box. Surely you wouldn't want any prospective clients of the Howard law firm to be so unduly tempted, so perhaps I should find a safer place for it."

Mr. Eule Howard then entered Alex's office laughing. He had been standing just outside and had heard at least part of our conversation. He said, "I have been telling Alex that he shouldn't keep the gold in his office, but should put it in the safe in my office." He then asked me to come into his office and inspect his safe. I said I thought that was a good idea, as I didn't think the gold was safe where it was. I glanced at Alex and he looked as though he had been hit. It seemed odd that while the mean things I had said to him hadn't bothered him, my seeming acceptance of his father's offer had. I believed then as I do now that he longed for his father's approval and imagined that what his father said was a criticism of his judgment or ability.

Alex's father's safe was crammed full and to my mind there wasn't room for anything else in it, and even if it had been empty, it didn't seem large enough to hold all the gold. As Eule Howard emptied the safe to show me the size of it, he revealed two paperback books with my or my father's name printed on the covers. Laughing the "coincidence" off, Eule Howard reminded me that there had been a Downard family of considerable importance in Covington. The husband, I was told, was a broker in Paraguay tobacco. The Downard family had lived in a mansion in Covington which, along with a large piece of land, was given to the city of Covington for the site of Covington High School with the provision, I was told, that the mansion be kept intact on the property. Eule Howard then told me that Mrs. B. Downard Davison was or had been a client, and I gathered that his acting for her had something to do with the transfer of the Downard property to the city of Covington.

Whatever the Downard family's part in Covington history, seeing my father's or my name on the covers was a strange event, indeed—yet another significant happening that went unrecognized by me then. Had my perception been clearer and had I been more aware of the knowing sequence of previous events in my life, I might not have jumped to the conclusion that I did.

I might even have recognized that I was embroiled in yet another mystical Secret Society charade.

I decided to keep the gold coins in Eule Howard's safe until I read the Wells Fargo letter. I told Eule Howard that regardless of the letter, I might start selling the gold coins immediately. Thanking him, I went back to Alex's office and told him that I wanted to read the letter and then we could decide what to do; meanwhile, the gold would be in his father's safe.

The following day I was told that the Wells Fargo box had been taken from Alex's office. I then wrote Wells Fargo about the box. Their reply indicated that they had no information about said robbery reported in the Atlanta paper, and that Wells Fargo therefore had no claim to the box or its contents. However, the writer of the letter added, he would have enjoyed seeing the box. After reading the letter, I went to Alex without making an appointment and told him that fortunately I had kept some of the gold coins before he took custody of them and wanted him to have one. I put one on his desk and walked out. I then took thirty of the gold coins wrapped in the red bandanna and went to see Jim. I let him read the Wells Fargo letter and told him about keeping some of the coins before Alex took custody of the box. I also told him about going to see Alex.

"You shouldn't have done that, bud," Jim said. "Alex was just trying to protect you, and so was I. There are influential people involved in this. You just didn't realize what you were into, and we had to do what we did."

Handing him the red bandanna of coins, I said, "I have thirty gold coins for you, and besides what they may symbolize, they are gold and not silver."

I then went to see the "carpenter" on Grand Avenue and told him about breaking into the concealed room adjacent to the foyer, of finding the Wells Fargo box, etc. I then let him read the letter from Wells Fargo. After he read it, I told him about losing the box and said that he and the other two carpenters had a legitimate legal interest in the treasure, that he should contact the other two men and tell them what had happened, and then we should attempt to recover it.

He didn't seem surprised by what I told him and wasn't at all interested in doing what I suggested. He went so far as to say that he knew the other two men didn't want any part of it either. It didn't make sense, and when I asked for their names, he refused to tell me; in fact, since the old building had been demolished and the material removed, the other two "carpenters" were no longer around and he couldn't find out what their names were. He then went on to say that Garrison owned the property and had hired the three of them; that Garrison knew about the concealed room and had called their attention to it, telling them not to break into it, and that he wanted to do it himself when the time came.

I was astonished by what he told me. I had intended to give him the remaining gold coins to incite him and the other two "carpenters," but it was obvious that for some reason he wasn't interested. So I went to see Garrison, who came to the door looking belligerent, which was all right with me. I thought I might use his hatred for me to arouse him to recover the treasure for himself, so I told him about finding the treasure and other things that had happened, then gave him the gold coin to incite him further. I don't believe he was at all surprised by what I told him, but I believe giving him the gold coin did surprise him. Seemingly, I accomplished nothing in my attempts to get the three "carpenters" and Garrison to go after the treasure. The fact was that a quietus (*quieta non movere*) had been declared on the entire affair.

The orchestration of the Wells Fargo mystical charade began with Jim telling the P&G lawyer about my discovery and receiving the "legal advice" that set in motion the false problem regarding rightful ownership of the treasure, which stopped me from selling the gold pieces immediately and resulted in the treasure being taken from me. While I was deprived of a great deal of money, those who perpetrated the charade were not attempting to personally profit from what they did. For them, the great value of the coins was not in their market value but their *numism* value. [*Numism* or *numismatics*: the collection and study of coins, paper money, tokens and medals.] The gold coins were instruments by which an incident was orchestrated by the secret society *Secret Combination*.

My brother-in-law Jim Robertson was a member of Sigma Nu fraternity and Skull & Bones, an "honor fraternity" at the University of Alabama. Alex Howard was a Sigma Chi at Centre College, and a Freemason, as was his father Eule Howard. Skull & Bones fraternity was purportedly the reconstituted Southern fraternity once called Kuklos Adelphon (1812–1866), identical to the Ku Klux Klan. To some degree, the Skull & Bones fraternity at the University of Alabama sought to parody Freemasonry. For example, at one time a recognition question in Freemasonry was, WHICH WAY DOES THE WIND BLOW? Using the same question, Skull & Bones at the University of Alabama chose to answer it with, ALL AROUND THE CAMPUS AND UP THE FRESHMEN'S ASSES.

Eule Howard's partner Harvey Myers was a Roman Catholic. Soon after the Wells Fargo box was taken from Alex's office, I talked to Mrs. Harvey Myers who said she had often seen me coming and going to my brother-in-law's apartment, and wondered why she hadn't seen me in some days. I told her that I had been looking for an old Wells Fargo box that I had misplaced. She then said, "I don't know what anyone would want with such a thing, but Harvey has one he might let you have. He had it in our bedroom and I told him he would have to get it out, and he took and put it in his vault in the basement."

In the past, Harvey Myers had taken me into the concrete room with the steel door, which he called a *vault*, and had with considerable pride showed me his stock of wine, pointing to a row of bottles that he said were worth more than all the rest. He said that the day before the federal prohibition law was passed, he had bought most of the wine in there. I remarked on the value of the wine and was told how safe it was because of the electric lock on the door and the well-hidden switch that turned it off and on. Some time after that, I had spent perhaps thirty minutes finding the switch that was near the cellar door entrance, and had entered the vault just to see if I could.

After Mrs. Myers told me what she did, I entered the vault again, but there was only wine in the vault at that time. I then took several bottles of the wine that Harvey Myers prized most. In a remarkably short time, he discovered their loss and bemoaned it to me. I told him that I had been told by a fortuneteller—a woman fortuneteller often called on Mrs. Myers—that there was a Wells Fargo box in his vault. He hadn't been around and so I had gone to see for myself if it was true. While in the vault, knowing he wouldn't mind, I had taken several bottles. I don't recall seeing Harvey Myers and his wife after that.

I didn't attempt to discover any symbolical occult design on the part of my brother-in-law or Alex Howard or his father or his father's partner Harvey Myers. But the convergence of several events—my brother-in-law's moralizing, the legal irregularities of the books with the same name as mine or my father's on them, and Harvey Myers having a Wells Fargo box— prompted me to wonder if they had all conspired against me. If so, they had not done so for monetary gain but for something else. In some way, a secret extraneous influence had been exerted on them. I theorized that my father, the great moralizer, also had something to do with first my brother-in-law's moralizing and then Alex's.

Moot questions were: Did Alex really get a letter from Wells Fargo? Was the treasure then sent to Wells Fargo without my permission? Was it just a coincidence that Harvey Myers had a Wells Fargo box, according to his wife? While I didn't have the answers to these questions, I did realize that individuals I had trusted were all part of a conspiracy of silence and would tell me nothing. What I did know was that I had discovered the treasure in a building I remembered having been taken to in a horse-drawn coach. If that was déjà vu and I had actually found the treasure by chance, then Chance had memory, intelligence, and a mean sense of humor.

Because the Wells Fargo box and its contents were an important Masonic sorcery symbol, my taking them was considered a Masonic crime, the commission of which is declared by Masons to be a heinous offense for which drastic punishment must be meted out. It is always considered a Masonic crime for a non-Mason to discover the occult secrets of Masonry, such as the evil perpetrated by Masons in their mystical public charades. Certainly, something more dreadful was being planned for me.

Chapter 16

Into the Tomb
Fort Thomas, Kentucky, 1931

At this part of the book, readers should now have a grasp of the design of "mystical incidents" so as to perceive them for what they are: Masonic charades.

Secret rites/rituals were largely designed to be part of mystically ordained incidents designated as "Mysteries," hence the term, Mystery Religions. The dogmas and doctrines of Mystery Religions invariably concerned fertility, abuse, violent death and resurrection of a god, and were taught only to the initiated who had been subjected to a series of abuses designed to induct the acolyte into a symbolical death and equally symbolical resurrection.

The representation of death finds its analogue in the Third Degree of Masonry, also known as the "Death of the Mysteries." Hazing, also a central aspect of the first several degrees of Freemasonry, is designed to impose humiliation, as in many military organizations and fraternal orders.

Masonic dogma alleges that Masonry is a Mystery of Life; it is a symbol or allegory of death, death followed by the great mystery of resurrection. Masonry provides three mysterious steps (F., *les pas mysterieux*) with the allegorical meaning, in the 3rd Degree, of leading from life to death (*i.e.,* the grave) where the source of all knowledge is alleged to be found. It is further alleged that "we must descend into the sacred vault of death before we can find the sacred deposit of truth" (*Mackey's Encyclopedia of Freemasonry*).

Well, such depositories aren't always easy to get into or out of alive. For example, consider the mystical Masonic sorcery charade that had to do with the Kramer mansion in Fort Thomas, Kentucky. Also please consider the three mysterious steps to a tomb said to be that of Dr. Simon Pendleton Kramer, a noted surgeon and scientist who served as major in the Medical

Corps Staff of the U.S. Army during the first World War. He was also in charge of the military hospital on Bivouac Street that once occupied the old Altamont Hotel building.

The Kramer mansion is found in back of the remains of the Fort Thomas military installation on the south side. Sitting on the brow of a hill from which there is a picture-postcard view of the Ohio River, it is now occupied by the nuns who operate the Carmel Manor Home for the Aged. The Carmelite Nuns have been described as a female order of Penitentes and were once known as the Sisters of Penance. In Truchas, New Mexico, they are closely aligned with the Penitentes who in January 1947 were granted the Catholic Church's blessing and protection by Archbishop V. Byrne.

The Carmelite Order (male) was said to have been established on Mt. Carmel in Syria in the 12th century; whereas the Order of Carmelite Monks, whose mystical origin is attested to in occult dogma, is said to have pre-existed the birth of Christ. It is alleged that in the 13th century, these Carmelites became part of the 3rd Order of St. Francis, also considered to be a mystical Order by numerous well-informed people. I include this information because I believe that the Carmel Manor Home occupies a mystical site (toponomy, the geography of witchcraft) having to do with a Masonic sorcery charade of great importance. The Carmelite Manor Home's location represents a type of *supplanting*, just as hundreds of Catholic "missions" in Mexico were built on sites of ancient pyramid temples as a method of symbolic supplanting.

The brother of a boy with whom I had gone to Highlands High School relayed Dr. Kramer's son's request for me to come to Dr. Kramer's estate. I had already inspected the old mansion when my parents said they were thinking of buying a house in Fort Thomas and suggested that I see a certain real estate agent for listings. Immediately, he had advised me to see the Kramer mansion before I looked anywhere else, because the age of the mansion and style of its architecture had made it hard to sell and so it could be bought cheaply. He had given me the keys to the place. I assumed that Dr. Kramer's son wanted to see me about buying the property, so I went to see him hoping that something might still be worked out.

I parked my car in front of the mansion. Halfway between the mansion and the servants' house, I saw a human skull. I picked it up and hollered, "Poor Yorick, I knew him well." The door to the servants' house opened immediately and the man standing in the doorway said, "You don't scare easily, do you?"

"Yes, I do," I said, "but it is not the dead ones I'm leery of. It's the live ones that cause me trouble."

I asked what the skull was doing there and he said that it had been in his father's laboratory in the big house and that he had put the skull out to scare kids who wanted to break in. It was true that the vacant Kramer mansion had the reputation of being haunted. "Kramer's son" knew who I was without my having to tell him and invited me inside the servants' quarters, where I asked him what he was asking for the property and he mentioned a price far more than I could even hope to make its down payment. When I asked him if he would be willing to lease or rent the property, he said no, adding that he and his sister owned the property, and that she wanted him to join her in Paris as soon as he could sell the family property. I attempted to convince him that he should lease the mansion to me to be used as a boarding house for old people, and outlined the things I would do to improve the property. He responded that he didn't think I could get the money from my father to do the things I proposed doing.

It sounded reasonable that he would know my father, given that Father had rented adjoining garages behind a number of stores on Fort Thomas Avenue near the Kramer property. Father had turned the adjoining garages into one big laboratory. It seemed a little strange to me that my father hadn't told me that he knew "the doctor's son" when I was talking to him and my mother about the old property.

The doctor's son suddenly did an about-face and said I could use the property for no charge if I would do something for him. When I asked what, he said that his father's tomb was in the St. Stephen's Cemetery and that there were goods in the tomb that he wanted me to get for him. I asked him why he didn't get them himself, and he said that he had promised his father that he would never enter the tomb. I gathered from the way he talked that it was a deathbed promise that he considered sacred.

It flashed through my mind that he could be setting me up as a dupe in a practical joke. Despite my skepticism, I went on with the idea, mentioning that I would be seen in the cemetery if I carried a light with me. He replied that I could go there immediately, for there was no cemetery watchman. I expressed doubts about getting into the tomb, thinking that a key would be necessary or that the door would have to be pried open, but he explained that it would be easy to open the door.

He got out a large cemetery map and penciled in directions to the tomb. To open the door of the tomb I was to go to a right-angle road marker near the entrance to St. Stephen's Cemetery and raise the extended part straight up and down; then, the door of the tomb would open. He reassured me that because it was his father's tomb no fuss could then be made about my entering it in case I was caught.

I can't say that I actually believed that the tomb door would open if I followed his instructions, but I was certainly intrigued by the possibility. I drove immediately to the cemetery and upon entering saw the right-angle road marker, then located the tomb approximately half in the ground, with three steps leading down to the door. I walked back to the right-angle road marker, raised the extended part so that the two pieces were straight up and down, and then ran back to the tomb. To my amazement, the door to the tomb was open.

In Masonic sorcery, the tomb is synonymous with vault, crypt, grave, masoleum, depository, labyrinth, cave or cavern. From the *Encyclopedia of Freemasonry and Its Kindred Sciences*: "In the earliest ages, the cave or vault was decreed sacred and from this arose the fact that the ancient mysteries were almost always performed in subterranean edifices and when the initiations were above ground, as in some Egyptian temples, the approach to its internal structure was so constructed as to convey to the neophyte the impression that he was in a vault. As the great doctrine taught in the mysteries, the resurrection from death—to die and to be initiated were synonymous terms—it was deemed proper that there should be some formal resemblance between a descent into the grave and a descent into the place of initiation."

A Masonic 3rd degree initiation is synonymous with death. A candidate for initiation into the Mysteries was supposed to receive enough valid information to get across the threshold (L., *limen*) of the sacred temple, labyrinth, cave, cavern, tomb, vault, crypt, depository, etc., *alive*, for such initiation places were booby-trapped and any uninformed, unsuspecting person would, of course, be killed.

The three steps from ground level to the door of the "Kramer tomb" represent the three mysterious steps (F., *les pas mysterieux*) whose allegorical meaning derives from leading from life to death. They also symbolize the first three degrees (Apprentice, Fellow Craft, and Master Mason), the 3rd Degree signifying Death and Resurrection.

I approached the tomb and could see clearly through its open door. Just inside was a bier on which was a shrouded corpse, and beside the corpse, and behind it, were grave goods in boxes of various sizes. I hesitated before entering the tomb, fearing that I might be trapped once inside. So I went back to my car for a jack and jack handle, and once back to the tomb used the jack handle to test the firmness of its steps. The first two steps were solid but the third step was a heller; pressure on it triggered the release of a sharp spike from the doorjamb that came out as though driven by a powerful spring. Anyone descending the steps would have surely been impaled.

When I recognized the danger I had been duped into, I became angry with "Kramer's son" and decided to hurt him. Despite the danger I had escaped, I decided to grab the grave goods, and keep them for myself. The protruding spike still scared me, given that it was electrically operated and might be retracted to spring out again if it once again triggered when I started up the steps. I considered breaking off the spike, but that looked too difficult, so I wedged it.

Finally, I entered the tomb and opened the shroud. The desiccated body had been beheaded; around the neck was a circular metal band. On the desiccated body was a wide leather belt with opals on it; leather slippers decorated with feathers and hair adorned the feet. Removing them and closing the shroud, I proceeded to take the grave goods to my car.

> By means of the Mummy, mankind it is said,
> Attests to the gods its respect for the dead.
> We plunder his tomb, be he sinner or saint,
> Distil him for physic and grind him for paint,
> Exhibit for money his poor, shrunken frame,
> And with levity flock to the scene of the shame.
> O, tell me, ye gods, for the use of my rhyme:
> For respecting the dead what's the limit of time?
> 　　　　— Scopas Brune

After loading my car—and it really was loaded—I removed the jack and wedge and then went to the road marker and returned it to its former right-angle position. Running back to the tomb, I saw that the door was closed and the spike retracted. As I drove out of the cemetery I saw "Dr. Kramer's son" near the entrance. He asked me if I had gotten the things out of the tomb. I said that I had, and he told me to put them in a car that was parked nearby. I cursed him and accused him of attempting to murder me, then told him that I intended to keep everything that I took from the tomb. He protested that he hadn't tried to kill me and that he really liked me. I called him a liar and threatened to have him arrested for attempted murder.

Driving away, I stopped at the home of Dr. Ross, a dentist and a neighbor and got permission to put some things in an old barn next door to his house. I opened several boxes of the grave goods and found them to contain books: an old Bible; a *Franklin Despenser Prayer Book*, written by Benjamin Franklin and Sir Francis Dashwood (AKA Hell-Fire Francis, Lord *Le Despencer*); Milton's *Paradise Lost*; Dante's *Divina Commedia*; Goethe's *Faust*; a book called *De Magnete, Magneti*, written by William Gilbert (1540–1603), with a snake on a *tau* cross on the cover. There was an old book entitled *When Tin Swept London*; old prophetic books with devices on them so they could be chained, scientific manuals and cipher/code books with the name James Shelby Downard on them.

Sir Francis Dashwood, Lord Le Despencer (AKA Hell-Fire Francis) was the reported founder of the Hell-Fire Club, AKA Monks of Medmenham and Friars of St. Francis, with headquarters on Dashwood's estate at West Wycombe, England. The Hell-Fire club was a witchcraft society whose members practiced sex magick (L., *magica sexualis*). A huge cave that was excavated on Dashwood's estate was the site of sex magick rites, and the earth that was dug out was used on the road from West Wycombe to High Wycombe, the site of Brunel University. Benjamin Franklin (1706–1790) holed up with Dashwood on his West Wycombe estate and there they wrote a prayer book called the *Franklin Despencer Prayer Book* in England, and the *Franklin Prayer Book* in the United States. Franklin was a member of the St. John Masonic lodge in Philadelphia, Pennsylvania, and in 1734 was elected Grand Master of the Provincial Grand Lodge of Pennsylvania. Franklin and Dashwood were, of course, intimate buddies.

F.H. George, Ph.D., is director of Brunel University's world-renowned Cybernetics department. George defines cybernetics as a "science concerned with all matters of controls and communications and to this extent it trespasses what we have come to think of as the established sciences." Cybernetics, of course, is intimately concerned with artificial or machine intelligence. This concern is predicated, to a certain degree, on human cooperation with machines. Symbolism is a cybernetic science.

I took some books home, along with several other things from the tomb, such as a small crystal skull and the large leather belt with the huge slab opals on it. I put them all in my "den," a maid's room on the third floor of our apartment that our maid didn't want to live in. By the way, the belt was most certainly an Australian aborigine witch doctor's ornament that indicated his calling, and the slippers were of a type worn by *kaditcha*, Australian aborigine ritualist killers who go in a group of three, similar to ritualist Masonic assassins who do what they do in imitation (*simulacrum*) of the three Assassins who reputedly assassinated Hiram Abif, the so-called architect of the Temple of Solomon, in the legend of the 3rd Degree. *Kaditcha* are adept in bone-pointing, which is quite important in Australian aboriginal whammy circles.

When I burned the slippers, I hoped that I had given some *kaditcha* a hot-foot.

Death Certificate of James Shelby Downard, author James Shelby Downard's father.
"Strangulation while mentally ill."

Chapter 17

The Dayton Witch and the State Department's Black Chamber

Washington, D.C. and New York City, 1931

Keeping in mind the Masonic allegories having to do with "sacred depositories" such as tombs and vaults, the tomb in St. Stephen's Cemetery was a sacred depository for things of symbolical and worldly importance, but the things of greatest importance and value were the books with the name James Shelby Downard on them.

I thought long and hard: books in that tomb would have been ruined had they been there any length of time; even a moderate rain would have flooded them. It is reasonable to assume that the grave goods were taken out after each murderous rite and then replaced before the next rite.

What about the headless desiccated body? Did the skull that "Kramer's son" said his father had in his laboratory belong to the desiccated body? Did the man die a natural death and then have his body beheaded? Was he killed upon trying to enter the tomb, and then beheaded? Sorcerers were often killed by decapitation. Had the man been a sorcerer, and if so, had he opposed Masonic sorcerers? Did the circular band at his neck symbolize that he had been cursed to be a thrall in the afterlife by Masonic sorcerers? Did it symbolize anything at all?

There was an unrecognized message for me concealed in cryptograms and ambiguous multiple meanings. For example, MELILOT can mean sweet clover, mildew, and honeydew, just as each can symbolize the other in cryptograms. Masonic sorcery goes in for cryptography in the practice of the Science of Symbolism, wherein occult expressions are transmitted by means of esoteric symbolism. The cryptograms left for me were:

- The crypt
- One book had an author named James Shelby Downard
- An old Cincinnati newspaper stuffed in the Downard book that had an ad for Procter Rendering Company advertisement for dead animals. The key words here are *Procter*, my brother-in-law's boss, and *render*.

Render \Ren'der\, v. i.

1. To give an account; to make explanation or confession. [Obs.]

2. (Naut.) To pass; to run;—said of the passage of a rope through a block, eyelet, etc.; as, a rope renders well, that is, passes freely; also, to yield or give way. —Totten.

Render \Ren'der\, n.

1. A surrender. [Obs.]—Shak.

2. A return; a payment of rent. In those early times the king's household was supported by specific renders of corn and other victuals from the tenants of the demains.—Blackstone.

3. An account given; a statement. [Obs.]—Shak.

Source: *Webster's Revised Unabridged Dictionary (1913)*

Father was quite upset when I showed him the grave goods and explained how I had entered the tomb. I then went to see Chief of Police Cook and told him what had happened. His only comment was that he would check into it, and when he verified that the man who had inveigled me to enter the tomb was indeed the son of Dr. Kramer, I didn't realize that he was withholding the most important fact of all: that Dr. Kramer was still alive and was in fact practicing medicine in Cincinnati, Ohio, just across the river. Dr. Kramer didn't die until April 12, 1940, and he wasn't buried in St. Stephen's but in Arlington National Cemetery. That Dr. Kramer might be alive had not occurred to me. I knew that people have tombs built long before they die, and that even then they may not be put into that tomb, though someone else may be. Elvis Presley owned an elaborate tomb in a Memphis graveyard, but was buried in the yard of his home, Graceland.

In a box of grave goods were several books with the name James Shelby Downard on them, along with a peculiar-looking instrument with a metal nameplate riveted to it saying DAYTON WITCH. A paper tag tied to it had "Brunel University" written on it. At first, I thought it was some sort of adding machine that had been manufactured in Dayton, Ohio.

The Dayton Witch was in excellent condition, and it couldn't have been if it had been sitting in the tomb for any length of time. Its power cord could operate on a 110-volt house current. There was also something on it that looked like a dry-cell battery (a powerpack, maybe?) Just for the hell of it, I turned it on and it chattered away like it was possessed.

I showed the Dayton Witch and cipher/codebooks with James Shelby Downard on them to my father and asked him if they were his. He denied that they were. I believed that he was telling me the truth in a certain sense, but was concealing the actual origin of those books. I asked him to help me figure out how the Dayton Witch worked, but he abruptly refused and left the apartment immediately.

All that day I tried to figure out how to work the Dayton Witch. I guessed it might be a war surplus instrument for coding and decoding. When I made some cipher settings, it made sounds that I imagined signified recognition at the very least, but that was as far as I got. The following morning I wrote a cash register company in Dayton, Ohio about the Dayton Witch. In my letter I requested information about getting an instruction manual for it. By then, I figured that it was more than just a cipher/code instrument and that it might also be a calculator for Army logistics and hence of considerable value for use in some large business.

When I went back through other grave goods, it occurred to me that all of it might well be used as stage setting for an alchemist's laboratory or that of a Hollywood version of a crazy scientist. Because some of the things were indeed weirdly symbolic, it also occurred to me that they might be a cherished collection of someone who practiced symbolism.

When I showed my father the grave goods over his protests, he just looked at the things from a distance and recoiled in horror from whatever I approached him with. It's true that he was fearful of things he considered contaminated. For instance, he thought old paper money was dirty, so when he cashed a check at a bank, he always asked for new money that he would then carry in an envelope in his inside coat pocket. In fact, he carried toilet paper for handling old paper money.

After my father returned to his laboratory, I went to see Dr. Ross about the things that had been added to the grave goods, thinking they must be his. But he said they had been brought by three men who told him that they were from the old hotel—the Altamont—that they were tearing down, and that they belonged to my father. I said my father had told me differently, after which Dr. Ross told me grimly to get all the things out of his barn.

So I took everything to my den and inspected the entire haul, piece by piece. Much suggested the occult to me, especially prophetic books that I thought had been faked until I realized that some predictions had actually come true. There was a fascinating incongruity in the mélange of books: Tom Swift and Edgar Rice Burroughs' Mars books hardly belonged with the old Bible and prayer book by Benjamin Franklin and Sir Francis Dashwood. Perhaps the latter had been intended to play a more symbolical role in the tomb than the other books, given that bodies are sometimes buried with a Bible, psalm or prayer book.

Wanting answers about the tomb, grave goods, and books with the same name on them as mine, I went back to the Kramer estate to have a talk with "Dr. Kramer's son," but he was nowhere to be found. Since the tomb opened and closed electrically, I asked the electric company for installation or wiring records, but could get no information. I decided then to go to the tomb, get the headless desiccated body, and take it to the offices of the newspapers. When I got to the cemetery, the tomb was gone, the ground filled in, and the entire area sodded.

I inquired of the Downard families in that area as to whether any relatives were named James Shelby; apparently none were. I did locate and talk to one of the three men who had brought the grave goods to the old barn. He was a Spanish-American War veteran who had been shot in the abdomen and wore a colostomy bag. He was also a Mason, and the two men he worked with were Masons. A little later I learned that the Spanish-American War veteran shot and killed himself. I also learned that "Dr. Kramer's son" had gone to Paris to live with his sister because he had been shot on the Kramer estate.

It might be said that with the disappearance of the tomb, the status of the grave goods had changed and they were no longer grave goods. I finally got Father to look at some of the cipher/codebooks with the same name as ours on them, and it surprised me when he asked me if he could have one of them. I was pleased that he had found something that interested him and told him that he was welcome to it.

As I continued to inspect the declassified grave goods, I once again encountered Million Dollar Gold Certificates in a box. Because of my keen sense of humor that is seemingly unappreciated by everyone but myself, I decided to send J. Edgar Hoover a number of Gold Certificates in a Hoover vacuum cleaner bag.

One of the books with my name on it had to do with telepathy and mind control, and surveying as an alleged mental communication pertaining to the earth's magnetism and terrestrial magnetic lines (ley lines) and angles in accordance with geometric concepts. One book surveyed a fantastic type of mathematics; another was about atomic piles, energy, and bombs; others were cipher/codebooks that I believed the Dayton Witch tool could decipher. I am quite sure my father was incapable of writing them.

Up until then, I had placed *the occult* in one category and *science* in another, but the books and the Dayton Witch changed that perception. I began to awaken to the question, what's in a name (*onomancy*)? Does the name Dayton Witch on a cryptograph and/or computer suggest an occult procedure? And what of the U.S. Department of State's Cipher Bureau (cryptography) being called the Black Chamber? Did it suggest the occult, too?

Herbert Osborne Yardley purportedly organized the Cipher Bureau of MI-8 (Military Intelligence Division, Section 8), directed by the State Department's Black Chamber. The U.S. Department of State's Cipher Bureau that had been under Yardley's supervision during and after World War One was officially closed by Secretary of State Henry Lewis Stimson (1867–1950) on October 31 (Halloween) in the fateful year of 1929. It so happened, though, that some people in the State Department and the Black Chamber just didn't get the message that the Black Chamber was officially closed.

A year after I entered "Kramer's tomb," I sent a cipher/codebook to the State Department with a letter in which I mentioned the Dayton Witch and suggested that material in the book be decoded. Not receiving a reply as soon as I thought I should, I wrote another letter. Finally, I received a long-distance call from Herbert Osborne Yardley. After expressing interest in the book I had sent to the State Department, he asked me to come to Washington, D.C. for a talk, saying in effect that it might be very much in my interest to do so. According to Yardley, the State Department had given him my book to decipher, and the type of report he made—as well as his personal recommendation—could affect my future. So at Yardley's request, I made a trip to Washington, D.C. and met him in the State Department, but he immediately took me outside the front entrance of the building to speak to me.

A Yardley book called *The American Black Chamber*, published June 1, 1931 explains the closing of the Black Chamber. Maybe Yardley was retired and was given a special assignment in regard to me and my book. But he led me to believe that he was with the State Department.

He asked me a number of questions that I answered as best I could, and then we quarreled about something to do with my being taken outside the State Department building to talk. That the State Department's top cryptographer who inveigled me to come to Washington and then acted rudely bothered me, and I asked for the return of my book. He said that a friend of his in New York City had the book and he would see that it was returned to me. I said that I was going to New York City for a few days and would pick it up if he would give me his friend's address. Yardley then gave me an address on East 37th Street, probably 131 East 37th Street, the address of the Black Chamber in New York City.

The following day I went to New York City and the address Yardley had given me. I knocked repeatedly on the door. After a while, a man came to the door, opened it about three or four inches, and peered out. I told him that Mr. Yardley had given me his name and address so that I could get my book. He said that he had just talked to Yardley and that he hadn't said I was coming for a book. He then closed the door, which I kicked a number of times.

After being given the brush-off, I went to see Mr. Harry K. Thaw (1871–1947) and brought several of the fabulous Million Dollar Gold Certificates with me. I then presented him with one of the Gold Certificates and told him that I felt he was justified in shooting Stanford White (1853–1906).

[Ed.: Harry Kendall Thaw was the son of a Pittsburgh coal and railroad baron who became a folk hero after dramatically shooting and killing noted architect Stanford White for having deflowered his wife Evelyn Nesbit several years before when she was sixteen and a Florodora (chorus) girl. The story was popularized in the 1955 film, *The Girl in the Red Velvet Swing*, and photographs by the talented Rudolf Eickemeyer, Jr. attest to Evelyn Nesbit's considerable beauty. The girl who had swung in White's red velvet swing died January 17, 1967 in Santa Monica, California.]

Thaw was amazed by the Gold Certificate and said he would like to show me something. I thought he was going to invite me into his home, but he came out and asked me to come with him. Together, we walked a few blocks and entered a brownstone mansion. The interior architecture and furniture were beautiful, and of fantastic concept. Everything was spotless and smelled of ozone; I wouldn't be surprised if professional cleaners cleaned the mansion several times a week and had just finished cleaning it. He took me to the third floor where a red velvet swing was hanging from the ceiling. I am quite sure that Thaw was involved in the occult, and that the secret red velvet swing in the beautiful but peculiar interior of that brownstone mansion was of symbolical importance to him. I then walked back with him to his home where we stood on the walk to talk for a few moments. I asked him how to get to the Morgan library. After telling me how, he asked me to mention his name to J.P. if I saw him.

I then headed for Madison Avenue and East 37th Street, the site of the J.P. Morgan (1867–1934) mansion. His father, John Pierpont Morgan (1837–1913), who had acted as America's central bank and Federal Reserve when none existed, had a mansion on Madison Avenue and East 36th Street. The two mansions were connected by a tunnel that also connected to the

Morgan Library. The architect of the Morgan Library was Charles McKim, a partner of Stanford White whom Harry K. Thaw is said to have shot. The mansion and library were constructed with fitted marble blocks without mortar. In Masonic dogma, such construction is called dry diking, and a person who does such work is called a dry diker, which is synonymous with cowan. As I've said, cowan is said to be a purely Masonic term that signifies an intruder, a profane person who has the temerity to know about Masonry.

When I arrived at the Morgan compound, a large luxurious sedan driven by a non-uniformed driver with an elderly man sitting in the back, pulled out. Taking a chance that it was J.P. Morgan, I shouted, "Wait a minute, you old pirate, I want to talk to you about Jekyll Island." The car stopped and I walked up to the back side window, holding out a Million Dollar Gold Certificate and saying, "Look what I have for your money collection."

J.P. Morgan took the Gold Certificate and looked at it knowingly. "What do you want for this?" he asked.

I said, "I want a guided tour through your library."

Without batting an eye, Morgan asked me to get into the car and instructed the driver to take us inside the enclosure. Once inside, we got out and went into the library. He then took me into what I assume was the main reading room where a number of young people were presided over very strictly by an older man. With the exception of one distraught-looking girl, the students looked deadly serious, surrounded as they were by books suggesting considerable age. It occurred to me that perhaps they were studying ancient tomes of mystical import.

After allowing me only a few seconds in that room, Morgan took me into the East Room where I saw a large book chained to an antique bookstand, similar to the prophetic books I had with chaining devices on them. I took that moment to give him Harry K. Thaw's greetings and to say that despite the trials and tribulations he had had, I thought him quite likeable, to which Morgan replied, "Most people who really know him think so, too." A man then came in and whispered something to Morgan. Of course, people generally talk quietly in a library, if they talk at all, so I shouldn't have thought it strange, but I did. Morgan then said that the man would show me around and left the room.

No sooner had he left than I walked over to the open chained book and recognized immediately that it was the same type of prophetic book I owned. I ruffled the pages, turning to a page near the end of the book. I had caught the man unawares, and he then protested that I shouldn't look in that particular book, as Mr. Morgan generally kept it in the West Room. I told him I was disappointed not to have gotten the opportunity to talk with Mr. Morgan about the Jolly Roger flag, or rather the Skull & Bones flag, that he always hoisted on his yacht the *Corsair* just as it approached Jekyll Island. He couldn't tell me anything, and so without further ado I turned and walked into the main reading room and sat down by the distraught girl. I asked her what was wrong.

She said, "I hate this place and want to leave, but they won't let me."

"You know that couldn't be so. If you really want to leave, you can go with me." She then alleged that Morgan was a wizard and would never let us leave. Jokingly, I said, "If he tries to stop us, I will get Hetty Green, the witch of Wall Street, after him."

[Ed.: Henrietta Howland Robinson Green (1835–1916) was the first female financier. Inheriting $1 million at age thirty, she increased her wealth one-hundred fold by grasping the magic of compounding interest. She lived in boarding houses and took public transportation to her Wall Street office.]

At the door of the West Room, I saw yet another "face-off": Morgan and another man were standing toe to toe, just looking at each other. Deliberately, I crossed the threshold, apologized for my intrusion, then returned to the East Room where my guide was still waiting as though chained to the spot. He then took me to a moderately sized but elegantly furnished bedroom and asked, "How would you like to have this room?" I didn't know why he said that. I replied something to the effect that the room was beautiful but I needed to see what kind of food went with the room before deciding. My humor was wasted on him, too, as it is on so many people.

He then took me to a tunnel. Before we had walked more than fifty feet, I saw a ticker tape stock market device that had a yard of paper tape with old stock market quotations hanging from it. Apparently, the device was just being stored in the tunnel, as it wasn't connected. Thinking it odd that the paper tape hadn't been removed, I tore it off, which greatly upset my guide. According to him, he didn't know what Mr. Morgan would say or do when he found out. Grabbing the tape from me, he walked hurriedly in the direction from which we had come. I waited several minutes for him to return and when he didn't, proceeded on into the tunnel and to the mansion where John Pierpont Morgan had resided. After walking through several rooms and not seeing anyone, I decided it would be advisable for me to leave, which I did.

Chapter 18

FDR and the Million Dollar Check

Fort Thomas, Kentucky, 1931

hen I returned home, I felt that my trip to see Herbert O. Yardley as well as my effort to recover my book were what I call a water haul. The book I had sent to the State Department was never returned to me, despite my letters. I even wrote William (1891–1969) and Elizebeth Smith Friedman (1892–1980) who had been employed by "Colonel" George Fabyan to decipher the Francis Bacon code and had thereby developed their talents in cryptography until both became recognized experts. They answered my letter immediately, and I gathered from their reply that they didn't think much of Yardley as a cryptographer or as a person, and that I should have known better than to deal with him. I don't recall now why I didn't seek the Friedmans as allies, but maybe I did and have just forgotten it.

[Ed.: Fabyan is celebrated for having established the first think tank. It should also be noted that the National Security Agency—founded 36 years after Fabyan's death—presented a plaque to the Riverbank Acoustic Laboratory that reads, "To the memory of George Fabyan from a grateful government." An eccentric (*i.e.*, visionary) millionaire, he employed equally eccentric men and women to study everything from acoustics to perpetual motion machines and the true authorship of Shakespeare. His 300-acre Fox River Valley estate called Riverbank, 40 miles west of Chicago, was certainly well-named in terms of toponomy (the geography of witchcraft) and onomancy (the doctrine of names), given that foxes, like the oaks in Oakcliff and Oaklawn, are pregnant with pagan lore. Did Fabyan have access to books such as those that Downard acquired?]

I started disposing of some of the tomb acquisitions by sending some of the old books to the New York City Public Library, including several cipher/codebooks with my name on them. In an accompanying letter, I suggested that cryptographers might be interested in deciphering the codebooks. I received a reply from the library thanking me for the gift. Meanwhile, I continued to resent how the State Department and Yardley had appropriated my book and kept trying to come up with some way to publicly denounce the high-handed, dishonest way I had been treated. While thinking along those lines, I decided to send some books to President Franklin D. Roosevelt, along with some Million Dollar Gold Certificates, old stamps from the tomb, and several other items. Among the books I sent were a few on atomic energy and bombs. In my accompanying letter, I wrote about the Dayton Witch as well as how much I admired him.

In a short time, things started to happen.

I received a telephone call from the White House. The caller asked if I was James Shelby Downard, and when I said I was, the caller said, "The President of the United States, Franklin D. Roosevelt, wants to talk to you." I thought someone was playing a joke on me until I heard President Roosevelt's wonderful voice. Still, I said, "Mr. President, just so I know that you are you, will you please say, 'My Friends,' for no one can say it with the feeling that you do." So he said it and then we talked like old friends. He thanked me for the things I had sent, then asked about my letter and what it said about discovering things that might once have been in an alchemist's chamber. I remember telling him about the paper tag on the Dayton Witch that read "Brunel University," and that I had been unable to find out where Brunel University was and wondered if he knew. I talked about the crystal skull, the Million Dollar Gold Certificates, and some of the novelties in the mélange. I also mentioned the book that the State Department had virtually stolen from me. He asked if I still had all of the other things that had been in the barn and a number of other questions, not as an interrogator, but in a friendly, interested way.

Later, he called again with more questions, including did I think that my father might have written the books with his and my name on them. I told him that it seemed to be a deep dark secret, and that one of the fables I had been told was that an "Uncle Brad" had written the books, though no one could identify "Uncle Brad." I said that I had been told that the James Shelby Downard designated as author of the obscure books was me and not my father. FDR then said that he'd have all the barn goods picked up and I that I would be paid for them. I thanked him and said that the stamps and Million Dollar Gold Certificates I had sent him were gifts for his stamp and currency collections. He then swore me to secrecy regarding the whole matter and proceeded to administer an oath, which I spoke with sincerity.

After the oath, we said goodbye and hung up. That very instant, there came a knock at the door. A man stood there with credentials identifying him as a Secret Service agent (*i.e.,* Treasury agent, White House Security Force). He said he had been sent to pick up some things I had. Waiting for him in a sedan was a man who I assumed was a member of the White House Security Force, too, though I didn't ask to see his identification. Their arrival must have been timed to the very second.

Their car was too small to carry everything, and the man with the credentials said that a large vehicle would be there soon. The words were hardly out of his mouth when an armored car arrived and parked in front of the sedan. Two men got out and the four of them went with me to my den. After the first load was carried out, one of the men who had arrived with the armored car stayed with the car while the other three went back to get more things. After several trips, everything was loaded.

The man with the credentials asked me if that was all of it and I assured him it was. "We had better look around to make sure before we leave," he said, so the three men returned to my den to examine my personal possessions. One of the men picked up a small ceramic skull with a cavity in it where incense was burned. He asked, "Does this go?"

It struck me that their attitude had changed as soon as they had possession of the things, and the man's tone of voice irritated me, so instead of explaining the ceramic skull, I just told them to take it and get out. Surprised, they hesitated, then turned and started to leave. In an apologetic tone of voice, one of the men said, "We were told to get everything."

As the days went by, I daydreamed about what I would do with the money I was to be paid and speculated as to how much it might be. At first,

I thought it might be as much as five thousand dollars, but as time passed I kept increasing the amount and what I would do with it: I would buy a car, new clothes, I would take my family on a long ocean voyage, etc. Finally, an envelope arrived from the United States Treasury. Showing it to my mother, I said, "Hold your breath," then opened the envelope and took out the check. I looked at the amount and silently handed it to Mother, then hollered in joy and jumped as high as I could. The check was for one million dollars.

Mother was flabbergasted and turned pale, staggering as though she might fall. I put my arm around her in affection as well as to support her, and we both sat on the couch. Then she said, "You must not let your father see this or tell him about it. We must keep this a secret between you and me." I couldn't understand it as I should have and resolutely said, "Of course I am going to show the check to Father, it wouldn't be right to do otherwise." I now wish that I had listened more and talked less, and heeded what my mother requested.

When I showed the check to my father, he became enraged and said that what I had done was "immoral"—a favorite expression of his. By saying this, he played his role as a moralist of great integrity. Though this role-playing often contradicted reality, I sheepishly accepted the part he played as factual.

For the next day or two, my father approached the check with a new tactic, that a mistake had obviously been made. Certainly, he explained, the things I had given the president's men couldn't possibly be worth more than a few thousand dollars, if that much. To deposit a check of this size would be viewed as possibly felonious conduct. It was decided that the right thing to do was to write the Treasury Department and inquire whether the amount was correct. Like a fool I did as I was told. It took considerable time before I received a reply, which in effect said that the check should be returned for verification. So I sent it back.

Time passed and the check was not returned, nor was another check for another amount issued. I wrote a letter of inquiry and received an immediate reply from the Treasury Department, the essence of which was, did I expect some payment from the government? If so, explain what the expected payment was for. Having been sworn to secrecy, I couldn't reveal what the expected payment was for, nor that President Roosevelt had personally arranged that I should be paid. I was stymied by the goddamn oath and my admiration for President Roosevelt.

Not being able to answer the Treasury Department as to why I was expecting a check, I therefore wrote several letters to FDR without actually explaining in my letter the dilemma I had put myself in, for I knew that letters to the President are opened and read before being brought to his attention. When I didn't hear from FDR, I assumed that he didn't get my letter, although I now know that he probably did, for I was being hornswoggled in a mystical charade. For a long time afterward, I couldn't imagine that President Roosevelt had been even remotely connected with such a thing, just as I couldn't believe that he had been connected with the attempt to kill me in front of Antoine's Restaurant in New Orleans on April 27, 1937.

The only thing I thought I could do to solve the dilemma surrounding the one million dollar government check was to go to Washington and see President Roosevelt, believing as I did that he would have the check returned to me if it was for the proper amount, and if it wasn't, would have another check issued. I talked to my parents about making the trip but they refused to finance it. Mother said they had already financed a trip to Washington, D.C. for me to see Yardley, and that I had gone on to New York City without telling them and accomplished nothing, etc. Though it didn't exactly qualify as an accomplishment, I had discovered the prophetic book in the Morgan Library that was similar to the prophetic books I had. I was unable to go to Washington to see President Roosevelt until the summer of 1933.

Chapter 19

Procter Takes A Gamble

Fort Thomas, Kentucky, 1931

My family ties to William Cooper Procter of the multimillion-dollar household products corporation was threefold: first, "because of friendship" he had bankrolled a small company that based some of its success with Patent No. 1662377, owned by my mother, Mrs. N.W. Downard; secondly, my brother-in-law James Eley Robertson was his executive secretary; and thirdly, the Procter Rendering Company advertisement that I had found in one of the books with my or my father's name on it. Though I had only met Mr. Procter once, I was incessantly regaled with stories lauding him in glowing terms, which I accepted as being fundamentally factual. His sense of humor was said to be particularly outstanding.

With this in mind, I telephoned the multimillionaire and told him I had some bones for sale that might be suitable for rendering, and I thought he should have first chance at them. He laughed at that, possibly picking up on the idea that some of the products made long ago by P&G were produced by rendering.

"How is it you are willing to part with them, as you must value them highly?" he asked over the phone.

I laughed and replied, "You see, Mr. Procter, when I was looking through an old book in an old barn, I found a newspaper advertisement seeking animal carcasses for rendering, and the name of the advertiser is the same as yours, and the name of the author of the book is the same as mine."

"What's the date of the advertisement?" he asked. Having the ad in my hand, I told him what it was. "I see," he said. "Now tell me where you get your bones."

"Oh, I don't have them now, sir, but I can obtain them for you, if the price is right."

Jovially, he said, "I'd like to know your source of supply, though."

Without hesitating, I said, "The source of supply is the Skull and Bones fraternity."

Without hesitating, he replied, "Is there anything to those bonesmen and anything on the bones?"

"I'm not sure about that, Mr. Procter, but I'll bet you've got some employees who could tell you, if you could get them to talk."

Despite being a very busy man with numerous commitments, Procter went right along with my "joke" and asked to meet so we could discuss the price of the bones. So early the next Sunday morning, I met Mr. Procter at the Mount Adams incline in Cincinnati. There are five inclines in the city: Mount Auburn, Clifton Heights, Price Hill, Fairview Heights, and Mount Adams. All five are of symbolical importance to those of the symbolical persuasion. It is often said that Cincinnati was built on seven hills like Rome, and the inclines are five of them. In the course of our meeting, I showed Procter both the advertisement and the cipher/codebook in which it had served as a page marker.

"May I borrow the advertisement and the book, Shelby?" the tycoon asked.

"You may have the advertisement, Mr. Procter, and I will loan you the text. Maybe you are a cryptologist along with everything else and you can make some sense out of it; I haven't been able to."

"No, I'm not a cryptologist, but the book looks interesting and I would like to see what I can do with it. Shelby, why don't you ride the incline with me to the Rookwood Pottery place on Mt. Adams?"

Rookwood Pottery was founded in 1880 by Mrs. Maria Longworth Storer and took its name from a peculiar feature of the famed Longworth Estate: the persistence of crows (rooks) roosting in great numbers in the area. The original pottery was on Eastern Avenue until it moved to the more spectacular Mount Adams in 1893. A great deal of pottery turned out by Rookwood bore numerous marks and symbols, some of which were decorative, others the trademarks of particular artists. In 1962, a booklet by Edwin J. Kircher catalogued these marks and symbols and discovered that trademarks and decorative flourishes do not account for all of the signs on

Rookwood pottery over the years. In my opinion, the esoteric symbols on Rookwood pottery form a story in themselves.

I was eager to accompany Procter but reminded him that it was Sunday and Rookwood probably wouldn't be open. He said he could get us in, even if it was closed to the public. Such is the life of the rich and connected. So we boarded a streetcar for the ride up. Just as it began its ascent, before Procter and I had even taken a seat, he became embroiled in a violent argument with a man who boarded the streetcar at the last minute and was standing up against him. I don't know how the argument started, but obviously Procter was slightly intimidated, so the streetcar stopped about fifty feet from where it had picked us up and Procter and I exited, after which he said, "This is actually neither the time nor place for continuing our trip to the pottery, Shelby, but we'll do it again at a more auspicious time." Perhaps our not continuing to the top was the better part of Procter's valor, given that the belligerent man might have been waiting for us at the top of the Incline. I agreed and thanked him for our time together. He thanked me for the advertisement and promised to return the book "in the near future."

Time passed and Procter failed to keep his promise. I asked my brother-in-law to please remind him about the book as politely as he could and suggest to him that I was anxious to have it back. I wanted it returned because I was certain by then that it was involved in some way with the Dayton Witch.

"You know, bud," my brother-in-law responded, "I'm reluctant to say anything to him about returning the book because I have never seen anyone so interested in anything as he is in that book. He spends literally hours every day poring over the cryptographs on every page, then takes it home with him."

"I have no doubt it fascinates him, but I want it back," I replied.

He winced as if my words caused him actual pain. "That will be difficult, bud, and I was hoping that you would let him keep the book. I fear that asking for its return, even in the most respectful way, might reflect on me."

I thought to myself, *All this over a book?* Aloud, I said, "When you put it that way, I can't refuse you." (I loved my brother-in-law.)

A few days later, I learned from Mother that Jim had received a gift of Rookwood pottery bookends fashioned into whimsical bears from Procter. I knew that he sometimes gave Rookwood pottery as gifts to his friends and trusted employees. When I asked Jim about the Rookwood bear bookends, he informed me, "Mr. Procter wants you to go to Rookwood Pottery on Saturday at 2 p.m.

I kept the appointment. Craning my neck for several minutes, I caught no sight of Procter. The pottery was open but deserted, so I decided to have a look around. I walked through the office and out into the shop where two men were standing near a kiln/furnace. One man ran as soon as he saw me, but the other remained. I asked him if he had seen Mr. William Cooper Procter, as I had an appointment with him. He grinned and opened the furnace where a corpse was engulfed in flames. "That's not him, is it?" he asked with gallows humor.

I left. All the way down the incline, I wondered what I had witnessed. Maybe a crematory's furnace had broken down and Rookwood Pottery was doubling as a crematory; maybe Rookwood Pottery was going into the "bone china" business; or maybe an esoteric society was turning bone into ash for going into special pieces of pottery (*My father's dust was turned into pottery.— Omar Khayyam*). Other questions nagged me even more, sticking to me like a Band-Aid to hairs around a wound that you just can't pull off because you know it will hurt too much: Why had I been shown the body? Why had Procter asked me to go to the pottery and then not shown up? What did he have to do with the cremation? Did the bear bookends my brother-in-law had been given contain human ash? These questions gnawed at me like berserk Vikings in bearskins.

A few weeks after I had witnessed the cremation, Jim approached me with a look in his eyes that some men have when ambition is making them do things they know are questionable. In other words, he had about him a bit of the wolf and a bit of the sheep. "Mr. Procter is really sorry he couldn't meet you at Rookwood Pottery and hopes you're not upset," Jim said sheepishly.

What should I say? Actually, I wasn't angry. I was just puzzled by what had happened and told Jim so.

"Oh good, bud, because Mr. Procter wants you to do something for him. He wants you to go to a kind of pantheon in a Cincinnati cemetery."

"That sounds like fun," I said cynically. "What does he want me to do, drive a stake in the heart of some corpse to keep it from going out on the town at night?"

"C'mon, Shelby, Mr. Procter likes you and has a lot of faith in you. I don't know why he wants you to go there, but I know it means a lot to him."

I shrugged. "I'll go, why not?"

I arrived at the cemetery, and came across the pantheon that I found to be bright and immaculately clean. In a corner was a pedestal holding a large brass urn, probably intended to hold ashes. On a hunch, I looked into it and was greeted by the sight of something that was turning up as often as the rabbit during Alice's trip to Wonderland: a thick wad of Million Dollar Gold Certificates. I took them, assuming they were why I had been sent, and departed the exclusive burial ground. I sent one of the Certificates to Procter via Jim. Soon afterward, I was told that Procter would like to have all he could lay his hands on. I sent him another.

Musing on the "money" in the vase, I recalled that in ancient times a coin was placed in the mouth of a cadaver to enable it to pay Charon the ferryman to transport the dead across the River Styx to Erebus. The Chinese also have a custom of leaving "soul money" for the dead, of burning it or throwing it into the sea. What the Masons do with symbolical money pertains to their religious symbolism. By taking the money of the dead, did I interfere with their rite of passage and strand them on this side of the Styx? I decided that if the ferryman accepts Million Dollar Gold Certificates, he was taking phony money, and any Styx ferryman that accepts such things is looking for trouble.

Procter and Gamble Corporation had a controversy in recent years having to do with the symbolism of its famous trademark: a man-in-the-moon caricature with thirteen stars. Some individuals allege that this trademark is a thing of witchcraft, an opinion Procter and Gamble has taken legal action to stifle. William Dobson, director of Public Information for the Procter and Gamble conglomerate, has attempted to explain the company's use of this frankly bizarre sign by saying that the design was first used on boxes of "Stars" candles. Dobson claims the stars represent the thirteen original colonies.

It is true that the P&G trademark is over one hundred years old, and perhaps the thirteen stars do symbolize thirteen colonies, and the man in the moon is a stand-in for a loony Uncle Sam. But it would be naïve to assume that there are other less benign interpretations of the man in the moon, the number 13, and interplay of starlight (the "thousand points of light") and corporate America as symbolized by EPCOT (Experimental Prototype Community of Tomorrow), a "utopian city of the future" at Walt Disney World in Florida that opened October 1, 1982. Such symbols may just as well represent the secrecy, silence, darkness and/or hoodwinks relevant to Masonry's Master Plan.

William Cooper Procter was a Mason with a serious passion for the occult. But what about my brother-in-law and my father? What was their ranking in relation to Procter, given that my brother-in-law set me up for the individual cremation at Rookwood Pottery, and my father who would set up a correspondence between that individual's cremation and the mass cremation I would subsequently witness. My father's association with Mr. Procter was not just through my mother's ownership of the patent, but had to do with Million Dollar Gold Certificates long before the ones I procured.

Before seeing a mass cremation, I semi-jested with my brother-in-law about it. "I'll bet that the RP on Rookwood Pottery is synonymous with RIP—Rest In Peace—and there is a little bit of bone in all their pottery."

"Shelby!" my brother-in-law gasped. "Don't talk like that. People don't know you're joking and you don't know what they'll think."

"Well, I'm only half-joking, and I don't care what they think. Something is wrong about that cremation at Rookwood. Besides, what would people think if they knew you were a member of the Skull and Bones fraternity?" He was startled that I brought it up. I went on. "Anybody who is a member of that macabre funster club ought not to object to a somewhat macabre comment about Rookwood Pottery, especially when I tell them what I saw there."

Jim was uncomfortable with what I was saying. Isn't that human nature for you? Here all of these Masonic-type fraternities practically make a religion out of poking fun at the uninitiated "profane ones," but when they get targeted with a joke, suddenly it's all "beneath their dignity."

At least Father saw some gallows humor in my jesting about Rookwood Pottery, especially when I said I had heard that it might be appropriate for such a rook to take up residence at Rookwood Pottery and scream *NEVER-MORE! NEVERMORE!* Father then recommended we take a little motor trip to Rookwood Pottery. I was pleased to go with him anywhere, given how little I saw little of him. He made a telephone call, then as we started to leave, he said, "Don't bring your gun, Shelby, or I won't go." I thought it was peculiar, but since there was one in the car, I didn't ask him why not.

When we got to Rook Pottery, Father got out of the car, went inside, and marched right out. When I asked what he was doing, he gave no explanation but smiled his enigmatic smile and told me to get back in the car. Sensing a mystery in the making, I stayed sharp and alert as we drove back into the city to a huge facility with a vast area for parking cars and trucks, though none were there. It was the city incinerator. I couldn't imagine why he was taking me to such a place, given his obsession about dirt.

Inside, a broad-of-beam man with a brutal, sadistic air about him stood near the door wearing a sidearm and toting a pump-action shotgun. Behind him was a row of incinerators or furnaces tended by prisoners. Their roar was dreadful and the heat overpowering. They were going full blast, all stoked up—but with what for fuel? The men looked ill and as if they might fall on the ground or even into the incinerators at any moment. Taking the scene in, I said to the guard, "You mean to tell me that Cincinnati garbage is so valuable that an armed guard is needed to protect it?"

The guard said nothing to me, but immediately said to my father, pointing to me with his shotgun, "Is he the one?"

My father said something in reply that I couldn't hear and then they started talking, which gave me the opportunity to walk quickly to the workers tending the first incinerator. Nearby were several desiccated bodies. One of the men opened the incinerator door as the other prepared to place a body inside it. Inside the incinerator were the remains of other bodies.

Recognizing that I was in a death trap, I bolted away from the incinerator past my father and the guard, my skin a-tingle. As I passed them, I heard the guard say, "He hasn't been prepared right, he's seen too much."

When I got to the car, I was breathing hard but not from exertion. I grabbed my single shot .20-gauge shotgun and faced Father and the guard as they slowly walked toward me. At about ten feet, the guard said with menace in his voice, "Go back inside. We're going to put you to work." When I stood my ground, he made a threatening movement with his shotgun that almost cost him his life then and there, given that I was pointing my shotgun at his belly.

"Get your ass in the car and let's get out of here," I shouted to my father, my tone of contempt feeling good. Prior to that moment, I had always treated my father with the utmost respect.

When Father got in the car, I ordered the guard to walk back to the incinerator. When I had driven only a few feet, I looked in the rearview mirror and watched the guard go inside. I stopped the car and told my father that I was going back to have a little talk with his friend. Cautiously, I walked back and peered into the gloomy incinerator area. I saw the guard hit one of the prisoner/workers with the barrel of his shotgun, at which I yelled, "You have no right to do that!" Hearing me, the prisoners grabbed the guard and incinerated him alive, after which they hightailed it.

As Father and I drove back to Fort Thomas, I wondered why he had insisted on making the apparently symbolical stop at Rookwood Pottery before taking me to a city dump incinerator where cremations were underway. Where did the desiccated bodies come from? Did they come from the type of graves that are called ovens? I recalled hearing that desiccated bodies were taken from "oven graves" in New Orleans. If that was so, then bodies might desiccate in the Cincinnati area. Was there an occult symbolical difference between a body being cremated at a pottery and in a dump incinerator? I longed to ask my father such questions, but I had only to look at his ashen face to see that it wasn't the time to ask him anything.

When my father was a young man at the University of Michigan in Ann Arbor, he had joined first the Delta *Tau* Delta fraternity and then a secret society known as the Illuminati, alleged to have originated in Bavaria—a quasi-Masonic society and thus as kinky and perverse as anything one can imagine. Father was one of those well-bred, exceptionally able young men who are regularly selected from among their classmates for indoctrination and training in specialized esoteric fields in preparation for executing the Master Plan behind the scenes. He was, as they say, a Big Man on Campus, part of the rising managerial and executive class. A young man such as my father was known as an *agentur* as portrayed in the Hollywood film, *The Brotherhood of the Bell* (1970).

In his early twenties, he was well on his way to taking over the Nickel Plate Railroad by means of a stock proxy reorganization (shakedown) that used women (blackmail) and Illuminati skullduggery to control stockholders. But then he had a falling-out with the secret society or at least associates with whom he shared membership. Due to fear of reprisals for not carrying out certain orders, he relocated to Indian Territory. Father claimed he didn't realize that he was being used for ulterior purposes by the "Illuminated Ones."

The book that I loaned and eventually was cajoled into letting William Cooper Procter keep was definitely part of the mysticism surrounding the Illuminati. Books like those are emanations of mystic power.

Chapter 20

"Uncle Brad"

Covington, Kentucky, 1931

I began to realize that the determining factor of my tribulations were the books with my name on them. Discovering who that James Shelby Downard was seemed to me to be the mystery I needed to solve. Maybe that James Shelby Downard was a member of the Downard family of Covington, Kentucky—the branch of Downards that Eule Howard had mentioned when I spotted the books in his safe.

Not only did my parents insist that we were not related to the Covington Downards, I was told, contrary to my memories, that we had never been in northern Kentucky before. Discovering that the Downard mansion was part of the Covington High School complex, I decided to go there and find out whether a James Shelby Downard was a member of that Downard family.

When I arrived at the mansion, a woman was sitting at a table in the foyer. I introduced myself and told her that I had memories of being in that house when I was little and would appreciate looking around to see if I could retrieve any more dormant memories. She wasn't rude, but told me that touring the house was not convenient at that time, for she was the only one there except for some workmen, and couldn't leave the desk to show me around.

So I made my way to Mrs. B. Downard Davison's home. I told her that I had some memories of being in her former home when I was little, and showing her one of the books with the name James Shelby Downard on it, I told her I was trying to find out about the author of the book and thought he might possibly be related to her.

Mrs. Davison was certain there was no one named James Shelby Downard in her family's genealogy, but that it was possible that I visited her home in the past. Then she offered to take me to see the old home. When we arrived there, the woman in the foyer repeated what she had told me before.

Mrs. Davison introduced herself and said that we just wanted to walk through her old home and was quite sure we would not be in anyone's way.

We walked through the downstairs and then went upstairs where some men in white overalls were just hanging around, not doing anything in particular. It took just a few minutes to walk through the rooms with Mrs. Davison making comments about the rooms and furniture that occupied them years earlier. We went downstairs; the woman at the table was gone. Mrs. Davison asked me if I could remember being in the house before.

I went to a series of panels in a wall and proceeded to press and shove several panels. Just as Mrs. Davison asked, "Do you think you should be doing that?" one panel gave way. Behind it was a small repository in which there was a bulging velvet purse about four inches wide and six inches long standing upright against a parcel of papers. I reached in, took out the purse, and handed it to her as she stood speechless. I removed the parcel of papers and immediately closed the panel, for I expected the woman who had been at the desk to come in on us at any moment.

Mrs. Davison stared at me as she clutched the bulging purse.

"Aren't you going to open it and see if it is all there?" I asked. Before she could say or do a thing, I rudely reached over and opened the clasp on the gold frame of the purse so that the jewelry protruded.

Mrs. Davison gasped. "Can you imagine Benny leaving all of these things when we left? He is simply so absorbed in his business that he doesn't pay any attention to anything else." She then suggested that we not let anyone see what we had because she had rather not make any explanations. Then she asked me what she should do with the purse. So I put it in my outside coat pocket and the papers in my inside pocket.

As we approached the front door, the woman who had been at the desk entered to say ask Mrs. Davison that would she care to go over to the school for just a few minutes, since everyone would be so happy to see her. Mrs. Davison demurred and before we got back in the car I handed her the purse and papers.

On the way back to her home, she said that she hoped no one would hear about our little adventure. I don't believe she knew about the repository or had ever seen the velvet purse or jewels before, which might have belonged to her mother or grandmother. As for the papers, I have no idea what they were about, but most were letters in envelopes.

After I hurried home I found that Mrs. Davison had called my mother to tell her about my discovery of things that her husband had thoughtlessly left behind when they moved, and how much she appreciated it. Her call gave me the opportunity to rebuke my mother—given that Father wasn't home— for trying to convince me that I had never been in northern Kentucky before.

I reminded her of when we first arrived at Fort Thomas and stayed in the old Ross home that had become a boarding house. I remembered climbing through a dining room window a number of times, carrying things and burying them between the old Ross home and the apartment house. And when we moved to the apartment house next door to the old Ross home, I had told her that Father had gotten some Negro men to dig for me, and after a few minutes they found a lime- and dirt-encrusted "tea service." When we couldn't clean it, one of the Negroes said he had a friend in the plating business who could clean it in a few minutes, so I let him take the stuff and you know what happened: I never saw them again. And when I checked with the Newport employment agency through which Father said he had hired the Negroes, they claimed to know nothing about them.

Mother's response to my remembering where things were, such as the "tea service" and Mrs. Davison's jewelry, was that there are people who can discover hidden things psychically or by divining. She suggested that this might be my condition. "However," she finally admitted, "your father was so very proud of you when you were little that he took you with him everywhere he went, and it is possible that he was in that area long ago and had you with him. As you know, whenever he went to a town or city on business, he would look in the telephone directory to see if there were any Downards listed, and if there were, he would often call them and sometimes go to see them, so perhaps he took you to see the Downard family in Covington." In this instance, at least, she was no longer trying to convince me that my memories of being in northern Kentucky were illusions. I pressed further.

"If Father did bring me to northern Kentucky in the past, why the hell doesn't he say so? It's strange how he never talks to me and never stays in the same room with me for more than a few minutes at a time."

Mother replied, "I will tell you something if you promise that you will say nothing about it to anyone, and if you promise not to ask me any questions about what I tell you." I promised. Mother then proceeded to transform meaningful information into yet another enigma. "After the Ku Klux Klan people took you and your father out to Caddo Creek and nailed your hands to the tree, they brought you both home. Later, they took your father someplace and did something to him. He wouldn't talk about it, even to me, but he blames you for what they did to him. For a short time after you were exonerated of killing the Ku Kluxers in the Ardmore trial, your father stopped blaming you. When we moved to Dallas, he started blaming you all over again, and I imagine he still does. He doesn't want you to recall certain things. While your father has told me a number of times that I must not tell you certain things, but I am going to tell you who wrote those books that have your name on them. It was Uncle Brad."

I sighed. "If you tell me who Uncle Brad is, then we will be getting somewhere."

"You promised that you wouldn't ask me any questions about what I have told you, and I expect you to stick to your promise."

The identity of "Uncle Brad" was a family secret that has been and is still hidden from me. He was purported to have been insane, imagining that he owned valuable property in Ardmore, Oklahoma that was taken from him through connivance. Reputedly, he would stand on street corners and buttonhole people to tell them his grievance. According to him, public records that proved his ownership had been burned with other public records by the "Courthouse Gang." That he identified the Courthouse Gang as Masons and accused them of arson distressed some people who wanted to get a court order to send "Uncle Brad" to the insane asylum, but my father interceded in his behalf.

Given that my father claimed not to have any brothers or sisters, and none of my mother's brothers and half-brothers were named Brad or Bradley, "Uncle Brad" might have been an uncle by marriage (one of my mother's sisters had been married five times)—but I don't think so. My provisional acceptance of my mother's story that "Uncle Brad" had written the books and used my name as author was simply a basis for further endless theorizing.

Chapter 21

Graduation
Highlands High School, Fort Thomas, Kentucky, 1932

ort Thomas was a maze of overt and covert malice and hatred. Most
confusing was the iniquitous spread of misinformation and defamatory
rumors about me that was intimately connected to an organized network of
crime and skullduggery that was in turn part of a much larger maze that led
nowhere.

I didn't know which way to turn. Still, the maze was not unknown to me,
nor was I a stranger to malice and hatred, so I made my way in and out and
about, leaving telltale marks that enabled me later to remember it unerringly, though I wondered how and why I had become the victim of such cease-
less abuse.

Tellingly, the pall lifted for a brief window of time when I was once
again asked to join De Molay. I told the boy who encouraged me to join
about the experience I had had in Dallas, and he told me that De Molay in
Fort Thomas was not like that, at all. So I said I would join and he said that
I needed a Mason in the Scottish Rite to sponsor me. I suggested that his
father sponsor me, but he gave me some reason as to why he couldn't. When
I mentioned it to my sister, she said she would talk to Alex Howard about it;
Alex and his wife were cherished friends of my sister and brother-in-law.
Several weeks later, when I saw my sister again, she gave me a gold De Molay
pin set with thirteen seed pearls on the shield and a tiny saber marked "De
Molay." and said that Alex would be glad to sponsor me and for me to wear
a De Molay pin until I was recognized.

"Recognized for what?" I asked.

My sister replied that she was just relaying what Alex had said.

So I started wearing the De Molay pin. After several weeks, the boy who
had initially urged me to join told me that there was going to be a De Molay

dance and that he would like to borrow my pin to wear to the dance, so I loaned it to him. A couple of weeks later, he told me he had lost the pin. He brought me a pin cut out of a piece of copper and told me he had had it made for me because he couldn't buy another pin. I thought about the loss of the pin for weeks while carrying the copper pin in my pocket. Then one day in the chemistry laboratory, in front of the De Molay boy, I poured nitric acid into a beaker and dropped the copper pin into it. We watched it go up in smoke as I voiced opinions about secret societies.

When I told Alex about lending the De Molay pin and not getting it back, he reminded me that he had sponsored me and that I should have come to him and he would have had it returned to me. I told him that if taking my pin in the way it was done was part of De Molay symbolism, then shit on it.

Several months later, the boy to whom I had lent the De Molay pin "found" it and returned it to me. In that interval between losing and finding the pin, malice and hatred for me had begun to manifest again and I thought I knew the source: an Knights Templar man named Hunt who had a son in De Molay. Hunt sold tea, both wholesale and retail, so when I went in I said I was a real Tea Taster. (The 99-year-old Board of Tea Examiners—it was just closed in 1996—employed "tea tasters," but many suspected they were actually engaged in espionage.) I elaborated on my ability to find things out and told him that I had traced some of the malice and hatred of me to De Molay boys, and that I just wanted to let him know that I knew.

It wasn't so much the students who were stand offish at Highlands High School; the teachers gave me the hardest time, including the principal Foeman H. Rudd. At first, he was friendly enough—I even loaned him my car to take out a young girl said to have been a "roundheels." As they drove away, I took a picture of them that turned out surprisingly well, so well in fact that their faces could be clearly seen. When he began to castigate me for no apparent reason, I retorted by telling him that a girl student at another high school alleged he had "knocked her up." Rudd didn't answer me, he just stalked off.

Rudd was attached to one teacher who was skilled in a number of crafts, including photography. There were rumors that this teacher performed fellatio with some of the students and made little attempt to hide it, despite the fact that homosexuality was not flaunted back then as it is today.

One day after being kept after school, I went to see the principal. Looking through open door to his office, I saw a teacher down on his knees with his head between Rudd's legs. I spoke without thinking, and the teacher jumped up and scurried out of the room.

It was getting close to June graduation and school was out for the day. I wanted to ask Rudd's favorite teacher if his open hostility toward me had anything to do with my interrupting his "conference" with Rudd. Then I saw Mrs. Moery, the teacher who had been acting as principal until Rudd arrived on the scene, who told me that my teachers had decided not to let me graduate.

Then I said, "But Mrs. Moery, I am going to let you find something out for yourself. Go into that classroom," I pointed to the general science room, "tiptoe to the cloakroom, then open the door and look in." She asked what was in there and I said I would go with her and she could see for herself. We then went quietly into the general science room and I opened the cabinet door and there was the pervert teacher and a pervert student performing fellatio on each other. Mrs. Moery exclaimed, "Oh my God!" and left as fast as she could.

I left, too, and went to see attorney Eule Howard about the high school teachers and their continual harassment of me. I told him how they conspired to keep me from graduating. I thought he might talk to Foeman Rudd about my being harassed and the conspiracy to prevent my graduation. I told him about the sexual perversion going on, as well as the debasement of a little girl who was often taken to the boiler room and made to suck and fuck. I told him that I intended to cause trouble if I was prevented from graduating, and if the newspapers refused to publish the truth about the high school, I would have circulars printed and distributed throughout Kentucky and Ohio.

Eule Howard said, "You don't need to go that far," and he looked up a telephone number and called it. He talked for several minutes and during that time repeated some of the things I had told him. After hanging up, he said, "You will graduate, but you will have to take a test before graduation—just a matter of form."

I thanked him and left. The next day, I visited Mrs. Moery and learned that what we had seen in the cloakroom had been "taken under advisement."

(Neither the pervert teacher nor student ever returned to that high school, as far as I know.) Assuming that Eule Howard might have spoken to Principal Rudd, I went to see him after school. I had learned that the "roundheels" girl whom he had taken out in my car was pregnant, so I thought I would partake in some psychological warfare.

Upon entering his office, I asked him if he had decided whether or not I was going to graduate. He replied that my graduating was not up to him but my teachers. He said he would talk to me about it. but first he wanted to discuss my attitude. I said, "By all means."

"You have ruined the career of a fine teacher," he said. "If you had only come to me when you found out what was going on, I would have been able to handle the matter without letting it go as far as it has. Do you know what it has done to the family of the boy involved? His father was so angry at you for exposing that unfortunate affair that he was going to come and get you, but I talked him out of it."

I responded, "You shouldn't have done that. I would have enjoyed seeing him. He is in the Woodmen of the World that is so mixed up in the Ku Klux Klan that it has sometimes been difficult to distinguish one from the other, and Freemasonry is mixed up with both of those outfits. I know a WOW of a story about that threesome that is as queer as what was going on in this school." I then launched into a tirade about people whom I considered aberrant at the high school, from the janitor to some students to him. I included Freemasonry, Knights Templar, De Molay, Ku Klux Klan, and Woodmen of the World, for I was cognizant then that the harassment I had undergone was secret society-oriented. After denouncing all of it, I demanded to know if I was to graduate or if the whole sordid mess would have to be made public.

Rudd said, "You are going to graduate."

The commencement ceremony took place in the high school gym. After the usual proceedings, Rudd handed out diplomas, accompanied by short favorable comments about those graduating. When he called my name, I stepped forward and was handed a folder with a diploma. Rudd then started to say that they had not wanted to let me graduate, but had decided ... I interrupted him and faced the audience, saying loudly that I had been harassed continually since I had enrolled in the high school, and that what

Rudd said was an insult, and that I would take no more of it, and that I had graduated because I knew something about Rudd and others in the school.

I continued with, "Do you parents know about the things that have been going on here? Do you know about the perversions, the little girl who has been continually molested in the boiler room? Do you know about the girl who became pregnant?" Then I held up a picture of Rudd in my car with the girl, then said, "Where do you think Rudd was taking this girl?" Then I handed Rudd the diploma and said, "You should have kept your damn mouth shut. I will pick this up after I take that goddamn test."

The audience was thunderstruck. There was bedlam for a minute, and when things quieted down the passing of diplomas continued silently.

The following morning I went to take the graduation test, but before doing so I said to Rudd something that no one had ever said before, including the accusation that the pervert teacher was sucking him off when I walked in on them unexpectedly. A teacher, Miss Baker, was sitting nearby and most certainly heard what I said, and looked ashen. She then handed me the test and answers to the test. I copied the answers, then wrote, "That is the way I was told the questions should be answered and so I am complying." After finishing the "test," I received my diploma from Ms. Baker.

People who at the commencement, including those who graduated, kept what had taken place there a secret, or perhaps they contracted lacunar amnesia. I questioned some of them about what I had done, and they would not or could not answer me. I consider those I questioned to be part of a conspiracy of silence that blighted the entire town.

Chapter 22

Mr. Zangara
Danville, Kentucky, Nassau, and Miami, 1933

In the fall of 1932, I went to Centre College in Danville, Kentucky, where I was sponsored by Alex Howard to join Sigma Chi fraternity, and I lived in the fraternity house. My parents had been doing quite a bit of travel that year and if Mother's glowing letters on different hotel stationery were to be believed, they were having a wonderful time. While in California, they had suddenly decided to go to St. Petersburg, Florida, so I sent letters to general delivery in St. Petersburg. It was usually some time before I got a reply, which I assumed was due to Mother not going to the post office box every week. But always I got a letter with a check the first of every month.

Then on February 13, 1933, I received a large envelope from Mother with considerable cash in it, with a letter saying she needed my help with a desperate predicament, urging me to come to Nassau immediately. She instructed me not to let my sister know where I was going or where they were. Sending a large amount of money by mail seemed peculiar, as Mother didn't usually believe in sending so much as a dollar by mail.

When I arrived in Nassau, I went to the address she had sent me and found her alone in a nice little yellow brick house that she said they had bought. There was no furniture in the house except a bed. In the driveway was an old Rolls Royce, apparently in excellent condition. Mother said Father bought it without talking it over with her first, adding, "I am hopping mad about what he has done, but your father wouldn't have done the things he has done if he was himself."

Just then, Father walked in. Mother kept right on talking, but about some type of business difficulties that involved their house, car, and bank account in Nassau. What brought on the trouble was such a touchy subject that Father, who didn't seem pleased to see me, left as soon as I asked him about it. Mother was so indefinite that I was at a loss to figure out what was what.

Apparently some men were causing them trouble, but Father refused to recognize it. The Nassau bank where they had deposited a large sum of money refused to honor their checks, and they had only been able to get along because Mr. White of the First National Bank in Cincinnati sent them money. It occurred to me that this trouble was something like the kind they had had in Windsor, Canada and Detroit, Michigan in the first part of the previous summer. They had purchased a house in Windsor from a Canadian tunnel guard only to discover that some men laid claim to the property, but instead of producing evidence, these men just huffed and puffed. Apparently, they were or had been connected with a place called the Look Out House in Fort Michael, Kentucky, where Mother and Father had gone occasionally to drink homebrew those Prohibition days. I met my parents in Detroit at the Fort Shelby Hotel. Mother said Father was terrified by the men claiming the Windsor property because they were real gangsters who threatened to kill them if they didn't hand off a large sum of money. This was about all the information that I could get out of her, except the name of the Canadian guard, whom I went to see.

He was expecting me. At first, he was reticent, but finally got around to disclaiming any and all responsibility for the trouble Mother and Father were having. He warned me that the men who had threatened my parents were very dangerous, then gave me their names and Detroit addresses. Every address turned out to be a beer parlor, gin mill, or gambling joint, and as soon as I entered, shooting would start. I was quite sure that the Canadian guard had telephoned the "gangsters" to tell them I was on my way, which would account for the timely shooting. Nassau seemed to be a similar setup.

When Father returned, I asked him to explain what was going on. He said he hadn't wanted Mother to send for me, that he could have handled the matter himself. But apparently there was a man from the Masonic lodge on Bay Street who was trying to help him. He had just been there, and if I talked to him, he would explain everything. Father then handed me a piece of paper on which was written *Tyler.* So I went to the Masonic lodge and handed the only man there the piece of paper.

Tiler is a symbolical title for the Mason that guards the door of a Masonic Lodge and supposedly prevents the intrusion of any "profane" person (*i.e.,* non-Mason) from entering. The Tiler has a wavy-looking sword, like the flaming sword alleged to have been placed east of the Garden of Eden that turned every which way in order to keep the way of the Tree of Life.

"Before I talk to you," the man said, "there is something that I need to do and I would like you to help me." He then opened a drawer of his desk and took out a small human figure, and tied a string about its neck. He then asked me to accompany him. We climbed some wooden steps to the roof and walked to the front of the building where there was a flagpole with no flag on it. He tied the end of the string to the rope by which the flag might be hoisted or lowered and told me to pull the human figure to the top of the pole. I told him I wouldn't do it, and so he proceeded to do the symbolical hanging himself.

We then started back to the office. When we got to the stairway, he started to laugh, saying how the figure he had just hung looked like me.

That son of a bitch was in a mighty poor position to badger me, for when I roughly shoved him, he fell down the stairs. There were thirteen of them. Historically, gallows had thirteen steps. He lay at the bottom whimpering, saying something about the hanging being a joke. Then I pissed in his face, and walked back to the yellow house.

I had begun to tell Mother what happened when a woman came in the front door without knocking. Mother introduced us, saying that she was a neighbor without whom she couldn't have managed. The woman then said something peculiar: "We just heard what happened in the Masonic Temple and want you to know that we are all for you," and then she turned and left.

Then a car drove up onto the lawn. Two men got out and came in the house as it they owned the place. I don't know why I didn't rush them as they came in, but I didn't. One of them rebuked me for what I had done, that a brother was in the hospital and was going to sue, that I would be punished, etc. Finally, they got in their car and left.

After making Mother a stiff drink, I asked her neighbor to watch her as I went to the hospital. On my way there, I ended up on a street that I recalled encountering some time in the past, perhaps when Mother, "Count" Eugenio, and I were on our magical mystery tour. I remembered that an eight-sided building was a jail, and a few blocks later I recognized a huge old vacant house with a cannon in its front yard; I had stayed there overnight and a shooting had occurred while we were there. I remembered taking a wad of Million Dollar Gold Certificates from "Count" Eugenio's briefcase and stuffing them into the cannon and firing it. In my memory, I kept confusing "Count" Eugenio with my father.

On my way to the hospital, I passed time with an old Negro woman, asking her if she knew that white Masonic witches were practicing witchcraft on the island, and that if she wanted to see evidence of it, she could go and see the human figure hanging from the flagpole at the Masonic Temple. She said she knew that what I said was so, and then making some symbolical gestures, said, "That will protect you." I thanked her.

No one at the hospital answered to the name of Tyler. But a doctor took me to a bed that had the man who fell down the steps. In a loud voice, I denounced him as a witch and said that he had given me to understand that his name was Tyler, and that he and at least two others had been trying to extort money from my parents and I wasn't going to stand for it; that if he and those helping him continued with their bad behavior, I was going to expose them as Masons practicing witchcraft.

Then I visited the bank that refused to honor my parents' account. After being told that the president wasn't there, I denounced the bank in a loud voice and said that my parents were being persecuted by Masons who were practicing witchcraft. I said that if they looked across the street at the flagpole on the Masonic Temple, they would see a small figure of a human being hung. (Note: that human figure or one just like it hung on that flagpole for at least forty-two years.)

Back at the little yellow house, Mother wanted me to know that everything I had done was all right with her, but that I must leave immediately. I told her that I knew of no way I could leave Nassau until the next day. She then said I should stay there that night and that she would stay with her neighbor. I asked where Father was going to sleep, and she said that if I saw him to join her at the neighbor's house.

The following morning Mother brought me breakfast and an address of a lawyer in Miami she said I should see as soon as I arrived there, that he had some important information for me. I insisted she tell me how Father got mixed up with the Masons in Nassau, for he had been opposed to all secret societies for years. She said he had told her that Masonry in Nassau was not the same as Masonry in the United States, because the type of Masonry practiced in Nassau was English York Rite Masonry.

I swore and said, "Even if Masonry differs some in different countries, it should be obvious even to him that all Masonry is secret society stuff and as treacherous in one country as in another. If you don't believe that, just read up on the history of the French Revolution and revolutions in Mexico, Central and South America, the Philippines, and a lot of other places."

When I was made slighting remarks about Father, she looked like she was going to cry, so I kissed her and left quickly.

When I got to Miami, the lawyer said he couldn't see me until the next day, and that because all the hotels were full due to the speech that President Roosevelt was going to make in Miami's Bayfront Park, he would call the Alhambra Hotel and see if some arrangement might be made for me. He told me that I should just go there immediately and ask for ———. I followed his instructions and upon obtaining a room I called and thanked him.

When I arrived at the lawyer's office the next morning, expecting to get information about my parents' business difficulties in Nassau, he instead told me to go to a hotel on Miami beach and talk to a man named Zangara who would actually give me the information I came to get. Frustrated by the runaround, I took a cab to the hotel and found Mr. Zangara in a room above hamburger joint where we had a burger and drank a half-pint of whiskey. He didn't speak English very well and basically I didn't know what he was talking about, so I said goodbye and left. The rest of the day I just roamed around downtown Miami.

After an early breakfast the next morning, I went to the Bayfront Park where a few early birds gathered to get good seats for FDR's speech. Gradually, more people drifted in until all the seats were taken. At 9:30, FDR arrived in an open automobile that stopped in front of the grandstand. On the grandstand he made a short speech. It was then that I walked toward the automobile FDR was in and saw Mr. Zangara standing in front of the car with a pistol. An instant later, shooting started.

It was reported that Zangara stood up on a bench and shot Margret Kruis and William Sinnott in the head, and Mayor of Chicago Anton Cermak and Mrs. Joseph Gillk, wife of the president of Florida Power & Light Company, in the abdomen, and that a "bullet nicked the forehead of Russell Caldwell, a Coconut Grove youth." Of course, eyewitnesses to accidents and other violent incidents often see things differently, and it is true that sometimes the same incident, seen from different positions, can be perceived differently. Even pictures taken at the same time from different angles can sometimes convey differing impressions. During the many years since then, I have seen some films represented as having been taken of that incident, and while the theme (*i.e.,* the attempted assassination of FDR) was the same, they differed in every other way. For example, one film shows Zangara standing in front of the automobile FDR was in. If some of those films were shown side by side, it would be logical to assume that one or more was intended as a reenactment but for some reason or other turned out faulty by chance, *or by way of connivance.*

I left Miami shortly after the Bayfront Park shootings and returned to Danville, Kentucky. Immediately upon entering the Sigma Chi fraternity house, several boys wanted to know where I had been. One of them said, "Some men have been here asking questions about you, and they just left." The others maintained this was so, and implied that I must have done something wrong. One of the boys even said he wouldn't want anyone who looked like the men asking questions about him. I thought they were pulling a practical joke as I had been the butt of many jokes since moving into the Sigma Chi house, and accepted them without rancor, despite many of them being cruel and done without regard to possible consequences. Such practical jokes were considered to be part of hazing, but the other pledges were not hazed as I was, which I attributed to my being the only pledge living in the Sigma Chi house at that time, something represented to me as a "special privilege." That of course was fallacious and I knew it, as much of what I was told in the Sigma Chi house was misinformation. So naturally I thought the story about men asking questions was just more of the same. Later, I questioned those who had told me the story, but they were all evasive.

Chapter 23

The Hanged Man
Oxford Retreat, Oxford, Ohio, April 6, 1933

One week later, I received a call from Mother saying they were at the Vinoy Hotel in St. Petersburg and were never going back to Nassau. I asked her what they had done about their bank deposit, house, and car, and she said it was a long story and would tell me when she saw me. A few days later, she wrote about what a good time they were having, how nice it was at the hotel, how liquor was delivered to their room every day and she had hired a girl to accompany Father to the beach to dance with him. I couldn't believe it. While Father might drink a glass or two of homebrew, his idea of a large drink of whiskey was a full tablespoon. I wondered if Mother were secretly trying to tell me something.

A week or so later my sister called, saying she didn't want to speak about it on the phone but that she had been to St. Petersburg and Father was now at her home, and I should come over as quickly as possible. When I got there, Father was on a walk, which gave my sister the opportunity to tell me that Father had threatened to kill Mother in their hotel room in St. Petersburg. Father and Mother had always seemed devoted to each other, so I couldn't believe what I was hearing. Mother was still in St. Petersburg and would return home in a few days.

When Father returned he asked me to walk with him. As soon as we started out, he said some people were trying to kill him.

I replied, "If by chance it is those people in Nassau, we can settle their hash in short order."

Father shook his head. "The Nassau business is just part of something that began long ago. I could have handled it in Nassau if your mother hadn't sent for you. I knew what those men were and how to deal with them." I asked for more information about the "Nassau business," but he would tell me nothing about it.

When I returned the next day, my sister said that some men from Cincinnati had taken Father to the insane asylum for observation. I said that deputies cannot legally cross state lines for such a purpose, that a court order for commitment was legally necessary, etc. My sister suggested we wait for our mother and talk to her.

Mother arrived the next day and it was evident that she had done considerable crying. Almost immediately, she asked me to go with my brother-in-law to see how Father was doing. At the ward where he was being held, my brother-in-law and I saw an attendant push Father and abuse him verbally. I cursed the attendant and threatened him, which made my brother-in-law mildly chide me, saying, "Bud, that isn't the way to get things done." We then went to see the superintendent of that crazy house, but he was too busy to see us.

Mother had already made arrangements to transfer Father to the Oxford Retreat in Oxford, Ohio, where alcoholics are sent for treatment. She had talked to Mr. Procter of P&G and Mr. Charlton Wilder of the Crown Rock Asphalt Company about Father being held for observation. Both of them had alcoholic friends who had been in the Oxford Retreat. Mr. Procter personally called the doctor in charge to help make arrangements for Father to be treated there. Mother said I should go back to Centre College, as Father would be safe and sound at the Oxford Retreat.

Because of an unguarded remark Mother made, I learned that she had been registered at the Sinton Hotel in Cincinnati for several days before she was supposed to have arrived. I checked it out and found that it was so. Perhaps she had rented the rooms before actually occupying them; after all, my sister said she had met the train when Mother came in from St. Petersburg.

When I returned to Sigma Chi house, I wrote Eule Howard, the attorney who had assisted me before. In my letter, I said that Father had been forcibly taken by some men from Covington, Kentucky to Cincinnati and imprisoned there against his will in an insane asylum. I asked him to help find out who the men were who had virtually kidnapped my father with the idea of bringing suit against them, and if they were deputies, suing the city and department they worked for. He did not respond by letter, but told me subsequently that he had made inquiries and in so doing had upset some people.

A few days after I returned, Mother called to ask me to return to Covington immediately, which I did, and we drove to Oxford. The retreat had been built as a residence on "landed property" near Western College that a relative was said to have been instrumental in founding, and where my sister spent her sophomore year of college after attending Southern Methodist University in Dallas. Inside and outside, the Oxford Retreat looked like a luxurious residence. There was only one patient besides Father, a very elegantly dressed woman in her late fifties or early sixties who came down the stairs to greet me as if she were a dowager welcoming a guest in her own home. She ignored Mother entirely, and after we exchanged a few polite remarks she glided off like a lady ghost.

While Mother talked with the doctor in charge of Oxford Retreat, I went out to search for Father, who was walking with his attendant/nurse. I found him, and when he and I had walked a little distance away from his attendant, he declared that he was to be killed. I asked by whom and he said he didn't know, that there were people who made their living killing people, and that such a person or persons might have been hired to do it for all he knew. But he said, "They are not going to kill me. I am going to escape, and you can go with me if you want to. You are the only one in the family I trust."

"You can trust Mother and Sister, you know you can," I said naïvely. Father responded, "Not now." He then asked me if I had any money and I said I had a little, and thinking that he wanted it, I offered him what I had in my billfold. But he said he meant did I have enough money to take a long trip and meet him? I said, "No, but how are you going to make a trip? You can't possibly have any money on you, for patients are not allowed to have money in their possession here, or so I was told."

He then told me that he had access to enough money to take him where he was going, and that when he got there he would have access to a great deal more. He said he had lots of money in a bank in Oxford, but couldn't cash a check there. If he tried, they would apprehend him and bring him back, for

Mother had stopped payment on any check he might write. Abruptly, he then asked me, "Do you know where you are?"

I said, "Of course, we are on the grounds of the Oxford Retreat, and over there is Western College where Sister went for a while."

"No, that isn't what I mean. Do you *really* know where you are?" he asked. But then the attendant/nurse walked up hurriedly and announced that we had to get back. He was holding a gadget by which he supposedly received the signal to return, despite the fact that pagers would not be on the market for years. When we returned to Father's room, he and the attendant started quarreling for no reason that I could discern.

On the way back to Cincinnati, I told Mother about the quarrel I had witnessed. She suggested that the attendant might be angry because a boy who attended Miami University in Oxford would take Father on trips into town, as well as to the Delta *Tau* Delta fraternity house. Possibly the attendant was angry about not making the money that boy was making. Mother also said she had seen Father several times at the Oxford Retreat and what a wonderful time they had had one day. I silently wondered how that was possible, given the brief time he'd been there. But I didn't mention the discrepancies in her version of happenings. I took her to the Sinton Hotel and drove back to the Sigma Chi house at Centre.

Father died in the Oxford Retreat on April 6. He had hung himself. Mother said to come to Cincinnati by train and that she, my sister, and brother-in-law would meet me. While on the train, I had three brandies, not to assuage my grief but because I was tired. I had been on one frustrating errand after another since about the middle of February.

The four of us drove to the Oxford Cemetery on the 8th. After Father's burial, Mother and I went to the Oxford Retreat to see the doctor in charge. Immediately upon entering, a regal-looking lady appeared. Grief-stricken, she said to me, "He was killed, and he told me it was going to happen. Why didn't you help him?" She looked around fearfully, saying, "I don't want them to see me talking to you," then hurried away.

After expressing his sympathy for our loss, the doctor showed us a holographic will that Father had written. He had read it, thinking it might be a suicide letter, which it wasn't, though it did indicate that he had planned to commit suicide for some time. He then asked if we wanted to read it separately or if he should read it to us, and Mother said he might as well read it. I agreed, but asked to look at it first to satisfy myself that it was written by my father. I could tell by the beautiful style that it indeed was in my father's hand.

The preamble was beautiful, mentioning my mother, sister, and me, but the bequests were startling. First of all, the Delta *Tau* Delta fraternity was bequeathed a huge amount of money, despite the fact that Father never had any interest in it and spoke disparagingly of all college fraternities. Then there was a list of his alleged holdings with the names and locations of a number of banks, including a bank in Switzerland. The amount deposited in each bank was listed, and while the bank deposits were large, the amount deposited in Switzerland was vast and could only be accessed by number and code. Mother insisted Father had no money and that the will showed conclusively that he was unbalanced. In a sense, I supported her; as far as I knew, he only had the account in a Nassau bank—at which Mother grabbed my hand and squeezed it hard, which I interpreted as a signal to be quiet, so I stopped talking.

The doctor was impressed by the way the will was written and said in effect that a layperson reading the will probably would not believe that its composer was unbalanced. Mother then asked me to let her talk to the doctor alone, so I got up and walked out into the spacious front room. Changing my mind, I returned to the vicinity of the doctor's office. Looking in, I saw Mother hand the doctor a Million Dollar Gold Certificate and a hunk of cash. Certainly, it cost a great deal of money to be "treated" in the Oxford Retreat, but never to my knowledge did Mother pay large bills or any bill in cash, so I was puzzled by her paying for Father's "treatment" in that way. I was really puzzled by her giving the doctor a Million Dollar Gold Certificate—puzzled then, but not now. After the payoff, she rose from her chair while I retreated to the main front room. When she joined me, we drove back to Cincinnati where I left her at the Sinton Hotel and returned to Danville and the Sigma Chi house.

A number of the boys were playing poker when I arrived. I said something uncomplimentary to them and turned to leave, when someone asked where I had been. I cursed them all and said I'd been at my father's funeral and that I believed he had been hung. At that, they got up and apologized for giving me the silent treatment because I hadn't been attending classes and the dean had called that day to ask me to be at sa faculty meeting the next day.

I didn't know if it was a joke or not, but the next day I attended the meeting. When I walked in, all of the faculty members looked at me very sternly and asked why I hadn't been attending classes. I expected to be expelled and said as much, but then proceeded to narrate what had happened since Nassau up to my father's death. I stressed the hanging of the human figure on the flagpole over the Masonic Temple and how my father supposedly hung himself a few weeks later, adding, "If that is coincidence, then it is a strange one." Every member of the faculty stood up, and the dean declared that they had had no idea my father had died. He expressed his and the faculty's condolences, and volunteered help in any and every way possible, saying that I had only to ask for it. No group of men could have behaved better.

I stayed at Centre until the end of the term and received slightly better than passing grades, then returned to Cincinnati where Mother was still staying at the Sinton, since she didn't want to go back to our home in Fort Thomas or stay with my sister. She wanted me to return to our home in Fort Thomas, however, at least until it was time for me to attend the Citizen's Military Training Corps (CMTC). She said she was going to Europe for a while—perhaps Switzerland?—and that after I had finished military training I should go to Washington, D.C. and try to see President Roosevelt to straighten out the matter of the check that had been taken from me by the Treasury Department.

She insisted she was heartbroken that she had had to support my father's stand against me, but there was nothing she could do. When I had ridden away on my motorcycle after being told they would meet me in Detroit, she thought she would never see me again. When it turned out the way it did, she had begged "my father" to give it all up, but he had insisted on going on with it. To make amends, she then gave me a thousand dollars for the trip to Washington and a thousand dollars for clothes, then left for Europe.

Chapter 24

The Military Vendetta
Fort Thomas, Kentucky, 1933

I was one of the first to report for Citizen's Military Training Corps (CMTC) at the Fort Thomas military installation, and was quickly assigned to a company and tent, the location of which was practically within spitting distance of the site where I had been the intended victim of the Ku Klux Klan. Through the flap on the tent I could see the stars at night. After taps, soft music was played for perhaps fifteen minutes with the final recording always being the soothing "Moonlight and Roses."

> Moonlight and roses bring wonderful memories of you
> My heart reposes in beautiful thoughts so true
> June light discloses love's old dreams sparkling anew
> Moonlight and roses bring memories of you.
> —Ben Black and Neil Moret, 1925

One night after the music played, one tentmate suggested that we all take turns telling about our lives, past and present. Their stories were those of Depression kids. To a boy, the themes were poverty's privations and its struggles. Invariably, they talked about how they and members of their families were not able to find work, much less a steady job, how they didn't have enough food or were cold and unable to buy warm clothing, get shoes half-soled, or pay rent. All of them suffered from the emotional trauma and melancholia brought on by drab, difficult, unfortunate, unhappy lives. One of them, after telling of what had happened to him and his family, expressed the belief of a great many people during the Depression years: that his misfortune was due to people who were financially well off. I wondered how it was, with all of them being so unfortunate, that they should be in the same tent with me, for I was in a sense living high on the hog at that time. I always had good food, a comfortable home, warm clothes—in fact, all of the creature comforts that the other occupants of the tent never had.

Finally, it was my turn. I knew that I shouldn't tell them about the many nice things I had at that time, nor would it be wise to tell them about the obstructions, hostilities, and violent attacks made on me since my diaper days. So I told them about my father's recent alleged suicide, and that I thought he might have been hung. I didn't go into details and of course didn't tell them about how nice the Oxford Retreat was, but used the word *drunks* instead of *alcoholics* and by so doing struck a responsive chord, for several of them said their fathers were drunks, too, and had been put in "drunk tanks." They knew or had heard of people being hung in jails by the jailers or police officers. The story of my father's alleged suicide served to buffer me from further demands that I tell them more, for when I said that I didn't want to talk about it any more, they didn't insist that I continue.

The following evening just before dark, the tents were empty, due to everyone being in the Armory for the weekly picture show. Because of a hunch, I chose this time to investigate the areas between the tents. Between and behind the tents was a two-foot-wide space that no one to my knowledge ever entered, possibly because there was some rule against doing so. In the vacant space in back of the tent where I slept was a dictograph ready to record, its electrical cord plugged into an extension cord that ran into the tent adjacent to my tent. Something was going on, but just what I wasn't sure.

There was little to CMTC military training except drilling, but one day the company was taken to a firing range to shoot Browning automatic rifles. Different companies were all in a line possibly ten feet apart, each with their own targets, and as the names of those who were to shoot were called, they would take up their positions on the firing line and fire and stop when ordered. My company commander was the one who gave the orders. None of the boys in my company seemed to know much about shooting Browning automatics, so some shot wide of the targets.

After I had fired, my company commander ordered me to go to the target and count the holes, saying that it looked to him like one shot might have gone through the previous hole. At the instant I walked up to the target I had been told to inspect, the order was given to start firing. I jumped away from the target and ran back to the firing line where I saw a boy in a prone position with the Browning automatic rifle I had been using in the firing position I had been in. That night the boy told me that the company commander had given the order to start firing but that he hadn't fired, thinking he might hit me. At the time, I thought the order to fire when I was near the target was a dangerous practical joke and didn't make an issue of it.

A day or two later after taps, music, and the usual discussion in our tent, the boy with the cot next to mine went to the latrine, or so he said. When he came back, he quietly asked me to come outside the tent. When I did, he said, "The commanding officer and some others are talking about you in the officers' tent, and you should hear what they're saying."

I went to the far side of the officers' tent as quickly as I could, and sure enough they were talking about me, mentioning my last name coupled with curse words. The gist of their conversation was about "getting me" as they had agreed to do. My commanding officer said—as the basis for what he said afterward—that I had shot a soldier a while back and that regular soldiers wanted to get me. It was agreed that they had the right for a first go at me, but if they didn't get me, then the officers would. After hearing that, I returned quickly to my cot and started wondering what I should do next. I also wondered how the boy who had tipped me off happened to be near the officers' tent, the latrine being in the opposite direction.

The next morning at assembly, I went on sick call to the hospital where a doctor took my blood pressure, ascertained my pulse rate, then assigned me to a bed. Dr. Southgate, a Fort Thomas physician, was in the hospital at that time, as was a nurse who had often come to the high school. Both came by to see me separately and I had the chance to tell them that while I couldn't explain, I was in danger and must be discharged from the CMTC. A few minutes later Dr. Southgate returned with the Army doctor, and using a stethoscope, listened to my heart and lungs and declared that my heart had a "metallic sound," that I had asked for a medical discharge from the CMTC and it should be granted and he would accept the responsibility. The Army doctor then used his stethoscope to listen, but said nothing.

The nurse came in, called the doctor to one side, and they talked for a few seconds. Dr. Southgate, the Army doctor, and the nurse then left. A few minutes later, the Army doctor came back and pronounced me hale and hearty and said I was malingering, he saw it all the time. Hardly a day passed that a soldier didn't pretend to be sick in order to escape duty, and while he often gave them "cc pills" so they could spend their off-duty time in the latrine, he wasn't going to do that to me, he was just going to send me back to duty.

So back I went, knowing that I had to get away somehow. That night after taps, music, etc., I left the tent and went to see a girl I knew in Fort Thomas. Leaving the Fort at night was an accepted practice of CMTC boys, and while there were a few guards who were supposed to prevent it, they never seemed to see anyone taking off. I, however, had to take steps to be seen and apprehended. I returned at perhaps 2 a.m. A sentry was standing just about where the line of Ku Kluxers, including Chaplain Rogers, had stood when I was supposed to be "naturalized" into the Invisible Empire of the Ku Klux Klan.

I walked up to the sentry and announced happily, "You have caught me, I confess, I have been out carousing."

But the sentry was determined to be difficult. He said, "I haven't seen you, get to your tent quickly."

I had to explain to him that if he did see me and catch me after I had been out all night chasing fast women, it would go on his record and show that he was alert and doing his duty properly. We talked for a few minutes, but I was getting nowhere with him. Even though I insisted that he take me to the guardhouse, he refused. I finally had to pay him ten dollars to do it. So I was taken to the guardhouse and the following morning to a court martial.

The company commander who was part of the conspiracy to "get me" officiated. The final ruling of the court martial was that I should be discharged.

I stayed home in Fort Thomas for a few days, then packed a couple of suitcases and took my car to the Alms Hotel garage in Cincinnati for storage. I caught a train to Washington, D.C. and went to the Continental Hotel where Mother and I always stayed. After a couple of days there, I moved to the downtown YMCA. For the next few days, I just walked around sightseeing. Finally, I went to the White House gate and told the guard my name and that I wanted to see my friend, President Roosevelt. "I want to give him this," I said, and held out a Million Dollar Gold Certificate. Immediately, the gate guard was galvanized into action. He called on the phone and in an instant I was permitted to enter. That phony money is as impressive as the Million Pound Bank Note that Mark Twain wrote about.

Chapter 25

Immortals and Illuminati

Washington, D.C., 1933

I have not been ordinarily disposed to exalt any person, living or dead, but my boyish ignorance had invested Franklin D. Roosevelt with imagined qualities that I honored deeply. That foolishness was so ingrained in me that even today, when I see and hear him in old films on television, I have difficulty disliking that arch-criminal.

I walked from the entry gate onto the White House grounds in high spirits, confident that in minutes I would see President Roosevelt. When I got to the White House door, I didn't use the brass door-knocker but knocked with the knuckles of the clenched fist that held a Million Dollar Gold Certificate. The door was opened immediately. Standing by the door of the foyer were three men, and perhaps fifteen feet from the door was a table at which a woman sat. I introduced myself to all present and announced that I had come to see the President. Walking up to the table, I showed the Million Dollar Gold Certificate and said, "I want to give this to my friend, President Roosevelt." Immediately, I was ushered into his office.

With Roosevelt was a man who must have been a member of the White House Security Force, introduced to me as Mr. Gaston Means. (*Was that a joke?* I wondered, remembering the Gaston B. Means I had encountered on Jekyll Island.) After being cordially greeted by the President, I presented him with the Million Dollar Gold Certificate, then ventured to say that I had something of a confidential nature to discuss with him and perhaps it would be best if I waited and talked with him alone. Mr. Roosevelt then assured me that anything I said would be held in strict privacy. With his assurance, I then told him about the predicament I got into pertaining to the government check because of the oath I had taken. Consequently, I hadn't been able to explain to the Treasury Department why the check had been sent to me. He said he would see what could be done about it.

The rest of our conversation was banter. He asked if I would like to stay in Washington and I said I would but didn't know what I could do to keep eating, unless the government check I had received was good. (There were those who didn't think the government was solvent.) He asked me if I would like to work in the White House and I said that would be fine, but I didn't know what I could do unless I worked in the kitchen which I would rather not do just then, for I still had some walk-around money. He asked me what I would like to do and what my educational qualifications were, to which I responded, "I had a simply dreadful time learning my ABZs, but I am an Illuminati and got my enlightenment in other ways." I said it as a joke, but then Roosevelt said, "I am, too; what is your Order name?" Out of the blue, I responded, "Spartacus," to which Roosevelt said, "That is quite an Order name." [Note: Spartacus is the alleged Order name taken by Adam Weishaupt, the alleged founder of the Bavarian Illuminati.]

I was having a wonderful time, and Roosevelt apparently was enjoying himself, too. After talking about my qualifications in a joking way, he asked me if I could operate a dictograph, and I said I was thoroughly capable of turning one off and on. He had "Gaston Means" take me to a small office to see a large dictograph that must have been specially built. When I returned to the President's office, our conversation resumed. The president asked if I had ever had any experience in law enforcement and I said, "Of course. I am a member of the Real Prairie Dog Police Force." To "Mr. Means," Roosevelt said, "Well, that's good enough for me." I knew, of course, that President Roosevelt had had my background investigated as soon as he became aware of the importance of the grave goods, so the questions he asked me seemed to be just part of an amusing game he was playing.

Our conversation ended with him writing a note requesting that I be considered for Special Training in the Bureau of Investigation. I was then directed to see two men on the White House Security Force and to get them to put their names on the note. He also gave me the name of a man at the Bureau to whom I was to take the note. The prospect of presiding over the dictaphone or being a guard in the White House was quite pleasing to me and caused me to harbor great expectations.

Following President Roosevelt's instructions, I went to the desk at the front door and told the lady the names of the men I wanted to see. She got them for me so quickly, I believe they were in a room adjacent to the foyer. One man had a friendly expression and the other looked stern. I told them what President Roosevelt said about getting their signatures on the note. The friendly man read the note and signed it, then shook my hand as though he were welcoming me. I then handed the note to the stern man who, after read-ing it, handed it back to me and said he would have to find out certain things before signing it. I said something like, "Let's go see President Roosevelt and you can tell him why you don't want to endorse his recommendation of me; I am sure that he can tell you anything you need to know." He signed the note without further ado.

Leaving the White House, I took the note directly to the Bureau of Investigation that was then, I recall, on Folger Street. I was told that the White House had called about me, after which I was taken to an unfriendly man who talked to me for a few minutes without saying much of anything, then set a time for me to return the next day. When I did, he kept me waiting, and when he did finally see me handed me a questionnaire that was actually a deceptive psychological test designed to obtain my psychological profile. I recognized it for what it was and answered some of the catch questions in intentionally insulting ways. The next day I was made to wait for well over an hour, only to discover the unfriendly man—too "busy" to talk to me — sitting at his desk. I knew something was wrong. With President Roosevelt's recommendation and the endorsement of two White House Security men, I should not have been receiving this impersonal, almost abusive treatment.

The next day I was told to call on Hugo Black—a former Cyclops in the Ku Klux Klan—and on James Amos, a Negro Bureau of Investigation agent, the very man who had helped me get my single shot .20-gauge shotgun so many years before. I volleyed a tennis ball with Hugo Black, and then went to see James Amos who looked frightened to see me and would not let me in. He was so frightened that I thought someone might be holding a gun on him. He said, "I told you never to come to see me." Perhaps he did tell me, but I don't recall ever seeing him in Washington or even knowing that he worked for the Bureau. I tried to break the tension by saying something humorous about the Amos and Andy radio program and how they were members of the Mystic Knights of the Sea lodge. I may have said something like, "You look scared, and if you are in any danger and I can help, just tell me. In fact, you can consider me a member of the Mystic Knights of the Sea, the Terror of the Deep, if you want to," after which he turned even paler and closed the door.

I complained to the unfriendly man about not getting the special training I was supposed to get, after which he brought me to the Marine Corps school at Quantico, Virginia for target practice. I shot extremely well, but the unfriendly man criticized me anyway. The next day I had my picture taken with men who had reputedly had instruction in hand-to-hand fighting, but that was the only contact I had with them.

Fortunately, I also had pleasant encounters during those frustrating days, having open access to the White House. I met Mrs. Roosevelt several times and liked her as much as I did her husband. I also had a long talk with Bernard Baruch (1870–1965), a member of FDR's New Deal "Brain Trust," on a park bench in Lafayette Park while his bodyguard sat on another bench a short distance away. I arranged for a photographer to take a picture of us and it came out very well. When I got it, I sent it to my mother with a glowing report of happenings, leaving out the nasty way I was being treated by the Bureau of Investigation.

Finally, I decided to have it out with the unfriendly man and discover just where I stood with the Bureau. When I paid him a visit, I launched into a tirade about being treated as though I was a non-person. Despite the fact that I had been recommended by President Roosevelt, I felt like I was a "plebe" undergoing a fraternity hazing and being given the silent treatment.

He responded that they had a report about me, with signed and notarized statements from some people in Ardmore, Oklahoma, that they just couldn't understand. I asked him what was alleged, but he refused to answer. I then told him that according to my parents, my sister, and my birth certificate, I was born in Ardmore on March 13, 1913, and that my family moved from Ardmore to Dallas, Texas when I was nine years old; that I had stolen a few apples from a neighbor's tree there; that I was in a gas explosion in front of my home in Ardmore; outside of those events I had no idea what might have been blamed on me, but it certainly couldn't be very much.

I was not being disingenuous. At that time, I really did not recall many of the events that I have related in this book, nor did I recall how they had happened; all of the memory work lay ahead. Had I been able to recall even some of the incidents that had taken place in Ardmore, Dallas, Louisville, Cincinnati, Fort Thomas, etc., I might have ascertained what was going on at the Bureau of Investigation.

The unpleasant Bureau man was talking with three men wearing guns. He indicated one of the men as being a firearms instructor and was going to show me how to shoot. I said that I thought I had done right well at Quantico, but if anyone could show me how to shoot better, I would be glad to learn. So the three agents and I walked to the elevator. When the elevator stopped, I stepped to one side to let the agents out first. Two of them walked out immediately; the third agent waited in the elevator a moment or two and then whispered to me to be careful. I whispered back, "Why? What's going to happen?" He then spoke in a normal voice and said, "I don't know why they and some others don't believe the information they have about you, and they are going to do something." We then stepped out of the elevator and walked to some closed double doors.

I saw that we reached a large, dimly-lit room that might have been used for lectures or movies. One agent stood in the middle of the room and he told an agent with me to leave with him through a curtained doorway. The third agent, alleged to be the instructor, was standing by a table on one side of the room. On the table was an array of pistols. In a commanding voice, he ordered me to choose a pistol, saying they were all loaded. So I picked up a .38 revolver and looking at the cylinder saw that it was indeed loaded. He then told me in the same commanding tone to go to the middle of the room. I proceeded to do as I was told, but on the way I pointed the pistol I had taken at the floor and pulled the trigger. It didn't fire, so I kept pulling the trigger; the bullets were duds.

When I got to where he wanted me to stand, it didn't suit him. He ordered me to move several times. At last, I hollered at him to make up his goddamn mind as to where he wanted me. It was then that he decided that was where he wanted me to be. He then ordered me to hold the pistol at arm's length, raise it slightly over my head and slowly lower it to eye level, saying that was the right way to shoot. Well, if I had ever shot that way, I would never have lived beyond the fourth grade. However, I didn't say anything. I did as he ordered, always pointing the pistol in a direction away from him, and each time he found some fault in the way I did it and would scream at me in anger or pretended anger.

After he started cursing, I put the pistol with the dud bullets in my coat pocket and unbuttoned my double-breasted coat. My .32 automatic was well concealed behind my belt buckle, due in part to my thirty-inch waist and forty-five-inch chest. With my right hand directly on my automatic, I released the safety catch. The room was so dimly lit that he could not see what I had done, or that I had an automatic in my belt. Even if there had been more light in the room, it is doubtful that he could have seen the automatic or my hand on it, for the unbuttoned flaps of my coat were probably not more than six inches apart.

He had unholstered the pistol he wore in order to show me how I should perform the procedure of lowering a pistol from a raised position to eye level.

Every time he found fault with the way I did it, he would show me with his pistol how it should be done and invariably point it in my direction. I was not only suspicious of him but angered by his crude and belligerent treatment, and with my hand on my .32 automatic, I insulted him. If his rudeness and anger had been just pretense to see how I would react, as the unfriendly man from earlier tried to convince me the following day, he most certainly was not pretending when he started cursing and pointing his pistol at me. So I shot him.

The sound of the shot reverberated in the room. The instant that the sound died away, two agents rushed out of the curtained doorway where I believe they had been standing all the time. I was prepared to shoot them if they made an overt move. But they made it quickly known that they had no such intention, so I permitted them to pick up the "instructor" and carry him through the curtained doorway. I then went to see the unfriendly man. All of the personnel in the area were gone with the exception of one girl whom I told that I had had an altercation with an agent and wanted to report it, but that I guessed it would have to wait until the next day.

I spent the rest of the day and some of the night contemplating what had happened to me since arriving in Washington. Soon I realized that the Ardmore investigation had no doubt been done long before my trip to D.C. When I glimpsed the interconnection between events that indicate intentional perfidy and betrayal, I attached myself to the wrong conclusion because I believed the government of the United States was beyond reproach. Little did I realize that the government of the United States is a labyrinth of secret society iniquity.

When I saw the unpleasant Bureau man the morning after the shooting, he immediately insisted that I was being tested to see how I would react when a gun was pointed at me. He asked me if I really thought the instructor would shoot me, and added that a brave man would never have reacted as I did. I told him that if a person showing hostility points a gun in my direction, it scares me, and my response will be to hurt that person then and there if I get the chance. When I asked if I had wounded or killed the "instructor," he threw up his hands, turned, and took a step away from me, and announced that the shooting incident would be expunged from my record. I told him not to expunge it, that I would do the same under similar circumstances, whether I were in the White House or the Vatican.

He continued talking as if I hadn't said what I did, then announced that I was being sent to Boston, Massachusetts on a special assignment regarding cargo theft from ships in port. I said something about not having received the special training I was supposed to get, or any training at all for that matter, at which he went into a song and dance about some men not needing training, etc. Then I was handed an envelope with my Bureau of Investigation identification. I asked how soon I was going to Boston and was told that we would leave immediately. I said I had to pack a few things and he said it wouldn't be necessary, I could get work clothes when we got there.

Without further ado, we got in a car and started for Boston. On the way, the unfriendly man told me that everything had been arranged for me to go to work immediately. I was to go to the hiring place near the dock where the ship unloading would take place, and I was to call out the name "Garbo" when hiring started. That's all I needed to do to be hired. I thought it kind of silly to call out the name of a movie actress and said so, but the nasty Bureau man clammed up. After I made several attempts to start a conversation, I made a rough vulgar remark about his silence and let it go at that. The fact is that I was getting the treatment that Masons inflict on people whom they term *cowans*.

> "But Free and Accepted Masons shall not allow Cowans to work with them: nor shall they be employed by Cowans without an urgent necessity; and even in that case they must not teach Cowans, but must have a separate communication."
> —*Encyclopaedia of Freemasonry* by Albert G. Mackey

I want to stress to the reader that though my memory had been tampered with by government mind molesters and I had transit lacunar amnesia, the guardian of my subliminal memories was on the job and my eidetic memory was still functioning. Thus I could visualize objects and incidents precisely when recollection was prompted. As each memory was mnemonic to me and something or other started me remembering, I got on an eidetic memory binge on the trip to Boston.

It took us three long days of hard, fast driving to get to Miami. Once there, we went to a dock and met two men who were obviously federal agents—Bureau of Investigation, federal marshals, ATF agents, etc. They looked me up and down and one of them said to the Immortal in what I considered a deprecating tone, "So this is the one," then announced that he was going to have to search me. I was angry and don't know why I let him search me, but I did. He didn't find my concealed money, so I considered myself fortunate.

We walked to a boat about forty-five feet long. Its engines were idling and a man wearing a captain's cap told me to come aboard, and we cast off. The captain took up his position at the helm and as the boat moved away, I hollered, "I salute you" and thumbed my nose at the three men standing on the dock. What I did seemed to please the captain who smiled broadly. When I tried to engage him in conversation, he volunteered that he wasn't supposed to talk to me. When I ignored what he said and asked him about his boat, he said it wasn't his, that it was a very fast boat and he would like to have it, but that it was used for rum-running or chasing rum-runners, I don't remember which, but I do remember that when I asked him why he worked for such rats as those on the dock, he said, "They give me what I need."

It was indeed a very fast boat. When we got into open water, he opened it up and we got to Long Key very quickly. There we got gas the captain didn't pay nor sign for. We were offered drink, too, what I believe is called Planters Punch—very good. When we pulled away from Long Key, I felt sleepy and got on a bunk to doze. I didn't wake up until early the next morning, perhaps 4 a.m., and we were at Key West getting gas that the captain didn't pay or sign for. The captain looked remarkably bright-eyed, fresh, and happy for not having had any sleep—cocaine, maybe—and said he would show me how fast the boat would go, and he did. We arrived in the Port of Havana about noon.

Following instructions, I walked through the customhouse area without being questioned, as arrangements had been made for my entry into Cuba at that perilous time. It was August 12, 1933, and a revolution was in full swing. President Gerardo Machado would flee that very day to Nassau, with terrorists shooting at his plane as it taxied down the runway for takeoff.

Immediately, I went to a park. Every face I saw looked worried. I asked a man if he had a pocket knife that he would sell for ten dollars and if he had change for twenty dollars. He said he did. I told him I was a tourist and had put the money in the heel of my shoe and needed his pocket knife to get it out before I could pay him. He handed me the knife and I sat on a bench and loosened the heel. Taking the money out, I handed a $20 bill to him and got $10 change. I then asked him how to find a pawnshop and after he gave me directions, he took off from the park like he was scared. I went to the pawnshop and bought an old U.S. Army .45-caliber automatic and some bullets. The pawnbroker told me where police headquarters was.

Police headquarters was crowded and in a hubbub, but as I walked in everything quieted immediately. I made my way through the crowd until I found Police Chief Antonio Anciart's crowded outer office. I told an official my name, that I was a friend of Police Chief Anciart, and that I wanted to see him but would be back later, for I could see that he was busy. When I got outside, I took a deep breath and hurried to the cantina where I was to be contacted. Buying a sandwich and rum, I sat at an outside table and waited. There were no customers, and not a car passed on the street. With the exception of the few worried people I had seen in the park and the men in the police station and the bartender, I had seen hardly anyone since leaving customs. I tried to question the bartender about how few people were on the streets, but he pretended not to speak or understand English, yet when I said I was waiting for someone to meet me, his expression indicated that he understood.

I went back to my table and waited some more. Across the street a man stared at me. Figuring that he was my contact, I crossed the street. Unbelievably, it was Enrique Esquinaldo, whom I had known off and on since grade school in Dallas, Texas. We seemed to meet in "accidental" ways, the most recent having been in Washington, D.C. I asked him what the hell he was doing in Havana and if he was supposed to meet me. He said he was with the Mexican *porra* and was staying at the embassy. (*Porra* means stick and is what the Cubans called the secret police who worked for Anciart.) He had been in the police chief's office when I came in and had overheard enough to know that I had been sent to Havana to be killed by the *porra*.

I believed what he told me because of all that had occurred during my short time with the Bureau. I asked Enrique to let me stay with him until I could contact people in the United States and arrange to leave safely. He said he couldn't do that, so I asked him to loan me some money, as I didn't have enough to get out of Cuba unless I rowed a boat. He said he didn't have any money, either, and we parted company.

Nearby, I'd seen a nice-looking walled house through a steel gate on which a sign advertised a room for rent in English. I ran to it just as a man reached through the gate and took the sign down. I told him I wanted to rent the room. He looked scared and seemed reluctant to even talk to me, but after a few minutes I succeeded in convincing him that he should let me in. I paid him ten dollars for a very nice room and went immediately to sleep.

The next morning, August 13, 1933, I got something to eat at the cantina just as the bartender was going through the motions of closing up. He explained to me that a radio broadcast said there was going to be trouble. (An underground radio station seemed to be the one that everyone with a radio was always listening to.) I asked him about the location of the U.S. Embassy, and he said the National Hotel. Though I didn't believe the embassy would be in a hotel, I decided I would go there after waiting for the bartender took all the tables inside. Trying to look unconcerned, I kept my .45 automatic on my lap under my hat.

A man came by and beckoned for me to follow him. He looked quite sad, as though he was mourning the death of a dear old friend. I followed him, being prepared to shoot instantly if I found it necessary. We walked to one side of the cantina and then he started to unbutton his pants. For an instant, I thought he was a pervert who wanted to expose himself, but then I saw that he had been castrated not long before, for the scar tissue was still blood-red. The *porra* made it a practice to castrate men who opposed the government. A number of these castrated men formed a secret society to oppose the evil government then in power.

I asked the castrated man if he was supposed to meet me and he said no, that someone had called him and told him that a stranded American was at the cantina. I knew that he had reason to hate the *porra* and asked for his help in getting to the American Embassy. He said he couldn't do that. I asked him to help get me to the Guantanamo Naval Base and that I would pay him well. He said he did not have enough gas to get me there; the gas that he had been able to get he had been buying from soldiers at Camp Columbia, but their supplies had recently run out. He suddenly alarmed, as though he had received a warning. Looking at his watch, he said, "I have to go, I have to go," and took off.

I returned to the cantina, deciding on the best way to get to the National Hotel. A car with two men slowly motored down the street. The man sitting by the driver had his arm draped outside the window with a pistol in his hand that he fired in my general direction. The shot didn't even come close, which made it obvious that he just wanted to scare me, but I shot at the driver, anyway. This car had the older plate-glass window known as "killer windshield." It smashed to smithereens and the flying glass struck both men. The car seemed to hesitate for a moment before slowly careening into a wall.

Needing money and bullets, I ran to the wrecked car and quickly searched the bodies. Both men had old U.S. Army .45 automatics, bullets, clips and money. I considered taking one of the automatics but didn't. While I was confused by the directions I had been given for the National Hotel, I started out immediately. Then another car with two men attempted a drive-by shooting and the killer windshield got them, too. Again, the men had .45 automatics and a large amount of money, which I took.

Like lemmings, the *porra* killers kept coming and the killer windshield saved my life every time. In one case, a would-be killer was carrying a beautiful Ortigie automatic gun and Cuban money along with U.S. currency, and in one car there were four men; otherwise, it was the same each time. Finally, it dawned on me: the *porra* patrol did not have radio communication. Many people must have witnessed each incident from behind their boarded windows, for the *porra* had terrorized Havana and driven everyone inside.

Havana was locked tighter than a drum that morning. No one was in the streets except me and the *porra* patrols. My pockets were bulging with money and bullets I didn't want to part with, but when I got to the National Hotel, I hid my .45 automatic and bullets in some bushes before walking up to the guards at one of the entrances. Although I did not have any identification, I was admitted. After stating who I was and how I came to be in Havana, I was kept waiting for at least thirty minutes while some type of communication went on that was there for the use of Ambassador Sumner Welles. Finally, an embassy official said that I had to leave.

Remember: I broke the goddamn oath of secrecy when I revealed I had been sent to Havana, although I hadn't revealed that I was sent to be murdered.

The National Hotel was supposed to be U.S. territory, as it was embassy operations and the residence of Ambassador Welles. But the goddamn place was still pretending to be a hotel; in fact, a number of non-Americans were staying there at that time. Since it was being operated as a hotel, I asked the manager for a room, and he told me they were all taken. I offered a large amount of money, but was told that I just couldn't stay there.

Leaving the hotel, I retrieved my automatic and bullets and then approached some Cubans who were striking against unfair labor practices at the hotel. I suggested they have a campfire and make some coffee and food. They thought it was a good idea but didn't have any money, so I gave them some. Pulling it out of my pocket, I dropped a large amount of cash, but the man who picked it up for me was friendly, as were all of the demonstrators who gave me directions to the telephone exchange.

En route to the telephone exchange, I bought a boy's shoeshine box after some haggling. Perhaps there was something symbolical in my buying the shoeshine box. In the summer of 1921 I bought a shoeshine box in El Paso, Texas, where my parents had taken me because my father was supposedly supervising some paving job and putting bids on other jobs. I started shining shoes and carrying luggage to and from the trains that stopped near the plaza across from the Regis Hotel we were staying in. Most of the shoeshine boys and luggage carriers were greasers and ganged up on white boys around the plaza downtown area. One by one, the white boys were beaten and driven away. However, I had made myself a nigger-shooter—a slingshot—and started pelting greasers. I also had a place to run to when the going got too rough. In that El Paso plaza was a cage with alligators. For some time, I took food scraps from the hotel to the alligators. At times, I would climb over the side of the cage and stand on the back of the largest alligator. While holding on to the side of the wire cage, I would burp the 'gators by shifting my weight up and down. The 'gators loved what I did and I believe looked forward to my coming to burp and feed them. So whenever I had real greaser trouble, I would run and get in the cage with the 'gators, where the greasers were scared to go. One day the greaser shoeshine boys brought a kid who was at least twenty years old, and when I climbed the fence into the 'gator cage, he did, too. The largest alligator chomped on him and started to roll, then another snapped at him and started to tug. Together, they pulled him into the 'gator house and that was that. No doubt about it, I won the Shoeshine War.

In Havana, I put most of the money in the shoeshine box with the bullets on top; I also crammed several $20 and larger denomination bills in the heels of my shoes. At the Telephone Exchange, a guard first refused to let me in, but money did the talking. Then with more money I bribed telephone operators to make calls to the United States. I couldn't get a call through until I passed out more money and said I was a friend of President Roosevelt. I called the White House, the State Department, a Washington newspaper, etc., each time saying I was a friend of President Roosevelt on a special service assignment. I also tried to call a newspaper in Miami, but couldn't complete the call. I smashed that goddamn secrecy oath to smithereens, just like I did those killer windshields.

Then I called the American Consulate in Havana and told the man who answered that I had been sent to Havana by the Bureau of Investigation to perform a special service, had to get out of Cuba immediately, and wanted to talk to Ambassador Sumner Welles. Again, I said that I was a friend of President Roosevelt. At last, Sumner Welles came to the phone. I told him about the calls I had made to the United States and that I had blown the goddamn security oath for I knew that I had been sent to Havana to be killed. In no uncertain terms, I told him that he better get me out of Cuba safely. He asked me to hold the line, and I held for a long time and was about to hang up when he got on the line again and told me to go to Camp Columbia and see Sergeant Batista.

Every few steps I took, I looked behind me. Out of the corners of my eyes, I spotted another *porra* patrol and by then knew how they would attempt to kill me. I waited for them to get close enough to shatter the car's killer windshield and like lambs they came to the slaughter. I took their money, not having room enough for further bullets.

Walking on, I saw a parked car with a driver in it, who got out of the car and stood in front of it. When I got near, I said hello and, while still watching him, walked up to the car and looked in; no one was in it. I asked the directions to Camp Columbia and he said just a short distance away. He looked something like the castrated man but I didn't want to ask him to open his pants for identification purposes.

There must have been an unusual reason for him to have been out in the street at that time, and I liked the idea then as I do now that he was a member of the secret society of the castrated, all of whom were brave and trying to be of help to me. I remembered, though, that when it was common practice in the Near East to castrate some slaves with special duties, they were as often as not loyal to their masters. So I watched him every instant I was with him as he drove me to within a block of Camp Columbia. I thanked him and gave him a handful of money, and he seemed on the verge of tears as he drove away.

Taking the bullets from the shoeshine box, I put them in some tall grass near where I left the car, stuffed cash in my pants pockets, and walked on to Camp Columbia. When I got to the camp and told the guards that I wanted to see Sergeant Batista, I was admitted immediately without being searched. A guard took me to a room in an administration building where there were three men. I told the man named Batista that I wanted to leave the country immediately and that I understood there were no passenger ships going to the United States at that time.

The men in the room weren't friendly or unfriendly, they just didn't talk. Batista asked me what I had in the shoeshine box. Being in no position to refuse, I handed the box to one of the men and said, "You look." He gave the box to Batista who dumped the contents on the desk. Then the telephone rang and Batista talked in Spanish for perhaps a minute. Hanging up, he said, "It seems you have some importance." He said something in Spanish to one of the men, who then left the room. Batista put the money back in the shoeshine box and said, "We are going to help you leave, but this has to stay

possible. He said he was in the Marines and had taken his discharge there. Haiti was going to have a big tourist boom and he was going to marry a fine Negro woman and they were going to take the money he had saved and build a fine apartment house while building was still cheap. They would make a fortune when tourists started coming, for there was no decent place for anyone to stay in Cape Haitien then. He said all of his buddies were mad at him for taking his discharge in Haiti and would hardly talk to him.

I was anxious to board a cruise ship there that was going to Miami. Before we parted, I sold him the automatic for fifty dollars. I found that the ship's purser was reluctant to let me book passage, which seemed odd. But I finally paid for the entire cruise and gave him a large tip, to boot. I went to my cabin, showered, had food and a razor brought to me, sent my suit to be cleaned, and stayed in my room until the ship was well underway for Miami. I left my cabin to look around and was surprised by how few passengers were on board. Something prompted me to return to my cabin until the ship docked in Miami.

I wasn't questioned by customs officers and went directly from the dock to the train station, bought a ticket to Washington, and boarded the train and felt that I was under surveillance. When I discovered the possible surveillant, I asked a porter in a loud voice about the death of Senator Walsh. Politely, he said, "We have been instructed not to talk about it." So I tried another tactic. Again in a loud voice, I told about attempts to murder me in Havana, saying it wasn't the Red Menace that was a danger to me, it was the hired killers of a cabal in the U.S. government, and that maybe Senator Walsh had cabal trouble, too.

Senator Thomas J. Walsh was appointed Attorney General by FDR. He had flown to Havana in early March 1933 and had stayed in the National Hotel. While there, he married a Cuban woman much younger than himself and then they flew to Miami. On March 13, after a few days in Miami, they boarded a train to Washington where he was to be sworn in as Attorney General. Walsh died on the train. Many jokes were told about the reason for his death, even a funny little song told of how he had died with a smile on his face. Of course, the Cuban "Red Menace" was also blamed for his death.

About two weeks after I arrived back in Washington, I read that on August 14, the day after I left Cuba, Police Chief Anciart with members of the *porra* violently attempted to force business establishments to open. People came out of their houses and started demonstrating, and the *porra* killed a number of them, after which the secretly operated radio station in Cuba called for revolution.

Chapter 27

Mind Molestation

Washington, D.C., Memphis, and Lexington, Virginia, 1933

I was still under surveillance when I arrived in Washington, D.C. Surveillance is just one of the many tricks of the trade in the government's paranoia factory. I went directly to the Continental Hotel and checked in. For the next few days, I just walked around the city, wondering what I should do. Should I go back to the Bureau of Investigation and confront them? Should I visit President Roosevelt and tell him all that had happened since his "recommendation"?

I passed a place where secondhand cars were sold and saw a beautiful little Bugatti. I walked around it, kicked the tires, looked at the engine, sat in it and longed to own it. My Dodge Coupe was at the Alms Hotel garage in Cincinnati and would cost money and time to get. So I paid cash for the cheaply-priced Bugatti. With the bill of sale and title in hand, I drove a couple of blocks, parked, and walked to a drugstore to buy a box of candy for a woman who worked at the Continental Hotel and had extended me some special little courtesy. But the drugstore didn't have the type of candy I was looking for, so I walked back to where I had left the car, stopping only to look at a suit in a store window.

That was when a car drove up to the store and stopped in a no-parking area. The driver got out and walked around the back of the car onto the sidewalk. I remembered him as one of the two agents accompanying the agent I shot at the Bureau; I also recognized the other agent in the car. I walked up to the car to talk, and the agent who had gotten out of the car hit me, using some high voltage, low amperage shock device, for I lost consciousness instantly. I don't know how it was done, but I remember the incident clearly and know that there was contact with the back of my head.

When I regained consciousness, I was strapped to an operating table and wired up like Frankenstein's monster. Raising my head as high as I could, I saw a man standing with his back to me, facing an electrical device of some sort; I could see cables going to it. I turned my head to the right as far as I could and saw cables on the floor that apparently came from the device toward the wall directly behind me.

I asked the man where I was, what had happened, and how long I'd been there. At that moment, I thought I'd been hit by a car and had been taken to a hospital. He didn't answer me but kept staring at the instrument panel. I then asked why I was strapped down and he said, "You have been having seizures," to which I responded that I didn't have epilepsy and actually felt fine, so let me loose. Then the evil man said he wanted to talk to me first, he had some questions he wanted me to answer and he would know if I was telling the truth or not. That's when I realized that one of the wires connected to me might go to a psychogalvanometer that might indicate bioelectrical agitation if one tells a lie. His questions and my answers went something like this:

Q: Were you in Havana recently?

A: Yes.

Q. Why did you go to Havana?

A: I was sent on a special assignment.

Q. What was the assignment?

A: I wasn't told what it was before I left Washington, and after I got there I found it was to be killed.

Q: What did you do then?

A: You might say I didn't accept the assignment.

Q: Do you think that the government has to be right to send a man to where he will be killed for the sake of national security?

A: If you mean my being sent to Havana, hell no.

Q: Do you think the government has the right to declare war and draft men and send them where it is known they will be killed?

A: If a government is protecting all of its citizens and is what might be called a decent government, then it should have the right to draft citizens for service in the Army. But a government has no right to draft any citizen it doesn't protect, and a government that doesn't protect all of its citizens has no right to exist. If a decent government sends soldiers into a battle that is of great importance and it is recognized before they are sent that many of them will be killed, I believe that such a government has the right to that.

Q: Do you think you did right to break the oath of secrecy that you took?

A: Oh shit!

After the first few questions, the others were all alike in that they were "Do you think you did right?" questions. "Do you think you did right to shoot those men?" "Do you think you did right to take their money?" Time and again, I raised my head to see the evil man looking at the instrument panel. I am quite sure the same instrument gave me multiple orgasms because it could not only monitor bodily functions but stimulate and inhibit nerve cells and tissues, as well as produce electroseizures and electronarcosis (coma). After the orgasms, he said, "I am going to tell you now that you are in a program that is necessary for national security, and I am only able to tell you that because you won't be able to remember any of this. You are going to have a seizure and go to sleep." I was then given an electroseizure and went into a coma.

When I regained consciousness, I found myself in a hospital gown and room, with no immediate memory of what had happened. Getting up, I walked into the hall to try a door. It was locked. A male attendant saw me and called out. I returned to my room and sat on the bed as he came in with another attendant and a doctor holding a hypodermic syringe. I asked them why I was there and said I felt fine and wanted to leave. The two attendants grabbed me and when I struggled a little, they overpowered me while the doctor gave me an injection.

When I regained consciousness yet again, I recalled having walked into the hall and being given an injection; and the bed I was in had been moved to the other side of the room. Hair was hanging in front of my eyes, and using the fingers of my right hand like a comb, I pushed back the hair, and when I did, I discovered a wire sticking out of the top of my head at least an inch. Having no idea why I was in a hospital, I thought I might have been hit by a car and that wire had been used to stitch me up. Carefully, I felt around the wire, but there was no indication of a wound. Holding it close to my scalp, I pulled it quickly and it came out easily, but for an instant I felt as though I might have a seizure. The wire must have extended into my head about an inch and a half.

Getting up, I looked into a locker and found my clothes, hat, and shoes. I got dressed and cautiously looked into the hall. Not seeing an attendant, I walked quickly to the door across the hall and found it unlocked. I opened it and ran into the hall and down a flight of stairs to the main floor. There, I made my way to the office area and discovered I was in the Walter Reed Army Hospital.

Not realizing that it had been arranged for me to escape, I ran out of that goddamn place and got into a taxi and had the driver take me to the YMCA, as I believed I was staying there. When I discovered that wasn't the case, I had memory to realize where I was staying. There was more to my seeming momentary memory loss than I realized. I didn't recall other things that I should have; I didn't even remember that I had bought a Bugatti.

Back at my hotel, I was told that my suitcase had been put in storage, as they didn't know when I would be back. Upon getting my suitcase and room back, I had a bellhop get me a bottle of whiskey. After some drinks, I remembered the Bugatti and the attack. I went to where I had left the Bugatti; it was gone, as I knew it would be. Then I went to the police station and found to my surprise that they didn't have it and claimed to know nothing about it. The policemen who patrolled the area said they didn't recall seeing it. One policeman said that if I left the bill of sale and title in the car, I had just better forget about it. I went to where I had bought it to see if they had a record of it. They said they didn't, and the salesman who sold it to me was on vacation in Florida.

I spent about three days trying to find out something about the Bugatti and then gave up, deciding to go to Cincinnati and get my Dodge, and then travel to Memphis, where my sister and her husband had relocated in July when he became president of the National Cottonseed Oil Company. I checked out of the hotel and boarded a train for Cincinnati. When I arrived, I went immediately to get my car and the garage attendant told me that he had just seen my mother. *How could that be?* I wondered. She was in Europe.

I drove to Memphis where my sister and brother-in-law welcomed me. For possibly two weeks after I arrived, I wrote a number of letters about the things that had recently happened to me in an endeavor to expose people in the Bureau of Investigation and what was going on in Cuba. I sent a letter to the Yacht Club that had sponsored the American entry in the latest Lipton Cup race and told them about my escape from Cuba with the two Negro men and woman whom I believe I called a witch; I suggested that if they wanted to win the next race, they should hire those Negroes who sailed from the Havana area to Cape Haitien in a seemingly impossibly short time. I wrote the *Miami Herald* and *Reader's Digest*. I wrote Franklin D. Roosevelt, Henry Wallace, Attorney General Homer S. Cummings, and Ambassador Sumner Welles reiterating things about the perfidy of the double-dealing going on; I received no replies, but that doesn't mean that my letters weren't answered.

Then my brother-in-law Jim Robertson told me that I had received a letter from the War Department that he opened by mistake. The letter set forth that I had been discharged from the CMTC without honor and that I could never serve in any branch of the armed forces again. I asked him for the letter and he said, "I'm sorry, bud, but I can't let you have it."

"Why not? It's my letter."

"Please don't ask me, bud, I just can't," he responded.

I was angry. "I don't believe some people know what honor is, and as far as my ever being able to serve in the armed forces again, goody goody gumdrop."

While Jim and my sister went to Atlanta on a business trip, I was abducted. Somehow, I ended up at a small railroad station perhaps a hundred yards west of the *Commercial Appeal* newspaper building on Union Avenue in downtown Memphis. Only a few people were at the station, beyond the two men who had me on a stretcher. When I tried to get off the stretcher, one of the men gave me an intramuscular injection. I remember calling for help from a woman standing some distance away. Just before I lost consciousness, I heard a man say, "You shouldn't have given him all of that, it might kill him." I don't know where I was taken, how long I was gone, or when I was brought back, nor do I have any recollection of what happened to me while I was gone. I assume, however, that I was brought back just before my sister and brother-in-law returned from Atlanta. I just woke up one morning not remembering being drugged, abducted, etc.

My sister informed me that Mother was returning from Europe and she was going to meet her. At my first opportunity, I told Mother as much as I could remember about what had happened to me while she was away, but all she wanted to talk about was where I was going to go to college, to which I said nowhere. She ignored me and insisted I go to any college I wanted, despite my poor grades, but that she thought Washington and Lee in Lexington, Virginia would be best. In a remarkably short time, I was enrolled and arrangements were made for me to stay at the Sigma Chi fraternity house. Everything happened so quickly, it was as though it had already been planned.

When I arrived in Lexington for school, I remember it was a dark, dark night. At the Sigma Chi fraternity house, I was shown to an excellent room that I would share with a seemingly nice boy who already knew my name. After we talked a while, another boy who had been drinking came in and started quarreling with my roommate. The quarrel got louder and louder, and suddenly the boy who had been drinking took out an automatic and pointed it at the other boy who then knocked it out of his hand. They grappled with each other, rolling on the floor. I kept thinking it was a practical joke and just watched, until the boy who had had the automatic really hit the other boy. Finally, they stopped rolling around and got up. It was then that I picked up the automatic, took out the clip (there was no bullet in the chamber), and handed it back to the seemingly drunk boy who then left the room.

I didn't know whether all this was staged for my benefit, but I went outside to take a walk and think it over. I had been outside only a few minutes when a wild celebration took place right in front of me. It was riotous, licentious, and violent, what today would be called "street theater." I had seen just such a "performance" on a Lake Michigan cruise ship when I was on my way to see my parents in Detroit, and then again some years later in Key West,

Florida. Of course, I associated the wild celebration and its violence with what had just happened in the fraternity house.

The next morning, the boy who was drunk seemed worried and contrite and tried to rationalize his behavior by saying that he had epilepsy and wasn't supposed to drink, and that the one drink had upset him mentally. He begged me not to let the dean know what he had done, saying he would be kicked out. I noticed that the boys who came to breakfast were very quiet, and on my way to the office of the dean after breakfast, all of the Washington and Lee boys I saw were also very quiet, perhaps just in accordance with the polite behavior standard demanded, but perhaps not.

I got in to see the dean right away and told him about what had happened at the fraternity house as well as what the boy had said about having epilepsy. I said that I didn't believe him and felt that the gun incident and fight had been staged. I also told him about some of the bizarre things I had seen in town shortly afterwards. Comparing the previous night's celebration to Mardi Gras before Lent, he responded that there is always celebrating the night before school starts, and that now Washington and Lee would settle down to hard studying.

I told him that I was no stranger to irrational behavior, riotous drunkenness and licentiousness, but the only thing I could compare to what I had seen the night before was Mardi Gras in New Orleans, and even that didn't compare to the compulsive happening. I told him that something was wrong, all wrong, and I had no intention of staying at Washington and Lee. As for the Sigma Chi fraternity house, to hell with it, for if what had occurred there was intended as a joke, it was no joke to me.

I caught a train to Washington, D.C. and got a room at the downtown YMCA. In a few days, I registered for some classes at George Washington University but almost immediately had a quarrel with a professor and got my tuition refunded. For a while after that, I happily spent hours every day in the Smithsonian Museum and ate at various good restaurants. Then one day while walking on 16th Street downtown, I heard my name called. Turning around, I saw Jane Butler, a Fort Thomas girl who had gone to my high school. She said she and her family had been living in Washington for some time, and that her father had a government job. I asked her about Wade

Hampton, for I knew he had thought a great deal of her. She then invited me to come and see her, so I called on her that night. She and her family shared a nice little apartment, and after talking with them a short time about Fort Thomas and their life in Washington, I said goodbye.

As I was leaving the building, I heard a noise behind some shrubbery. I discovered a man standing in the darkness. Persuading him to come into the light from the apartment house entrance, I saw that it was Wade Hampton who was obsessed with Jane Butler in years past. As he was packing a gun, I assumed he had a job with the police force. We talked for a couple of minutes, but got no information from him at all, as he kept saying he had to go.

Soon after that strange incident, I got a call from Mother saying she was coming to Washington and wanted me to met her at the train station, which I did. After she had stayed at the Adams Hotel for a few days, we took an apartment at the Fairfax. I escorted Mother to various places, including an auction house where she went often. Then she announced that her friend Colonel wanted us to go to Harvey's Restaurant with him. Col. (Ret.) George H. Bunker was with the Interstate Amiesite Company of Wilmington, Delaware that leased patents that my mother held from my father's inventions, including Patent No. 1662377. He knew a lot of rich, influential, and famous people, some of whom he called his close friends, such as Gen. William Joseph "Wild Bill" Donovan (1883–1959), head of the Office of Strategic Services (OSS), precursor to the Central Intelligence Agency (CIA).

So Mother, Colonel Bunker, and I went to Harvey's. Before we were even served, Colonel Bunker asked me if I recognized one of the three men seated at a table near us. "Yes," I said, "that is Wild Bill Donovan," and I went over and said hello to him. But when he stood up, I said some things I thought were humorous but he didn't, and neither did the men with him. Then I returned to our table and proceeded to laugh at what I had just said. Minutes later, the three men left and Colonel Bunker hurried after them, then returned to our table almost immediately.

That evening I had internal convulsions that recurred throughout the night, after which I hiccoughed for two days and nights. I tried all the folkloric remedies for stopping hiccoughs, but nothing worked. It was truly an ordeal. Finally, Mother left the apartment and returned with a medicine she said a friendly druggist had recommended. It worked, and I went to sleep immediately. Not long after I went to sleep, I became faintly aware of some men putting me on a stretcher and carrying me through the doorway of the apartment and down the hall. But when I regained consciousness, I was in my bed and felt fine. I vaguely recalled the dream-like memories of the stretcher and the men, and asked Mother about it. She said that she had left the apartment immediately after I went to sleep but had come right back. She was positive that I had not been taken from the apartment, that I must have dreamed it.

Right away, I started having spasms in my guts and was scared that I would start hiccoughing again. I told Mother that I thought I should see a doctor as I might have gotten a peculiar type of fish poisoning after we ate at Harvey's. So Mother called a friend with whom she had traveled in Europe to inquire about a suitable physician. The friend suggested Mother call Alice Roosevelt Longworth who would certainly know the best physician to see. That name was rich in associations: Alice in Wonderland, my little Alice Blue gown so long ago, Franklin Roosevelt, and of course Maria Longworth Storer of Rookwood Pottery.

When "Alice" didn't answer, Mother called her friend again and was told that "Alice" often didn't answer her phone and was probably out in the yard. It was suggested that I just go to her home at such-and-such address. When I went, I found a delightful woman of friendly disposition in the yard. She gave me the name and address of her doctor and said she would call him and tell him I was on my way to see him.

His secretary/nurse ushered me in to see him right away. I told him about the gastrointestinal spasms and hiccoughing ordeal and my food poisoning theory, after which he performed the most ridiculous examination for a gastrointestinal disorder that can be imagined. He felt my prostate gland, then had me get on the operating table and lay on my stomach, after which he examined my rectum and palpated the space between my legs. I sat up and said, "I am going to tell you a story I heard at Fort Thomas that reminds me of your examination: A soldier went on sick call and the doctor gave him a prostate massage. When he told another soldier what had happened, the soldier asked him to describe it. The soldier who had received the massage said,

'Well, the doctor had me take down my pants, then he put his left hand on my shoulder and stuck the forefinger of his right hand up my ass, and then started to massage.' 'No,' he said, 'that is not the way he did it, he placed his right hand on my shoulder and stuck the forefinger of his left hand up my ass and started massaging' 'No!' the soldier shouted, 'that son of a bitch had both hands on my shoulders when he did what he did.'

"So doctor, I come to you because of an ordeal of hiccoughing and internal convulsions and you stick your finger up my ass, examine my asshole, and poke the area between my asshole and my balls, all for supposed diagnostic purposes to discover why I had the hiccoughs. Doctor, you might imagine that I feel like the soldier when he really understood what had been done to him."

The secretary/nurse turned blood red, and the doctor left and went into his office. When I got back to the Fairfax apartment, I told Mother about the examination and what I had said, but she maintained that the doctor must have had some reason for making this type of examination he had made.

(Note: In time, I learned his reason for such an examination, but it had nothing to do with hiccoughing or internal convulsions: it was to stimulate the *pudendal nerve.*)

I told Mother that I didn't want to stay in Washington any longer, and she suggested I go to Memphis via St. Louis, and that she would come to Memphis as soon as the lease of our apartment was up. Why she insisted I go through St. Louis made no sense to me. I must have done it, though I remember nothing of it.

As soon as I arrived in Memphis, my sister's husband Jim made it a point to tell me that I had received a letter from the War Department, the same letter he had told me about before, the one that said I had been discharged without honor. However, *I didn't remember.* The fact is, he mentioned the letter now only to test my memory for the mind molesters. We even went through the scene again of my asking for the letter and him saying, "Bud, I can't let you have the letter," and remembering none of it. I had no inkling of my brother-in-law's role in keeping me uninformed about the ritualistic persecution I was consistently subjected to over the years. I had even accepted without rancor the part he had played in depriving me of the Wells Fargo fortune. I did, however, write a letter to the Department of the Army about the CMTC "court martial," and about the Ku Klux Klan gathering at Fort Thomas that had set the stage for what happened later at CMTC. As usual, I didn't receive a reply, but that doesn't mean there wasn't one.

I was in Memphis only a short time before a succession of events occurred from which I should have deduced that I had ready-made enemies there. Sadly, I couldn't deduce anything because I couldn't remember my past experiences. For some reason, I got hostility from people I had just met or didn't even know. A vicious circle was operating, but I couldn't understand what I had done to cause such manifest dislike. Meaningful incidents were continually laying claim to my attention, and because my attention was constantly being diverted, my attention span for each incident was shortened and I couldn't recognize the all-pervasive, malicious influence I was up against.

Then an attempt was made on my life, and I permitted those who had attempted to kill me to get away without retaliating. Later, it occurred to me that by not retaliating I might have provoked further mistreatment. What I didn't realize was that all of the attacks and enmity were rooted in mystical charades in which quite a number of people were participating. I identified perhaps as many as ten Masons and Ku Kluxers who most certainly took part in giving me a hard time.

Among the Mason/Ku Kluxers was a group of rich, influential men, said to be eighteen7 in number, who fancied themselves to be the Knights of the White Camellia. Historically, the Knights of the White Camellia had operated during Reconstruction and supposedly went out of existence. Perhaps that is so, but despite their initial friendliness that indicated they may have been more or less innocently involved, they became enemies by secret association. I also wondered if all camellia were white.

Knights of the White Camellia Ku Klux Klan: The Knights of the White Camellia, a Texas Klan group led by Charles Lee, along with the Texas chapter of Thom Robb's Knights of the KKK, has been linked to a number of incidents of racial intimidation and harassment in Vidor, Texas. These incidents, which occurred in 1992 and 1993, involved efforts to prevent the desegregation of an all-white Federally assisted housing project in Vidor. Among the reported acts of intimidation was the threat to blow up a housing unit to prevent its integration; residents of the project additionally alleged that the White Camellia Knights carried automatic weapons on a bus they drove through the housing complex and that one Klan member offered white children $50 to beat up African-American children. The Texas Commission on Human Rights has brought a civil suit against both Klan groups in response to these incidents.

—http://www.jewishvirtuallibrary.org/jsource/anti-semitism/KKK.html

A third contingency was involved in the mystical charades to which I was subjected—people who were not apparently secret society-oriented but, like the people in the opera *Un Balloon Maschera*, simply took pleasure in tricking the gullible and being "in" with the insiders.

Chapter 28

Masonic Sex Circuses

Memphis, Tennessee, 1934

Sex circuses for public and private consumption are actually Masonic sex magick rites arranged by *gringo* Masonic sorcerers and greaser witches who are in the same business but work with different companies. The two sides have long had an unstable agreement but the different companies sometimes attempt hostile takeovers by way of their magical and mystical procedures. This is what occurred in Memphis when the sex magic, sex circuses, and *Rite of Memphis* were put on.

I now recognize the gap in my memory that pertained to Enrique and the sex circuses to be *localized amnesia* or the lack or loss of memory connected with a certain time, place, experience or event—an amnesia, in this instance, induced by the Mind Molesters via brainwashing. Some memories of people, things, incidents or events were able to persist, which means that the brainwashing done to me in Memphis was highly selective.

About the time that I began to take note of my situation in Memphis, I ran into Enrique Esquinaldo—by chance, I thought then—and was glad to see him. After all, he had warned me in Havana of the danger I was in. I recounted to him what had happened after he'd warned me about the *porra*, how I had escaped, and something about my present uncomfortable situation in Memphis.

He responded by saying that he'd thought I might be in Memphis, but didn't know where to find me. I wondered why he thought I might be in Memphis, but didn't ask. He said he had a desk in a real estate office on 2nd Street across from Court Square, but wouldn't tell me where he was living. If I needed to get in touch with him, I should call the Mexican Consul in Memphis and leave word; he then took me to the Mexican Consul and introduced me to them. Since he had told me he was working for the Mexican secret police when I saw him in Havana, I assumed his being in Memphis had something to do with that. He took me to the real estate office and showed me his desk. While I was there, I saw that he had a notary seal and watched him notarize two documents for a man apparently working in the office. Later, I checked and couldn't find any evidence that he was a notary. However, I surmised it may have been part of his cover and therefore was condoned by local, state, and federal government; otherwise, he couldn't have gotten away with it—or so I thought.

I took him home with me, wined and dined him, gave him a quart of excellent moonshine, then took him back to the Consulate. I wondered how he could be a Mexican national with special Consulate privileges given that he had lived in the United States since he was a child. I also wondered why he had never introduced me to his family, why he never seemed to have any money, and how it happened that I ran into him "accidentally" in so many widely flung places.

A few days after our meeting, Enrique called me and said there was something he wanted me to see and asked me to meet him at the real estate office, which I did. We went to a building on South Main and up a flight of stairs to a door. He knocked in a special pattern, and a Mexican opened the door into a large room. Another Mexican was standing by a table upon which a naked girl lay face down, her legs spread wide apart. Her hair was peroxide blond, and her body from her neck to the soles of her feet was decorated with highly creative colored designs often associated with the visualizations people have under the influence of such mind-altering drugs as mescal buttons, psilocybin mushrooms, ayahuasca, etc. As I approached the table, she was told to turn over, and when she did she put her left arm over her eyes so I couldn't see her face. The front of her voluptuous young body was also decorated but apparently not finished, or else the two Mexicans did what they did for symbolical reasons, because they both picked up brushes and proceeded to touch up certain parts of the design.

As soon as we left, I asked Enrique how he had ever gotten involved in such stuff, and he said he wasn't but thought I should see it for reasons he couldn't then explain. He said that the girl was going to perform in a "circus" that night and he thought I should see that, too, then told me the time and place and that I could make up my own mind as to whether to see it or not. After I left him, I went to a telephone and called the police. While I refused to give my name, I told the officer about what I'd seen and where I had seen it, then about the sex show that was to be held and where it would be. I suggested that detectives be sent and that I would be there but not to arrest me; I described the distinctive clothes I would be wearing. The officer asked me why I would be going to such a thing, and I said I had been advised by a friend to see it for reasons unknown to me, but that I had known him for years and thought he might know what he was talking about.

So I went that night at the set time to the appointed place. Quite a number of people were in a large darkened room standing around an illuminated roped-in arena. There the young girl with the painted voluptuous body performed sex acts with men—including a Negro—and women. Her face was pretty, with beautiful blue eyes that shown brightly as they reflected the light directed on her and her partners. Close to the arena were several men whom I assumed were plainclothes detectives. When it was announced that a dog was to be brought out, I left, thinking the place would be raided. A man guarding the door objected to my leaving and hollered to someone outside, but I got out by threatening him.

The Memphis papers said nothing about a raid the next day, so I assumed the raid wasn't reported because of the nature of the event. Enrique came to see me and asked if I had seen the "circus" and what I thought about such a thing going on in Memphis. I told him I had seen it and was amazed that a girl as young and beautiful would do what she did unless she was a dope fiend. He said he didn't think she took dope, but knew she was a powerful *bruja* ——, he used a word in conjunction with *bruja* that I can't recall. He also said there was to be another "circus" that night. That was when I realized that the "circus" had not been raided and wondered if the police were being paid off. I asked where it was going to be and Enrique said he didn't know but that if I wanted to see it, I should go to the Stockmen's Hotel at such-and-such a time and I would be taken to where it was going to be. Not revealing the location of floating gambling games was standard practice, so I wasn't suspicious.

I am often inquisitive about extraordinary things, and so my interest was aroused as to just what was going on in a city where the upper-class citizens boasted so often of their city's rectitude. So that night, I took my water pistol and .25 Colt automatic and my Bureau of Investigation identification, and went to the Stockmen's Hotel. Strangely, there was no desk clerk and the lobby was vacant. I went outside and stood by the door.

I had been there only a moment when a car drove up and three middle-aged men and a woman got out of the car. She was wearing a long evening wrap with a paisley scarf draped over her head in such a way that I couldn't see her face; the pattern of the scarf reminded me of the design painted on the girl's body. I followed them in and waited in the lobby while they went upstairs. Still, no desk clerk appeared by the time they came back downstairs. One of the men asked me if I was going with them and I said I was and followed them to their car. Two of the men got in the front seat and the other man, the woman, and I got in the back. We drove a short distance to a cattle-loading pen. A number of cars were parked nearby, and there was a pole with one light burning on the cattle pen.

The three men and woman walked through the gate in front of me while I stopped to pay. When I got in, I saw one of the men and the girl I had ridden with in the center of the pen where an old carpet was spread out. The girl took off her wrap and stood stark naked. She was the same girl as the night before, but the designs had been removed. Several men and women standing near the carpet were also naked, and at the command of the man who came with the girl a sex show began, a vile, evil sex rite. When someone in the crowd shouted, "Where is the pony? Bring on the pony," I made my way through some men standing at the entrance gate and started for a taxi parked a short distance from the pen.

Suddenly, a man blocked my way and insisted that I return to see the rest of the "circus." I started to walk around him, but he stepped in front of me again. When he did that, I had a strong urge to hurt him badly. Instead, I just threatened him and shoved him, then walked on to the taxi. The driver asked me if I knew whom I had shoved. I said no, and he said it was Bobby Berryman, the boss gambler.

The next morning I went to where the Mexicans had painted the girl; it was closed. I went to where the first "circus" had been held; it too was closed. From there, I went to the Stockmen's Hotel and it was closed as well, which was strange enough, given the many people in town needing accommodations. Going to a nearby business establishment, I inquired about the hotel being closed and the man I talked to said he thought that it had been closed for some time.

The following weeks were busy ones for me. I was determined to find out who the three men were that I had gotten a close look at in the hotel. Whenever I went to the real estate office to talk to Enrique, he was out, so I called the Mexican Consul and asked him to please tell Enrique that I wanted to see him if he called in. A short time later, Enrique called me and I told him that I needed to see him but didn't want to talk in the real estate office. I suggested we meet at the Peabody Hotel. He didn't want to talk there and suggested we meet at Court Square.

We sat on a bench and I told him about what had happened at the Stockmen's Hotel, what I had seen in the cattle pen, and about the man that the taxi driver said was Bob Berryman. Enrique cursed Berryman so vehemently that I thought he must have had some personal encounter with him. I then told Enrique how I had gone to where the girl had been painted and where the first "circus" had been held and even the Stockmen's Hotel, and how they were all closed. I told him that I wanted to find the three men. Then I told him I thought it was all fantastic, especially the beautiful white girl being sucked and fucked by the Negro man. With Memphis being so oriented to the thinking of the Old South, I just couldn't imagine such a thing being done and wouldn't have believed it if I hadn't seen it.

Enrique asked me if I could recognize the three men if I saw them, and I said that I could before much more time had passed, for I could visualize short-term past incidents with considerable accuracy. He then said that the three men were members of a Clandestine Lodge that met in Memphis. I knew that he meant a lodge concealed for illegal purposes, such as those organized to foment revolution. I said, "I can understand why that goddamn lodge is clandestine, for those sons of bitches would be tarred and feathered if people in Memphis found out what is going on." Enrique was obviously period of time, I even lost the memory of meeting Enrique in Memphis, or of his having steered me to the "circuses" and all else that had to do with them.

Chapter 29

Soul Money and Treasure Troves

Memphis, Tennessee, 1934

revious chapters have alluded to vault, cave and tomb symbolism of Masonry's secrecy, silence, and darkness—a symbolical hiding place for those outside the reach of law. There was Harvey Myers' basement vault and Eule Howard's wall safe into which my Wells Fargo box disappeared. There was the Kramer vault or tomb at St. Stephen's Cemetery whose grave goods I took that in turn were taken from me. Now, it was a bank vault with treasures like unto the grave goods, all of secret society, occult significance. If I had only been able to remember those other brushes with vaults, I might have realized what was going on, but I had been brainwashed and pro- grammed by the Mind Molesters.

John Austin and his family lived across from my sister and brother-in-law on Central Avenue; in fact, the Austins owned the property that my sister and brother-in-law lived on. I liked John and thought nothing of his going in for such things as needlepoint. One day, however, I showed him a Million Dollar Gold Certificate and noticed how his hand was shaking when he handed it back to me. He suggested I take it to a man at the Union Planters Bank and see what he had to say about it. He then volunteered to call and tell him to expect me.

When I got to the bank, just for the hell of it I decided to show the Million Dollar Gold Certificate to a teller and asked him to change it into bills of small denominations. Staggered, he was speechless until he called out for the man I came to see, who hurried over to see me, saying he had talked with John. I handed him the Million Dollar Gold Certificate and asked him if he could ascertain its value. Asking me to follow him, he led me out of the bank and onto Madison Avenue to a building on the same side of the street find out. I sent a Certificate with a letter of inquiry to a company in England that manufactured paper and printed banknotes for a number of countries. In my letter, I called attention to the wonderful paper used for Million Dollar Gold Certificates and asked if they had manufactured the paper, and if they hadn't, who might have. I also wrote the LePages Glue Company about the bow and the glue used in its making. I didn't receive a reply to either letter, but that doesn't mean my letter wasn't answered.

I also wrote several letters to custom gun makers in England, describing the shotgun and peculiar bullet and giving them the name engraved on the shotgun. Every custom gun maker I wrote answered me, and all of them expressed the desire to see the shotgun and peculiar bullet but none recognized the name on it. I showed the shotgun to several people who were all impressed. Perhaps because it was so valuable, I typed out a little statement that I was confident had some bearing on the shotgun, signed it in front of a notary, and had it notarized. Then I put the notarized statement in the hole under the butt plate of the shotgun and put the butt plate back on.

Sometime later, Jim told me that there was going to be a gathering of members of some club, society or organization that Boz belonged to, and that all of the men were bringing their shotguns and Boz wanted to borrow mine to show around. Jim went on, "I know you don't like Boz, but he is our friend, bud, and I would appreciate it if you would let him take it." As usual, I did as Jim wanted, so Boz collected the shotgun the day before his meeting. Then I got to thinking what a fool I was to let anyone borrow it. The next day I called Boz but he had already left for his meeting. Finding out from his wife where the meeting was being held, I went there as fast as I could. It was quite a gathering. Some men were listening to someone talk while others were standing by a large number of shotguns all stacked like U.S. Army rifles, with a tie around each barrel.

I looked for Boz but couldn't find him, and so with a couple of men watching over the shotguns, I went from stack to stack looking for mine. Of course, it wasn't to be found, so I concluded Boz still had it and just hadn't come to the meeting. Later I was told that Boz had arrived late and stacked the gun with some of his friends' guns, and that someone took the gun while he was listening to one of the speeches. Boz offered to give me the Civil War rifle, but I refused it. Anyway, I still had the magnificent bow and beautiful transit.

I decided to take the transit/theodolite to a surveyor to examine. I had noticed a business on Madison Avenue that offered surveying services, so I went there. All of the men in the office were interested in the transit. I told them that I had a hunch it had been used surveying the Winchester line, the boundary between Tennessee and Mississippi that supposedly went awry and caused a number of disputes. Some areas in Arkansas were called No Man's Land when the line became a baseline for a survey in Arkansas. One of the men said he thought he could find out. He had seen a picture of one just like it, but he would have to go to the library to look it up and be paid to do it. So I paid him ten dollars in advance and entrusted the transit to him. When I went back to get the instrument and information, I was told he had quit. Of course, his alleged address and phone number were bogus.

Well, I still had the magnificent bow. One day I made an arrow and shot it high in the air. While the bow still vibrated after the arrow was released, it had a different feel, and the vibration was just momentary—kind of a self-satisfied quiver, I thought. After losing the transit, though, I put the bow in the attic of my sister's home for safekeeping.

About that time, a Mexican boy about fifteen years old came to see me, asking if I was an *amigo* of Enrique Esquinaldo. I said yes, but I hadn't seen him for a long time. The boy said, "He's at the Western State Hospital in Bolivar [Tennessee] and wants you to come and get him." When I asked the boy who he was and where he lived in case I needed to get in touch with him, he refused to tell me. Perhaps he was an illegal alien; otherwise, why didn't he want to identify himself?

Immediately, I went to Bolivar to see what I could do for Enrique. I went to the office at Western State and asked for him. In minutes he walked in. When we went outside to speak I asked him why he'd been committed. He said he hadn't been committed, that some officers were holding him for observation. My father's fate in mind, I said, "To hell with that noise. Don't bother with that legal stuff, I'll just take you with me now and we'll get you a lawyer and sue those responsible for you being here."

He smiled and said, "There is something I want you to see before we leave," and he started walking in the direction of a large old building that was part of the crazy house complex. I wanted to get away from there immediately, but I followed him past the big building and entered a small house.

Inside was a girl with peroxide blonde hair sitting in a chair, staring at an ugly doll in her lap. I spoke to her and when she looked up with tears in her beautiful blue eyes, my heart went out to her. I had the feeling I had seen her before but figured it had to be a déjà vu; she was so pretty and sad that I was positive I would have remembered her if I'd seen her before. The memory of that girl had been wiped from my mind, which, like Jim with the letter from the War Department, may have been what Enrique was trying to determine.

Enrique and I went to my car and drove to Memphis. On the way, I questioned him as to whether he had done anything that would explain his being held for observation. I also asked if he knew who the girl was that he had taken me to see. But he was unresponsive. No sooner did we get to my home than Enrique called someone to whom he spoke to in Spanish for several minutes. Then there was a knock at the door. When I opened it, two men brushed past me and ordered Enrique to come along. I protested that they had no right to enter as they had and they flashed their police identification. Enrique didn't appear to be afraid in the least and went with them without protest.

As soon as they were out the door, I got my .20-gauge shotgun and several shells and hurried after them. Catching up with them, I said, "I am a Bureau of Investigation agent, and you had no right to enter my house without my permission." I then instructed Enrique to get in back of me, take my billfold out of my back pocket, and show my Bureau identification to the "nice policemen," which he did. Then I told those cops to get in their car and leave pronto. When they had driven about twenty feet away, I shot the rear tire on the left side and hollered at them to keep driving, which they did. Going back into the house, I called Memphis' Boss Crump and told him what had happened without asking him to intercede in any way, though I thought there might be trouble about my shooting out their tire.

But of course nothing happened. The fact is that my being suckered into going to the crazy house to help Enrique was just part of another mystical charade, and my confrontation with the cops was just a little something that those who arranged the mystical charade hadn't counted on.

Chapter 30

The Eastern Temple
Brownsville and Galveston, Texas, 1934

Mother didn't return to Memphis when the Fairfax apartment lease expired in Washington, D.C. According to her, she would have liked to have kept the apartment longer as she had some business to tend to, but it had already been leased. The admiral's widow had invited her to stay with her at the [now Marriott] Wardmen Park, and they had such a good time together that she stayed longer than expected.

When Mother finally got to Memphis, she immediately encouraged me to get a job on a cruise ship for a while, saying, "You don't know what you want to do now, and you might like to work on a luxury liner until you decide. Colonel Bunker might be able to help you—you know what wide contacts he has. In fact, he said some time ago that he would like to see you ship out." I wasn't sure what he meant by "ship out," as it was normally used in association with dying, but if Colonel Bunker could get me a job on a cruise ship, it might be fun.

The Colonel said he couldn't get me a job on a cruise ship right then, but if I went to Galveston, Texas and talked to a man named Segal who owned the Beach Hotel, he might be able to get me a shipboard job. So I went to Galveston. Mr. Segal said he didn't know a Colonel Bunker and couldn't help me, but that his desk clerk Eddy Hartling might be able to help, since he had worked on several ships. I liked both of them, and in a matter of a few days Eddie said he might be able to get a job on a sulphur ship that made trips from Freeport, Texas to New York. It was due to arrive the next day. The ship was called *The Eastern Temple* and was owned by two Greek brothers whose office was in New York City. The younger brother worked on the ship as chief engineer, and the other brother handled the business end in New York. *The Eastern Temple* was several days late in getting to Galveston from

Brownsville; it wasn't carrying any sulphur because something or other had to be done to the ship.

When *The Eastern Temple* finally docked in Galveston, Eddy took me to meet the Greek and I was hired immediately. The ship would leave the following morning and when it finally got underway the next morning, I was put to work as a wiper in the engine room. The engine was oil-fired and oil was all over the engine room and in the bilge. A lit match would have burned the ship up, if it didn't blow up first. Almost immediately, the engineer and engine room crew started giving me a hard time. The engineer was a Filipino, and his crew were dirty greasers. I was covered with oil within minutes, and one of the dirty greasers wiped his greasy hands on my back. I just laughed and let the affront go. At shift change, I discovered that everything I had brought on board had been stolen. I reported it to the Greek and he gave me some of his clothes to wear.

That night, I tried to sleep in the cabin I had been assigned to, but the bed bugs, lice, and odor of dirty greasers made sleeping impossible. The next day when I went to the engine room, the engineer gave me an iron object that weighed about a hundred pounds and told me to take it to the Greek in the machine shop. It was very difficult to carry that piece of iron up steep, winding iron steps, but I did it, and was watched every step of the way by the engineer and the entire engine room crew. Taking the iron object to the machine shop, I gave it to the Greek who pretended he was going to do some lathe work on it, but knowing that he had something to do with my having been told to haul it to the machine shop, I picked it up, took it to the railing, and threw it into the Gulf.

That night I slept in one of the coiled rope hawsers on deck. The rope was so large there was considerable room in the coil and I wasn't too cramped to sleep. Before I went to sleep, I heard a noise. Looking out of the coil, I saw the ship cook, a chink-greaser, go to the cover of the hold in the bow, unlock it, and dump something from two buckets into the hold. When he left, I got out of the hawser coil and went to the hatch. From below, I could hear angry voices and what sounded like scuffling. I tried to raise a door to the hatch and look in, for the moon was bright enough to have enabled me to at least see something, but the hinged metal fastening on it was padlocked.

Returning to my hawser coil bed, I speculated as to what I should do about the people imprisoned in the hold.

The following day, I hung around the machine shop while the Greek showed me how to operate a lathe. That evening the Greek, invited me to his cabin to drink ouzo, drink meant to incite lustful feelings, though perhaps only via word wizardry, given that *anise-anus* doesn't bring on a *lickerish* feeling.

After drinking the ouzo, the Greek asked me if I minded sleeping in the hawser. I said no, that it was far better to sleep there than in a room with lousy, dirty greasers, and that I liked looking at the stars, anyway. He agreed with me but said he could make up a bunk for me in his cabin, if I wanted to sleep there. I thanked him and said not at that time, but in a few days I might take him up on his offer. He then handed me a key to his cabin and said that if at any time during the day I wanted to take a drink, I was to help myself—he showed me where he kept several bottles of liqueur—or if I wanted to take a nap, just to sleep on his bunk.

When I left his cabin, I went to the machine shop and got a crowbar to pry the hasp off the hatch, then went to the coiled hawser and got in to watch for the cook. After a time, he came and opened the lock, dumped the contents of two buckets into the hold, closed it and left. I waited a while, then went to the hatch, pried the hasp loose, and raised the hatch. The odor that came from the hold was nauseating. When I peered into the part of the hold that I could see, I saw men eating slop that the cook had dumped in. One of them said, "Help, help, we are dying, there is a dead man here now." I whispered to them not to make any noise and that I would be back tomorrow night. I replaced the hatch and hasp by pressing the nails back into the holes I had pried them out of.

The next morning at the table with the captain, mate, radioman, two other white men and the Greek, one of the white men made a remark about me being in the cabin with the Greek. I proceeded to slap and choke him, if for no other reason than to make my position in the pecking order a little clearer. An hour or two later, while the Greek was busy in the machine shop, I went to his cabin and got a .22 rifle and a couple of boxes of shells. Taking them to the hawser, I concealed them in the coil.

That evening I went to the Greek's cabin and had several more drinks of ouzo while he tried to convince me to move in with him immediately. He also asked me what I had done, saying they had received a number of radio messages inquiring as to whether I was on the ship. He told me not to worry, though, for no matter what I had done, I was safe with him, he would protect me. I said I hadn't done anything wrong and didn't have any idea who could possibly want to find me. After talking with him a while longer, I returned to the hawser and waited until the cook came to dump his two buckets of slop into the hold. Then taking the rifle and crowbar with me, I went to the hatch and opened it, dropping an end of rope into the hold after tying the other end. I whispered to the men below that I had to leave to prevent anyone from discovering them while they were escaping, and that they would have to get out any way they could and hide and stay together until I came back for them.

With the crew all in their cabins, with the exception of those in the engine room, the only way the prisoners could be seen escaping was from the bridge, which was brightly lit. Since the hatch area was on the dark side, I didn't think they would be seen, but I took up a position where I thought I could take over the bridge if they were spotted. After perhaps thirty minutes, I went back to the hatch area and saw that most of the men had gotten out with the exception of those who were either too weak or scared to try. Despite their weakened condition, some were able to climb the rope; perhaps desperation gave them strength. I then had them walk quietly aft and put them in a compartment where a large amount of heavy rope was kept, along with a gasoline drum. It had never been entered by anyone except myself, to my knowledge.

The next morning after the crew had eaten, I assembled everyone on the ship aft, with the exception of the officers and the engine crew. Then I opened the door of the compartment and had the dirty greasers come out and stand where they could be seen by all. I said, "I am a federal agent and this ship is in an area owned by the United States. Look closely and you can see the Florida Keys." I then pointed to the greasers who had come out of the compartment. I told of how they had been imprisoned in the hold; how the heat of the sun on the steel plates of the deck had almost destroyed them;

how they were fed slop and had very little water to drink; how they had to shit and piss where they were, with no toilets in the hold where there had been sulphur; how they were illegal aliens being smuggled into the United States, etc.

The captain, who was standing at a rail on the deck above, cried, "This is mutiny!" and drew a pistol. I shot just inches above his head and made him drop the pistol on the deck below. I had one of the greasers that I had released from the hatch shove the pistol close to me with his foot so I could pick it up. It was then that four crew greasers tried to attack me, but I convinced them to stop without having to kill them. Enraged at what they had attempted to do after I had released the other greasers from the hold, which I thought should have earned me a friendly feeling from all greasers, I forced them into a lifeboat and had it lowered into the water, and then shot several holes in its bottom.

I told the assembled group what I would do to them if they didn't do what I ordered—threats that I certainly intended to carry out. Then I ordered them to get back to what they had been doing. I had demonstrated by my treatment of the captain and the mutinous greasers that I was cock-of-the-walk. No one could have been more ready to do battle than I, and I had no idea whether there was another gun on the ship or what attempts might be made on my life. So when the greasers I had freed started to approach, I ordered them to stop. The greaser who did the talking for the group said, "We thought you would tell us what to do."

"Tell the cook to give you something to eat, but first get the other men out of the hatch. Leave the dead man where he is."

The greaser said, "What if the cook won't give us food?" to which I replied, "You give him a beating and do the same thing to his helpers if he tries to interfere." I spoke in a harsh way because the situation called for it.

The Greek lingered nearby, possibly because he really didn't know if the threats I'd made applied to him or not, so I called him to me and told him that I appreciated his offer to protect me, and I was going to do the same for him as long as he didn't try to harm me in any way.

I went to the top of the stairs leading to the engine room and fired a shot at the metal ceiling and another at the boiler, then hollered down to them what the facts of their lives were. Next, I went to the radio room where the operator slept and found him back on the job. He told me that he had just received another inquiry about my being on board, that he had replied that I was and hoped he'd done right. I told him he'd done right and thanked him. He was genuinely pleased at what I had done onboard and said so. I told him that I was going to stay in the radio room until the ship got to New York City. He asked if I wanted him to leave and I told him no, but I would have to have the bed. He said that there were two mattresses and he could put one on the floor for himself, and I said no, I would sleep on the mattress on the floor. I said I was glad to have his company but that I was going to have to be very careful of everyone and everything on the ship and wouldn't hesitate to shoot him if he did anything he shouldn't.

And that's what I did: I stayed in the radio room, only going to the galley to get food, until the ship arrived in New York City. I came out as we passed the Statue of Liberty, then went back into the radio room until the ship docked. One man boarded and met with the Greek. I hollered to let them know that I saw them and stood watching while they talked for a few minutes. Then the man who boarded the ship almost ran to see me, saying that he had just talked to his brother who had told him that I was protective of him, and that there were two federal agents on the dock on the other side of the warehouse who wanted to question me. He then said that if I could climb down the front hawser and go around the far end of the warehouse to a telephone booth, I could call a taxi from there and leave without being questioned.

I left him standing there, went to the stern hawser and climbed down, holding the rifle in my left hand, my right hand on the hawser along with the longer part of my legs. But the hawser wasn't tight and when I got within four feet of the dock, it sagged. So I swung down on a timber bolted to a piling. Wiping the pistol, I put it on top of a timber close to the top of the dock. I climbed back on the dock and started for the telephone, but after walking a few feet changed my mind and walked to the bow of the ship to see the federal agents.

I had no sooner rounded the warehouse than I saw one federal agent. Standing some distance away near a taxi cab was my mother with another man wearing a gun. As I walked toward the federal agent, he asked me in a belligerent voice who I was. I told him and walked closer. He said, "Come over here," and took a few steps closer to the edge of the dock. I walked up to him and again in a belligerent voice he asked, "What happened on the ship?"

I said, "I'm too tired to talk now, but there are illegal aliens on the ship and a dead man in the hold."

"Did you kill him?" he asked, and without waiting for an answer put his right hand on my shoulder and said, "Give me the gun." I pushed him gently backward and he fell from the dock. The water there had oil on it, and as I looked down I saw that for about two feet above the water line the creosote piling had barnacles. I am sure he had a very unpleasant time for a while. I then walked toward my mother and the other federal agent who moved slightly. I said, "Don't" at which he stood stock-still. I walked up to my mother and said, "Let's leave," and we got into the cab.

Chapter 31

Colonel Bunker the Handler

New York City, 1934

efore Mother and I entered her hotel on Fifth Avenue, I took the .22 rifle apart and wrapped it in a newspaper that she had brought with her to the dock to read while she waited for *The Eastern Temple;* as she said, she didn't want to talk to the federal agents while she waited. We went up to the double room she had been in for several days. She said she had received a telegram saying I had been kidnapped and was on a ship. Immediately, she had contacted the Bureau of Investigation and called Colonel Bunker to ask for his help, too.

While I was in the tub taking a hot bath, Mother said she had to go out for a while. I asked her to get me something to drink before she left the hotel, and shortly after that a bellboy brought a bottle of Virginia Dare wine tonic in a sack—medicated wine with quinine in it, but it was better than nothing. As I drank it, I listened to Guy Lombardo being piped into the room. The medicated wine made me sweat profusely and sleepy as well, so I got into one of the beds and slept. When I woke, the bed was wet with perspiration and both sheets were dirty: I had given myself a sweat-bath with the medicated wine, and it had done a better cleaning job than the bath. I called for maid service to change the sheets, and while that was being done, I took another bath, then got back into bed and had room service bring me a large meal, then slept again until Mother returned at twilight. It was hard to believe she had suffered any ordeal at all, she was so carefree and lighthearted. Any other mother would have looked harried if her son had been kidnapped. She hadn't looked worried at the dock, either. But then my sister and I knew we had a very unusual mother—I just didn't realize yet how unusual.

The next morning, Mother remembered that she had gotten someone to drive my Dodge to New York City, in the trunk of which were a suitcase with clothes in it and my little two-cylinder Indian motorcycle—a Motorplane, only a few of which were manufactured, and mine was the 25th ever made. So she telephoned the hotel garage and had my suitcase brought up to our room very quickly so I could dress.

Again, she said she had to go out on business, and when she returned Mother told me she had been questioned about me by federal agents. Then she said, "When I showed them your federal agent identification and they checked on it, they were flabbergasted by the reply they got." Then she added, "You have nothing to worry about." Contrary to her view, I was sure that I had no standing with that Rat Bureau since my trip to Cuba, if ever I had any standing.

The next morning, Mother said she wanted me to have a wonderful summer after the dreadful experience I had had on *The Eastern Temple*, and that we were going to Cape Cod in a few days, but that I might enjoy sightseeing in New York City first. She had called Colonel Bunker to tell him that everything was all right and about our travel plans, and he had said there were some things I might like to see, beginning with boxing at Stilmans Gym where professional boxers worked out, and perhaps fencing at a club a short distance from our hotel. He also suggested I might like to see the Rockettes practice at Radio City Music Hall; he would make a phone call and all I had to do was tell the doorman my name. I told Mother I would like to see the Rockettes rehearse but had no desire to watch fencing or boxing. But Mother said I should go anyway in case Colonel Bunker ever asked me about it. So, of course, I went.

Hardly a minute after I was seated ringside at the gym, the announcer said that there would be a slight delay before the next match and that a volunteer was needed to spar with a boxer at ringside until the next match was ready to begin. He then pointed me out and asked if I would oblige them. So in my street clothes I got into the ring, and hardly had I touched the opponent's face when he fell to the floor, supposedly unconscious. Two men jumped into the ring and approached me, saying they were boxing managers and wanted to manage me. I recognized it as a joke of some kind and got out of the gym as fast as I could.

Then I went to the fencing club. Upon entering by way of a shabby-looking entrance, I saw a staircase going up to the main floor and down to the basement. On the banister by the newel was a kris, a short sword with a wavy blade like the one wielded by the Masonic Tiler at the east of the Garden of Eden, turning every which way to keep the way to the Tree (*tau*) of Life. (Masonry is full of such crap.) Thinking that I should take it to someone employed in the club, I picked it up and took it with me to the main floor. There I saw an elderly man slouched in an easy chair who looked to me like some of the cartoons I had seen depicting clubs in England. I said hello and asked where I could find the fencing instructor. He said to take the elevator to the second floor. When I got out of the elevator, I saw three men; the one who appeared to be the oldest was gripping a foil that didn't have a button on it. I rightly assumed he was the instructor.

Walking up to them, I smiled, holding the kris so that the point of it was to the side. I held it out and asked the instructor if it was his. He refused to take it and launched into a tirade, making threatening gestures toward me with his foil. I was apologetic and asked him to please excuse me for anything I had done to offend him. Backing away, I put the kris on the floor so that he could not in any way construe a threat. That did no good, however, and he took a step or two toward me in a threatening way. I was amazed by his attitude and equally amazed by the pugnacious attitude of the two men with him; it just made no sense. I was, however, armed to the teeth with my trusty water pistol and switchblade. Surreptitiously, I had taken out my water pistol, concealed in my right hand, when the instructor's torrent of abuse first began. I backed away again, but not because I didn't feel equal to an attack. I won't go into what occurred there at this time, but when I left to go to Radio City Music Hall to see the Rockettes practice, I was beginning to think that Colonel Bunker had set me up.

At the Music Hall, a man was standing at the entrance as though he were expecting sightseers. When I told him my name, he permitted me to pass. However, there were no spectators inside but myself. The pretty Rockettes were on stage, so I took a seat a few rows from the front. The music began to play and the Rockettes danced. After they had performed a while and were catching their breath, I went up on stage and told them how much I enjoyed their performance, then thanking them, I returned to the hotel.

Mother had a sandwich waiting for me that was big enough for a meal. As we sat and talked, I told her about the Rockettes, and that I had called at the gym and club that Colonel Bunker had wanted me to see—I said nothing about what had taken place there—and that I was ready to leave New York City. She said she had forgotten to tell me that the federal agents had told her that the captain of *The Eastern Temple* wanted his pistol back or to be paid for it, and she had told them that I didn't have a pistol with me. *How strange*, I thought, *that the captain should talk about the pistol—how very, very strange.* Mother then said she was going out to look at some dresses—not to buy them because they were frightfully expensive, but just look at them. This seemed strange to me, too.

Once she was gone, I had no sooner gotten into bed to listen to Guy Lombardo when the telephone rang. Answering it, I was amazed to hear the *Eastern Temple* Greek's voice. How could he have found out where I was? It just didn't make sense. Immediately, I told him that I wanted to see him to find out what had happened, and that I also wanted to return his rifle. He suggested that I meet him at a club within the hour. I said I couldn't do that, but that I could see him the following morning. So it was arranged that we would meet at a certain club in the Greek section on or around Eighth Avenue and 30th Street.

With the dismantled rifle still wrapped in newspaper, I set out the following morning about thirty minutes before the set time. I gave the taxi driver the name and address of the club, then asked him to wait for me. As soon as I entered the club, I saw the Greek sitting alone at a table and a number of Greeks sitting at other tables. With a friendly smile, I said hello loud enough to be heard by everyone. I attached the stock, barrel and mechanism (incidentally, the rifle could have fired without the stock on it) and held it out as though offering it to him, saying, "Here is your rifle," then laid it on his table. He then said something in Greek and the men at the other tables proceeded to leave.

I asked what had happened to him, the captain, the crew, and the men who had been in the hold, as well as the dead man. He said that everything was all right, that I had been wrong about him smuggling illegal aliens into the country, they had been stowaways and had been treated the way they were for that reason. He then said that if I would just work with him, he would make me rich quickly, that *The Eastern Temple* was registered in Panama and he had connections there. I could go to Panama in a boat that he would provide and pick up something he had left there. I would then bring it to The Eastern Temple in Brownsville, Texas, for which I would have more money than I ever dreamed of. I said I wasn't interested in any more voyages, that the recent one had been enough.

On my way back to the hotel room, I speculated upon what had and hadn't happened in regard to *The Eastern Temple*. When I got off the elevator on my floor, I was surprised to see Colonel Bunker and a man approaching the desk in front of the elevator, as though they had just come from Mother's and my rooms. I said hello and thanked him for the interesting places he had suggested, then excused myself quickly by saying I had to go to the toilet.

When I saw Mother, I told her about seeing the Colonel and asked her how long he had been in New York. She said that Colonel Bunker hadn't come to see her but to do business, and had called her when he arrived that morning, saying he was with Bob Fletcher, an Interstate Amiesite executive, and would be very busy, then apologized for not being able to see her. Her story seemed strange if not unbelievable. Saying no more about him, I told her I was leaving New York whether she was ready to go or not. She said she was ready to go, too, and so the next morning we left for Cape Cod.

Chapter 32

Wild Bill Donovan's
OSS Baker Street Irregulars
From Gardiner's Island, New York to
Chimney Rock, North Carolina, July 1934

When Mother and I reached Falmouth, who should be my contact for yet more books with my name on them but Norman Mattoon Thomas (1884–1986), the six-time Socialist candidate for president. As soon as we checked into our hotel, Mother called my attention to the fact that Norman Thomas was lecturing in a downtown theater, reminding me how much my father admired him. It did not occur to me that the unpleasant man at the Federal Bureau had sent me with a "detective" to seek out Thomas at Communist headquarters in New York City little more than a year before. Mother recommended that I call on him and have a talk, so I went to the theater where he was to lecture and as luck would have it, he was there.

During our talk, Thomas mentioned that he treasured books written by a man with the same name as mine. They were stored at a building, and he had intended to re-read them, but was so busy getting ready for his lecture that he wasn't able to go get them, and if I would do it for him, he would give me a pass to all of his lectures. I didn't give a damn about his lectures, but curious to see the books, I agreed to get them.

The small brick building outside of town had no windows and only one metal door. Norman Thomas neglected to tell me that a powerful electrical current was connected to that metal door. If I had tried to enter the building the way I was expected to enter, I would have been electrocuted. However, I cut an electrical wire leading from the junction box to the little building and touched it to the doorknob, which created an electrical display similar to an electric welder's arc, indicating to me that the current was at least 220 volts and of high amperage. The door then opened, which meant that the lock was a manual/electrical lock. Cautiously, I entered the building and found some books with my name on them, as well as several prophetic books either similar to or duplicates of the books I had taken from the tomb alleged to belong to Dr. Simon P. Kramer of Fort Thomas, Kentucky.

I returned to see Thomas who undoubtedly was surprised to see me. I told him what I had done and his response was to demand the books. Given that I had decided he had set me up to be killed, I refused to give him the books and punched him in the face.

At the hotel in Falmouth, I showed the books to my mother, and she suggested we go to Boston immediately. We were there for only a few days when she received a call from Colonel Bunker who was traveling to Boston to ostensibly talk business with Mother. While in Boston, Colonel Bunker asked me about my business plans. I told him I didn't have any, but would start looking for a job after my vacation. Colonel Bunker mentioned that he had been talking with "Wild Bill" Donovan; he and others were forming an organization that I might fit into.

Bunker had been in the Army Engineers during the First World War, and he and the men he commanded had allegedly built a bridge over a river that Donovan and his men reputedly crossed for a decisive battle. As a result, Bunker and Donovan had become great friends. I had heard the friendship-bridge story a number of times, as well as some of Donovan's other successes—and yet Colonel Bunker disavowed any and all knowledge of the Donovan organization. He called Donovan, and made an appointment for me to see him the next evening.

When I arrived at the house Donovan occupied, he only let me into a dimly-lit foyer where a grotesque life-size statue like a mummified body stood. As Donovan and I talked, I watched the statue out of the corner of my eye. It must have been on a rotating base because I am positive that it turned toward me as I watched. Years later, I learned that that statue or a duplicate of it was owned by Robert Leroy Ripley (1803–1949), creator of the "Ripley's Believe It or Not" cartoon strip and assisted Donovan and Morley in their *dessous des cartes* subversion activities.

Donovan told me to go to Gardiner's Island in the North Fork end of Long Island. Gardiner's Island was reputedly where Captain William Kidd buried his treasure in 1699. Donovan said I was to see Christopher Morley (1890–1957) about what position I might be suited for. Whether the man I went to see was actually the writer and editor, I do not know. I do know that I didn't like the idea of going to Gardiner's Island and felt somewhat rebuffed by Donovan's lack of hospitality and friendliness. What was supposed to have been an interview had amounted to nothing.

I spent the night in a tourist court and the next morning took the Bridgeport Ferry to Long Island where I rented a boat and went to a heavily wooded island with trees and underbrush. Being careful of my clothes, it was difficult to make my way to the center of the island. Somewhere along the way, I came upon an old vacant house. Just for the hell of it, I went in, thinking that the witch known as Good Wife Garlic, who reputedly lived on Gardiner's Island, might have occupied that house. Father sometimes jokingly referred to Mother as Good Wife Garlic because of her liberal use of garlic in her cooking. Outside the house was a number of graves.

I was getting peeved at Donovan for not telling me how to find Morley as I roamed around shouting, "Mr. Morley, where are you?" Coming to a clearing, I shouted for one last time, and out of the woods came Morley with a younger man dressed in army fatigues. I introduced myself and was a little surprised that Morley knew who I was and why I was there, for I had no idea that there was any way of communicating with the mainland. Morley's questions seemed vacuous. He asked how I felt about Jews and Germans and what was happening in Europe. I told him I wasn't really angry with any races or nationalities, including Negroes and Mexicans, and as for what was happening in Europe, I said I really knew nothing about it except what I read in newspapers and magazines, and that I didn't believe all that I read. He asked me if I'd give my life for my country, and I said no in a loud voice.

The fellow with Morley kept grinning and acted like macho characters tend to do. I was polite to the two of them, but did inquire in an abrupt way as to what kind of position I was being considered for. Morley said that the Donovan organization was looking for Soldier of Fortune-type men to take specialized training. Special forces were in the process of being trained by instructors in established camps, and if I qualified, I could be an instructor, too. He explained that after a period of training, the men had certain privileges, but instructors had even more special privileges that included introductions to beautiful women.

What Morley pitched didn't convince me. I suspected that Donovan and his associates were doing something illegal, even if "Wild Bill" was the great patriot that Bunker said he was. What's more, I recognized that I was not the Soldier of Fortune type. I hoped to find a position from which I could enjoy life without hardship or danger. I figured, however, that I could play at being a Soldier of Fortune for a few months if the pay was good, and the specialized training wasn't too strenuous. Morley said there wasn't any drilling.

Morley said he wanted some of his and Colonel Donovan's associates to pass on me at a meeting in New York City on July 5. Reservations would be made for me at the Ansonia Hotel, and if I wanted, I could go there immediately. I thanked him and said I would have to go back to Boston first, but that I would be at the appointed place at the appointed time. Morley gave me the address of a chophouse for the July 5 meeting.

Back at Boston, I shared my suspicions about the Donovan organization with Mother, who said Bunker had recommended me highly to Colonel Donovan, and that it wouldn't be fair to her Colonel friend if I didn't at least attend the meeting.

On July 4, in New York City, after watching some of the Independence Day parade, I located the chophouse, then checked in at the Ansonia Hotel. I had stayed there twice before, most recently exactly two years earlier. I was somewhat offended that such rich and prominent men as Morley and Donovan would send me to a hotel that was far from the best. The doors to the rooms were all ajar on my hall, which to me meant salesmen were relegated to the floor. Curious about what they were selling, I walked into several of the rooms. Upon entering, I would say, "Wrong room, excuse me" and leave. Two men occupied each room. In one room, the men were wearing shoulder holsters.

The next day, I met with as queer a group as you might imagine. This meeting was a mystical charade that had nothing to do with the Baker Street Irregulars (Christopher Morley's group of Sherlock Holmes aficionados).

Everyone looked as if they were attending a funeral, and a weird ceremony began almost immediately. I was served some foul drink that, after touching my tongue to it, I surreptitiously poured under the table as a speaker jibbered on about predestination and how we're here for a certain allotted time. While he talked, the members of the group one by one left through the door that opened onto the street. The preacher was the last to leave, and as he went out the door he beckoned for me to come, but I had no intention of following. Instead, I shouted to hell with you all and stalked out the locked door I had entered.

The name of the Baker Street Irregulars is taken from the group of men who sometimes assist Sherlock Holmes and Dr. Watson in the Arthur Conan Doyle novels. Many Baker Street Irregulars groups take fanciful names: The Speckled Band, the Five Orange Pips, the Maiwand Jezails, Order of the Blue Carbuncle, the Giant Rats of Sumatra—this last one has a symbolical headquarters in a Memphis tobacco shop. The Baker Street Irregulars are actually a cover organization for subversive activities of rich, influential, ruthless people in the United States, Canada, and England. (See *A Man Called Intrepid* by William Stephenson.) But of course I didn't realize all of that then.

I returned to my room in the Ansonia Hotel and was packing a few things when I heard a small noise outside my door. Taking out a .25-caliber automatic, I faced the door. A moment later, two men crashed through the door, their momentum carrying them almost to the center of the room. I shot one of them about an inch below the collarbone, then ran out of the room and into the lobby where I hollered for the desk clerk to call the police. An instant later, a number of men from the rooms with open doors rushed the lobby, so I ran out of the hotel onto the street with these men on the chase. I ran into stores and out of side doors and backdoors, down side streets and alleys. Even though I outdistanced my pursuers and tried to hide, they got wind of my movements.

Finally, I got to the Barbizon Hotel where girls attending the Katherine Gibbs School were staying. As the girls were about to enter their hotel, I flashed my Bureau of Investigation identification card and asked for their help. They got me into the hotel and past the front desk without my being seen, then stashed me into a room upstairs. A few minutes after I was hidden, I could hear pursuers in the hall just outside the room. I also heard the girls confronting them like avenging angels, screaming that men were in the prohibited area and raising such a ruckus that the pursuers had to slink away. I can't find enough words of praise for those young ladies.

I spent the night at the Barbizon and returned to Boston the next day. There I found Mother in her hotel room in a rage. She said that Colonel Bunker had called and sounded so upset that he wanted us to come to his home in Westchester, Pennsylvania immediately. I evaded this plan by saying that I had to go to New Haven to see about the job with the Donovan organization, and that I would return the day after next, which I'd keep open to pay the Colonel a visit. I put the books that I had gotten in Falmouth in my car and drove to New Haven, my plan being to store the books at the Yale Skull and Bones fraternity, if they would have them.

Misinformation guided me to Yale's Skull and Bones. I still thought of my brother-in-law James Eley Robertson, a member of Skull and Bones at University of Alabama, as a fine, upstanding man. He hadn't explained to me that Skull and Bones at the University of Alabama was not part of Skull and Bones at Yale University, nor had he told me that Skull and Bones at Alabama was connected to the Southern college fraternity Kuklos Adelphon, meaning it was quasi-Klan, like the supposedly defunct Knights of the White Camellia.

In New Haven, I quickly located the so-called Tomb, but it was locked. I had no success in finding Yalies who admitted to being members of the secret society. Pressed for time, I flashed my Bureau identification at the post office in order to get the address of Skull and Bones' sponsoring organization, the Russell Trust Association. When I found their office, I again showed my Bureau identification and recounted how I had gotten the books, how I had sent a cipher-codebook to the State Department, how I had been told that Archibald MacLeish of the State Department was a member of Skull and Bones—in short, I told those deadheads as much as I could during the short time I had to talk to them. In the end, of course, they took the books.

On the way back to Boston, I rehashed in my mind the things that had happened to me in such a short time. It appeared to me that each incident had sparked another incident. I had the unfortunate habit of wondering what

I did wrong to merit such treatment. When I got to the hotel, Mother was in a dither, so we drove all the way to Westchester without stopping to sleep.

When we finally arrived at Colonel Bunker's house, I parked across the street. No sooner had we gotten out of the car than he ran out in an angry dither, too, saying agitatedly that Irénée DuPont wanted to see me and I must immediately go to Nemours, his estate in Wilmington, Delaware. But I was tired and didn't know Irénée DuPont from a horse's ass, and said as much. Colonel Bunker took Mother aside and talked to her, after which she restated the infamous words, "Won't you go for my sake?" She was continually exploiting my love for her, and I always did what she wanted me to do, no matter how much I felt imposed upon. So I took my little Indian motorcycle out of the trunk and started for Wilmington.

The DuPonts were connected to Colonel Bunker through Senator Daniel Hastings of Delaware, a strong well-wisher of the Interstate Amiesite Company, who was married to one of the DuPonts. At one time, Senator Hastings offered to get me an appointment to the U.S. Military Academy at West Point or the Coast Guard Academy despite my poor grades, telling me that military academies were looking for other qualities in applicants than scholastic ability. Senator Hastings had also gone with Mother and Colonel Bunker to see one of the DuPonts who, Mother said, knew a great deal about horticulture and had taken her through a hothouse, showing her his rare plants. I wondered then as I do now if that hothouse visit had anything to do with Colonel Bunker calling Mother his "fair lady" (belladonna). One of the DuPonts was shot in a whorehouse in Louisville, Kentucky, and prior to the shooting had stayed in a hotel where Father often stayed.

In Wilmington, I was directed to Nemours. Before going to the gate, I put my .25 Colt automatic under the motor of my motorcycle and secured it with friction tape. The guards at the gate apparently expected me, though I had to suffer the indignity of being searched. Then I drove through but stopped before getting to the mansion and pretended to inspect the motor while I removed the automatic and put it in my pants pocket.

At the mansion, an unfriendly man directed me to a sitting room where I waited. Glowering men were moving about everywhere, inside and outside the mansion. I got up and started walking about silently. I found a woman whom I told that I was expected and couldn't wait any longer, that if Mr. DuPont wanted to see me, he was going to have to do it then and there. She then took me to a bedroom where he lay dying if not dead. According to the record, Alfred Irénée DuPont died April 29, 1935 at his Epping Forest Estate on St. John's River at Jacksonville, Florida, but he appeared to have croaked that day in July 1934.

Irénée DuPont was one of the wealthy men who provided financial support to the secret organization that became known as the Office of Strategic Service (OSS), headed up by Wild Bill Donovan. DuPont even provided a building for that organization's secret activities, since the U.S. government couldn't openly provide for an organization that was not supposed to exist. Government hierarchy supported the secret organization, as did the Bureau of Investigation and *eminence gris* families like the DuPonts.

On the way back to Westchester, I was so tired that I spent the night at a tourist court. When I arrived at Colonel Bunker's the next morning, Mother was mad as a wet hen about something or other and said the Colonel wasn't there. My car was parked where I had left it, so after I loaded my little motorcycle we left for Asheville, North Carolina. The entire trip, Mother was mean as only she knew how to be, telling me when to stop and when to go and where to turn, but after we arrived in Asheville, she settled down. We checked into Lake Lure Inn where we stayed until moving on to Chimney Rock where we then stayed until the weather started to cool. [Chimney Rock, North Carolina is one degree latitude difference from Chimney Rock, New Mexico. Five hundred million years old, Chimney Rock NC has a twenty-six-story elevator built inside it, as well as a complex of underground labyrinths.]

After several weeks, Colonel Bunker came to the Chimney Rock Inn for what was supposed to be a week or 10 days but ended up staying only one night and left in a hurry. Mother said that something I said upset him. The day he left—Halloween—Mother took me to the beautiful Grove Arcade in Asheville to show me one of the unoccupied stores she was using for storage. Giving me a key, she told me to go in and see what was there, because it all belonged to me.

Everything inside was covered with sheets. After finding a statue about three feet high, I thought that all the things stored here were what Mother and Sister bought at antique auctions, but then I raised another sheet and under it were two Dayton Witch cipher/computer mechanisms. I went out and locked the door and said to Mother, "There are two Dayton Witches in there, and I have a hunch that the truth about them would frighten more people than any Halloween story ever told." I asked her what they were doing there, where she got them, and how long she had them.

But she shook her head and said, "There is a record in there for you of everything. You will get it all at a certain time, but I can't let you have it now or tell you about the things that have happened. Your father and I kept records of everything our family was involved in. We wrote about them in the order they occurred; that is what we were doing your last year of high school. Do you remember how you would come home after school and find us writing and typing? We would tell you we were writing business letters because we didn't want you to discover what we were doing."

We stayed in North Carolina until Chimney Rock Inn was about to close, then returned to Memphis.

Chapter 33

Of Prophecy and Highbrow Deceit

Memphis and Miami Beach, 1934

ost of the grave goods books with my name on them were scientific manuals. Those having to do with telepathy, mind control, and atomic fission were my favorites. The atomic physics tome contained a drawing of an atomic pile and a bomb, and the book on mind control seemed to be a sequel to the volume on mental telepathy, having something to do with surveying and terrestrial magnetism. I only skimmed a book on mathematics, but saw enough to know it was no ordinary math text. The material in these books seemed outlandish to me, and the technology it described seemed like fantasy. But I had no doubt whatsoever that these scientific manuals were representative of a dangerous esoteric secret, even if the atomic bomb, mind control, and mental telepathy were pure science fiction.

But the prophetic books were something else again, for they detailed things to come. To assess the accuracy of these books, one had only to look into the previous pages and read descriptions of events that had already taken place. While contemplating how such a thing might be, I thought of racehorse gambling and how it had become a custom in cities and towns like Cincinnati, Covington, and Newport. Bookmakers not only placed gamblers' illicit bets and equine wagers, but many also sold tips drummed up by various touts or horserace analysts. Some touts went so far as to print up phony tip sheets showing winners they had allegedly predicted so they could fool the gullible into buying other tip sheets. I wondered if the same sort of fiction had been perpetrated in the prophetic books toward some unknown end, for it was difficult to believe that future events could be predicted so accurately. I was, of course, unaware that I was being continually manipulated in occult charades, some of which were possibly arranged to benefit me.

I was somehow induced to go to the Shelby County clerk's office. I have no idea why I went, but go I did. The county clerk wasn't there, but a chained prophetic book was. I examined the thing quickly to make sure it was what I thought it was. Then, a smiling lady suddenly appeared. She said she knew nothing about the book except that it was one of a number of such titles in the Goodwyn Institute, and that soon it would be taken back. And what she said was true: at the Goodwyn Institute were more chained prophetic books and more smiling women who seemingly wanted to be helpful but still couldn't find the record of the books they were sure the Institute owned.

I couldn't decide what to do about the prophecy books. For several days, I weighed the pros and cons and finally decided to use my Bureau of Investigation identification to take custody of these books. But after I returned to the Goodwyn Institute they books were no longer there. An uncooperative employee declared that she had no knowledge of the chained prophetic books. A cover-up was apparent, but I still didn't realize that government agents in Memphis were working in conjunction with Memphians who practiced Masonic sorcery. It was the opera *Un Ballo Maschera* all over again: those who took pleasure in fooling the gullible fool-savant. As Arthur Schopenhauer (1788–1860), the German philosopher, said, "Everybody's friend is nobody's." To make matters worse, I thought everybody I liked, liked me, and so treated them as friends long after they had proven not to be friends. Consequently, I was easily tricked.

At this time, a rich, socially prominent Memphian who pretended to be my friend asked me if I was interested in getting a fine job. He said that a man he knew named Diggs Nolan had seen me at Grisanti's Restaurant said he could have me working there. I said I wasn't especially interested in work but might if the price was right. He assured me that the job would pay well, for Diggs Nolan had a very lucrative business, and he looked at me closely when he said *Diggs*, which didn't mean a damn to me at that time but should have, had I known more about Memphis. This prominent Memphian then said he would make an appointment for me if I wanted him to, and I said to go ahead. So he gave me Nolan's address, a house near the Sears. The house didn't seem like much, but I assumed that it was just used for business.

When I knocked, the door was immediately opened by Diggs Nolan, who asked me to come in. Then he pointed a pistol at me, and locked the door behind me. He picked up a hypodermic syringe and ordered me to take off my coat. Feigning fear, I started to wring my hands as leaped up onto the divan, pleading, "Please, Mr. Nolan, don't stick me with that, I am a little coward and scared of needles." Then I jumped from the divan onto that evil man, knocked him down, injected him with the contents of the syringe, and hit him with my fist for good measure.

Several days later, I drove by the Nolan house. Seeing police there, I parked my car and went up to the house. I showed my Bureau identification to a policeman at the door and talked to him for several minutes. He told me that a telephone call had been received at the police station about something being wrong at this address. They had known for some time that dope was being sold there, but nothing had been done to close the place up. He thought the telephone tip had probably been made by some addict who had come to get dope and couldn't get it. When they got there, the front door was open and they found a man lying on the floor. The coroner pronounced him dead, saying he might have died within an hour of being found, but the policeman said he might not be dead, for he had seen a number of addicts who appeared dead but weren't. In fact, there was an addict held in the morgue for a couple of days while identification was being made, and it turned out that he hadn't been dead, at all.

Diggs Nolan apparently sold dope and was an addict. He hung out at a place called the Green Beetle and had a room at the infamous Stockmen's Hotel, where I had encountered Bobby Berryman, the boss gambler.

I made sure to confront the socially prominent man who set me up to be killed. He told me that he was forced to tell me to see Diggs Nolan and actually followed me when I did. Then he mentioned that he was glad to see me leave the Nolan house, as he hated what he had done. He said he knew that I would come after him, but no matter what I was going to do, he wanted to let me know some things first. He then related a nightmarish series of grotesque drug-induced incidents that seemed incredible to me then. When he finished his spiel, I got up and stood over him. "That sounds like shit to me, although some of it may be true. Anyway, I am going to do something that will show you how I feel." Then I hit him and left.

A fellow in his early twenties whom I had met here and there on several occasion asked me if I wanted to join a secret Cotton Carnival Society. Thinking of the fun and games associated with the word *carnival*, I said I would. He said they would come for me the next afternoon for an initiation, and since the Carnival Society was oriented to carnival security, I was to bring a shotgun but no ammunition, and if I didn't have a shotgun he would lend me one.

The next day I got out a few shotgun shells and my trusty .20-gauge and waited. At the appointed time, the man who recruited me and two others came for me. First, he asked to see my shotgun, examined it, and handed it back. They took me to a deserted house on the edge of town with a full chicken house in the back. I was told to keep the chickens from being stolen, and then the evil Memphians drove away. Suspicious, I loaded my shotgun. A few minutes after they left, I heard a noise. A Negro man was creeping up to the chicken house and pen with a couple of gunny sacks. It was obvious to me that he wanted to be seen. I pointed my shotgun at him and said, "I know that you have come here to steal my chickens."

"Boss, I have a wife and three children and I can't find work. We have no food at home and I just have to get them something to eat. If I could just have one chicken?"

Sternly, I responded, "You are not going about it the right way. Here is what you should do: Leave off the 'boss' and repeat what you said." When he did that, I said, "Take all of the chickens," and digging into my pocket past the shotgun shells, I fished out some change and said, "You will probably need some cornmeal and grease, too, and this ought to be enough to get both." I then watched him catch the chickens and put them in the gunny sacks. He looked stunned, so I said, "You shouldn't have let those dirty sons of bitches get you to play such a dangerous game."

He said, "It isn't supposed to be dangerous for me. You don't have any shotgun shells and you're the one who's supposed to get hurt." I told him that my gun was loaded and showed him one of the shells from my pocket. He then said, "I'm going to show you something," and stepping to the chicken house he showed me a section of it that was hinged so that pressure on it would knock out anyone in front of it. The Negro explained that his job was to get me into the chicken house and clobber me out with the trick section.

I told him that we were going to have some fun with those dirty white sons of bitches. I shot my shotgun, and in a couple of minutes, those dirty bastards drove up and got out of the car. I pointed the shotgun in their general direction and had the Negro search them for weapons; they had none, nor were there weapons in the car. After making the driver put the chickens in the trunk, I made the three of them get in the front seat with one of them sitting in the lap of another, while the Negro and I then got in the backseat, after which they drove the Negro and chickens to his house. I kept the sons of bitches in the front seat until we arrived at my home, when I had the driver get out of the car so I could club his leg with the barrel of my shotgun. Then I chased them off.

I had become a member of the Memphis Country Club of which Dr. Tenney, a Freemason, was the director. He exhibited antipathy toward me immediately. The time came for the girls to make their debut, and I was encouraged by members of my family to date debutantes. I wasn't so inclined, but agreed to do it. At what might be called an introductory dance, three elderly women interviewed prospective escorts. Two of the elderly women were charming and I would have rather taken them out, but the third woman was antagonistic and it seemed this was planned. I was asked what type of work I did and produced my Bureau identification, asking them to please not hold it against me. Then I was asked if there was anyone to recommend me and I said that they might ask my friend President Franklin D. Roosevelt, as he was the one who recommended me to the Bureau of Investigation.

The upshot was that I was accepted as an escort, but I had no intention of following through. I was soon asked by Mrs. Patterson, manager of the country club, to take one of the girls to a masquerade ball. I suspected that the dance was being arranged by the secret society chicken charade planners and tried to beg off of doing the chore, but couldn't.

The night of the dance I went at the appointed time to the home of the girl I was to escort, about two blocks from my brother-in-law's and sister's house. My costume looked like a little boy's sun suit and I brought a little tin bucket such as children use to play on sandy beaches, and in that bucket I put my .25 Colt automatic. I pointed out that it wasn't appropriate for me to take my date to the dance dressed as I was. She said the dance had already started and that I looked fine, so on we went. I was surprised when she directed me not to a hotel ballroom but to an amusement park with a shabby, dirty dance hall. A few people were in costume, but the rest were in street clothes and not very nice ones at that.

As soon as we started dancing—with me holding my little bucket with my automatic in it—I saw the men who had tried to injure me in the chicken charade talking to men at the end of the dance floor. When one of the three men came out to the dance floor and tried to dance with my girl, I refused. He hollered to the men for help, and the girl scooted away. I told the dirty son of a bitch that if I were attacked, I would shoot him first, then the others.

The bouncer came up and I showed him my Bureau identification and announced that dope was being used on the premises and that I would run everyone in if there were any trouble. He said that he would do something about it if I wanted him to. I said no, to let it go for now. On my way out, I saw the girl I brought with a man she had asked to take her home. I thanked him and we parted company. The next morning, I brought her flowers and that was that. What happened the night before had not occurred by chance.

I went to a celebration at the country club where Elaine Patterson, the daughter of the manager, was holding court at a large table surrounded by young men. Elaine had been the first Memphis Cotton Carnival Queen in 1931. I knew a fellow at her table and stopped by to say hello and comment about how none of them were drinking. When I got my bar bill at the end of the month, I found that a large number of drinks had been signed to my name. A nice bartender explained that he questioned the signing of the check, but a club member had said it was all right. Initially I thought it was a joke and that the bill would be paid by the joker, but that was not the case. Dr. Tenney insisted I pay the bill; I refused and we quarreled. Mrs. Patterson told me she would pay the bill, but I refused to let her. The bartender who had sided with me resigned or was fired. The bar bill quarrel might be considered a small thing, but it was one of a series of incidents from which a conclusion can be drawn.

A Firestone plant was being built in Memphis, and Raymond and Laura Firestone of the Firestone Tire family moved next door to my brother-in-law and sister. Unkind stories had circulated about Raymond's mother Idabelle Firestone (1874–1954), who was a composer of some talent as her compositions "If I Could Tell You" and "In My Garden" attest. Eventually, Raymond Firestone and I began to talk.

During one conversation, he said that some important men were having a party at the Firestone home in Miami Beach, Florida, and would I care to be one of the exceptional young men of fine families who would serve at the tables. I said something humorous like, "If there are a number of black sheep at the party, there is no telling what will happen if I am there." He asked me what I meant, and replied, "Black sheep are as traditional among fine families. I know about such things because I was declared to be a black sheep dressed in wolves' clothing long ago. However, for black sheep to wait on wolves is something I don't know about, so maybe I will go to your party, maybe I won't. I'll let you know tomorrow."

I told my brother-in-law about our conversation and had he ever heard of anything so ridiculous as Raymond Firestone implying that waiting tables at a party was some type of recognition conferred on exceptional young men of fine families. I told him what I had said about black sheep and wolves, and he said, "Bud, don't you realize that serving at the party will mean being introduced to vastly important men?" After talking with Jim, I told Raymond Firestone that I would go to Miami Beach and serve at the party. He told me when to be there and reminded me that it was confidential and I was being entrusted with private matters.

I called Enrique and told him about Miami Beach and asked if he would like to go with me at my expense. He accepted the invitation and we left for Miami Beach three days before I was to be there. Enrique did most of the driving, and I joked about being the only waiter from Memphis who had a chauffeur. I was surprised that Enrique seemed unnerved by what I had said. The fact is that I hit home, as Enrique was a member of a terrible occult greaser society.

We arrived in Miami, got a hotel room and located the Firestone Estate that is where the Doral Hotel is today. Beautiful trees and shrubs grow around the periphery. Anyone today would find it difficult to visualize how beautiful and vacant Florida tourist towns and beaches were some fifty or more years ago when the tourist season wasn't on. In Miami Beach, there were very few people on the main drag.

Enrique took me to the Firestone Estate. He would go back to our hotel room and rest, and I would call him when the party was over and he would pick me up. The gate to the Firestone Estate was locked, but that was no problem. I climbed over it.

I walked up to the front door and knocked. After some time, a man, whom I assumed was hired help, came to the door. I introduced myself and the reason I was there, but nothing had been done for a big party. Toward the beach, I saw a picnic table, and further out in the water was a large, beautiful yacht anchored some distance from shore. I wondered about water depth as I noticed two men on the beach who looked like workmen.

The man who answered the door left me to my own devices, so I walked out to the beach and asked the men if they knew the name of the yacht. They seemed quite friendly and said it was the *Nourmahal*. Returning to the house, I noticed that whiskey and mixers had been put on the picnic table. Inside the house, a couple of young men scurried away. Turning toward the yacht, I saw a number of men in a powerboat pulling away from the yacht and heading toward the beach. The two friendly men I spoke to on the beach watched as the powerboat arrived.

Enrique knocked at the door, telling me to get out of there fast. At that moment, things started happening. Men from the yacht came in, one with a pistol, and a number of young men from somewhere in the house also appeared. Several shots were fired and the man with the pistol was most certainly hit, and everyone fled the room except him. I ran out past Enrique and jumped in the car he had left running and as soon as he got in, we drove away fast. A couple of minutes later, I hailed the policeman. I told him that we heard gunfire at the Firestone Estate and he might want to check it out. Wisely, Enrique had put our luggage in the car and checked us out, so we didn't have to stop in Miami. We drove back to Memphis without stopping.

Harvey Samuel Firestone (1868–1938) might have been one of the "important men" who were supposed to have been at the Firestone Estate; then again, he might have just loaned his estate to others.

Back in Memphis, when I went to see Raymond Firestone I was told that he had gone to Akron on business. I wrote the Firestone Company in Akron in regard to the Firestone Miami Beach estate and learned that the estate had been closed for some time. I decided to go back to Miami Beach and see what I could find out. On the way, I stopped in Jacksonville to inquire about the *Nourmahal* and was told that Irénée DuPont owned it and it was docked at the Jacksonville DuPont estate on the St. John's River. I actually hired a man with a powerboat to take me up the St. John's River to see if the *Nourmahal* was docked at the DuPont estate. There was a yacht there, but it didn't look like the *Nourmahal*.

In Miami and Miami Beach I got very little information, but near the Firestone Estate I flagged down a police car and told him that I had attended a party the week before at the estate. The cop claimed that he wasn't notified of a party occurring there.

Yes, I was being stymied. Soon enough, I went to Tuscaloosa, Alabama to take three non-credit classes at the University of Alabama, my brother-in-law's alma mater. As usual, it was Mother's suggestion.

Chapter 34

The Chicken Caper
Tuscaloosa, Alabama, 1934–35

uscaloosa was deep in what was called Klan Country. In fact, the Klan had a huge gathering on the University of Alabama football field where the Crimson Tide practiced and played, a meeting that could only have happened with the tacit consent of university administrators and board of trustees. Many students and townspeople came to watch and listen to Klan speakers, but at least no Negroes were beaten or burned.

At the Sigma Chi fraternity house in Tuscaloosa I met Marvin S. Knight and his beautiful police dog, Duke. Neither were welcome at the Sigma Chi house—as one of the boys in the clique said with contempt, "He's a New Yorker and dresses like big-shot Ivy Leaguers. He wears Roger Peet clothes and drives a big car." Their antipathy may have been directed as much toward me as Marvin; I may have been born in Little Dixie, but I wore London-drape suits and liked Marvin and his dog.

Marvin was married to Agnes Torrey of Mobile, Alabama, a very pretty girl. She was supposed to stay in Spring Hill, a suburb of Mobile, while Marvin finished up in Tuscaloosa, but she had come ahead to attend the university. Marvin didn't know how they were going to manage their living arrangements, with him staying at Sigma Chi and Agnes with a friend. After I met her, we went out to a place called the Moon Wink for some beer and whiskey, and then to the hotel where I intended to stay while at the university.

Marvin and Agnes found an apartment but didn't keep it for long due to a then-unrecognized mystical charade. I assisted them by flashing my Bureau identification and lending Marvin some money to pay a fine. After it was over, they suggested that we lease a house together, hire a cook, and get two fraternity brothers to board with us. Marvin didn't want to stay at the Sigma

Chi house, given that he was a Northerner and didn't fit in. So we leased a nice two-story brick house. Immediately, Duke the police dog disappeared. Marvin was heartbroken, saying he wanted to leave and go to Florida, but things settled down. He and Agnes ran the house and bought the groceries, and we hired a Negro man to cook. Wayne Bomberger and Bob Vickers, two members of Sigma Chi from New York, came to live with us.

On my first day of class, I had a confrontation with a male teacher that I recognized as a planned harassment of secret-society origin. I stalked out of the classroom and after talking to the dean about it, didn't attend any of the three classes I was enrolled in. Still, I had a pleasant time in Tuscaloosa and was able to play a marvelous joke that made up for the confrontations to which I was subjected. However, I don't think the joke was appreciated.

My brother-in-law had often talked about an incident that took place while he attended the University of Alabama. The grounds of the Alabama Insane Asylum (later known as Bryce Hospital) adjoin the university campus grounds. Once a patient who was permitted to go outside the asylum for long walks (he hadn't actually been committed) was taking a walk on the street in front of the dean's house and saw a farmer with a huge load of chickens. He was taking them to town to sell at a ridiculously low price because he'd inherited them with the farm he'd just bought and wanted to get rid of them. When the footloose patient saw the farmer, he asked him if he wanted to sell the chickens. The farmer said yes and a price was agreed upon, at which the man pulled out his checkbook and paid the farmer. When asked where he wanted the chickens, the man pointed to the dean's house and said, "That is my home, just turn the chickens loose in the yard." Given that the farmer was new to the area, he didn't know it was the dean's house and did as he was told.

The hubbub was incredible, and when the dean called the police and they discovered that a resident of the asylum had purchased the chickens, the farmer was so disgusted that he tore up the check. But the asylum resident was actually a well-to-do man who ran a profitable business and was normally of sound mind, but every now and then he would become depressed, as many businessmen did during the Depression years, and would then check himself into the asylum where his longtime doctor friend would then give him physiotherapeutic treatments. He wasn't insane and his check was good.

One evening I too saw a farmer with a truckload of chickens as I was walking toward Moon Wink outside of Tuscaloosa. I thought of my brother-in-law's chicken story and figured that this truckload of chickens was an act of fate! So I hailed him and related my chicken story. He saw the delightful humor in it and said he would like to re-enact it, but was afraid he'd be arrested, and then I flashed my Bureau identification and assured him that I would protect him if it became necessary. So I paid him his asking price for the chickens and asked him to drive to the dean's house and turn the chickens loose in his yard. If anyone might ask why he turned the chickens loose, he was to say that Mr. James Shelby Downard bought the chickens from him and told him that Mr. Downard wanted him to turn the chickens loose to catch some of the cockroaches that were infesting the area.

So we drove to the dean's house and I helped him turn the chickens loose, just seconds before a large number of students exited the house. Again, a great hubbub turned into a great to-do, until it all quieted down and the dean asked me not to disturb anything more. The students who witnessed the chicken caper did not even find it amusing. Everything I did and said was intentionally funny with only a touch of malice. How nice it would have been if people could have seen the humor in it all.

Some Tuscaloosa incidents dreamed up by secret societies were not intended to be funny, though. About two weeks before Easter, I was told by a chickenshit Sigma Chi that Negroes were not going to be allowed to walk on the sidewalks of the streets downtown on Easter morning. "What do you have to say about that?" he added with a smirk.

I replied, "Easter morning is a mighty poor time for such a thing to be done. What's more, streets are public thoroughfares. Those who do such a thing are asking for trouble. However, it appears to me that you must be trying to trick me."

The following Sunday, I went to a large Negro church where I was treated cordially and welcomed by the minister from the pulpit. I felt sure that cordial treatment would have been accorded to any white person. I stood up and said, "I am a federal agent," and handed my Bureau identification to the usher, saying, "Please show this to the minister for verification and bring it right back." I waited for him to do what I asked, then said something like this to the congregation, "I didn't come to worship with you or listen to singing, as some white people sometimes do. I came to talk about trouble that might possibly be plotted for Easter morning." Then I related what I had been told by the chickenshit Sigma Chi.

After the minister inquired about what should be done I replied that if there was any old woman in the church who had cooked in the homes of white people and cared for their children who would be willing to walk a few blocks with me on Easter morning, and if a Negro cab driver could be found who would bring the lady to where we would start our walk and then stay some distance away but in sight of us, so he could pick up the brave lady if trouble started, I was prepared to try and hurt whoever attempted to stop her from walking. The minister then asked the congregation if they wanted to do it and the response was a unanimous YES! I then handed $20 to one of the ladies of the congregation and said that the money was for material for a dress for the brave lady to wear when she walked with me. A group of women said the dress could be made in time, and then we set the time and place.

On Easter morning we met at the appointed time and place, and the cab driver, after letting the woman out, stayed just behind us as we walked toward town. She wasn't wearing the new dress I had arranged for her to have. We walked uneventfully for a block and a half, until she said she didn't want to walk any further. I asked her if she was tired or her feet hurt and she said no. I asked if she was afraid and she said no, she just didn't want to walk any further. So the cab driver picked her up and when I gave him $10, he said, "Is that all I am going to get?" I was furious and told him some things in no uncertain terms.

Next Sunday I went to the Negro church and the entire congregation, possibly at a given signal, stood when I entered. I took them to task for not making the dress, for the woman not walking far at all, and the cab driver complaining about the money I gave him. I am quite sure now that they had all been told to act the way they did. However, I was disgusted with them and still am.

During college spring break, Billy Whyte had driven up from Dallas to make plans for the trip we were going to make. After we made tentative plans for two coming trips, Billy returned to Dallas.

Billy played a dubious key role in my youth. Several years after the Cagliostro ordeal, he and I both attended Culver Military Academy's Naval School for three summers. Strange things happened to me there, some of which had to do with memories, or more exactly *anamnesis*. It was again a case of my remembering having been there before, but everyone assuring me I hadn't. How could I remember a place I'd never been before? For example, I found a speedboat tied up at one of the school's docks on Lake Maxinkuckee exactly like a boat I once had that had disappeared. Given that it was a home-made boat crafted with professional skill, it didn't seem likely that there could be two such boats, but it was explained to me that the boat had been built according to plans obtained from *Popular Mechanics* magazine and that there might be many such boats in the United States. While there might be more than one such boat, it seemed strange that another boat should have similar distinguishing marks on it. My parents said I should not make an issue over it, and so I let the matter drop.

Then there was the old red Stutz Black Hawk roadster in storage. The keys in the car were on a key chain whose paper tag had the same name as mine. Did another James Shelby Downard attend Culver? My inquiry amounted to nothing.

The third summer, some boys made torches and then lit and threw them from the portcullis onto the roof of a building used for storage. Though the fire department quickly extinguished the fire, in so doing some of the things inside the building were drenched and had to be carried outside, which I helped to do. One of the trunks I carried outside had the same name on it as mine. When I opened it and inspected its contents, I found winter uniforms such as Culver Cadets stored for those who planned to return for fall term. I also found a considerable number of papers with "Continental Asphalt and Petroleum Co." embossed on them, a company that my father had worked with. I asked Major Stautenberg for help. He smiled benignly and said he couldn't answer my questions, but that I could have the trunk and its contents if I wanted.

With Billy's help, I loaded the trunk into his car and took it to the railroad station where we sent it to his home in Dallas, Texas, where I intended to visit him later in the summer. I never saw that trunk again, so any revelation it might have offered as to another James Shelby Downard whose path I continually crossed was forever lost to me.

PUBLISHER'S NOTE: Downard's memoir stops a few episodes and two years later, following mishaps in a Texas-Mexico border town. He never completed his book.

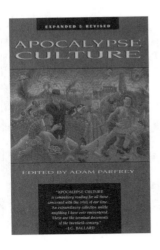

Apocalypse Culture
Edited by Adam Parfrey

"*Apocalypse Culture* is compulsory reading for all those concerned with the crisis of our times. An extraordinary collection unlike anything I have ever encountered. These are the terminal documents of the twentieth century."
— J.G. Ballard

"Parfrey has edited a new book of Revelation, a collection which is almost as awesome and terrifying as the original biblical text."
— Edwin Pouncey, *NME*

Enlarged and Revised Edition

5 1/2 x 8 1/2 · 362 pages · illustrated · ISBN 0-922915-05-9 · $14.95

Voluptuous Panic
The Erotic World of Weimar Berlin
Expanded Hardcover Edition
Mel Gordon

Voluptuous Panic's expanded hardcover edition includes the new chapter, "Sex Magic and the Occult," documenting German pagan cults and their bizarre erotic rituals. This edition also includes sensational accounts of hypno-erotic cabaret acts, Berlin fetish prostitution, gay "wild boys," sex crime, and descriptions and illustrations of Aleister Crowley's Berlin OTO secret society.

8 x 11 · 305 pages · hardcover · extravagantly illustrated throughout
ISBN 1-932595-11-2 · $34.95

It's a Man's World
Men's Adventure Magazines, The Postwar Pulps
By Adam Parfrey, with contributions from Bruce Jay Friedman, Josh Alan Friedman, Mort Kunstler, David Saunders, Bill Devine

It's a Man's World looks back at the last great run of pop illustrations, at least as brilliant as pulp's best. Contributions from Bruce Jay Friedman, Josh Alan Friedman, and David Saunders help bring us inside the offices, showing us how the writers, illustrators, editors, and publishers put together two decades of "armpit slicks."

8.5 x 11 in · 288 pages · hard cover · heavily illustrated
ISBN 0-922915-81-4, $29.95